TO MY GOOD FRIEND

SUSAN ROZENSHER

WITH BEST WISHES!

9-18-98

Managing Risk in the Foreign Exchange, Money, and Derivative Markets

Library of Congress Cataloging-in-Publication Data

Riehl, Heinz.
    Managing risk in the foreign exchange, money, and derivative
markets / Heinz Riehl.
        p.   cm.
    Includes index.
    ISBN 0-07-052673-7
    1. Futures.   2. Interest rate futures.   3. Foreign exchange
futures.   4. Derivative securities.   I. Title.
HG6024.A3R54   1998
332.64'5—dc21   98-6532
                                                            CIP

McGraw-Hill

A Division of The McGraw-Hill Companies

1 2 3 4 5 6 7 8 9 0   FGR/FGR   9 0 3 2 1 0 9 8

ISBN 0-07-052673-7

*The sponsoring editor for this book was Betsy Brown, the editing supervisor
was Patricia V. Amoroso, and the production supervisor was Pamela Pelton. It
was set in Palatino by Victoria Khavkina of McGraw-Hill's Professional Book
Group composition unit.*

Printed and bound by Quebecor/Fairfield.

Managing Risk in the Foreign Exchange, Money, and Derivative Markets

Heinz Riehl

McGraw-Hill

New York   San Francisco   Washington, D.C.   Auckland   Bogotá
Caracas   Lisbon   London   Madrid   Mexico City   Milan
Montreal   New Delhi   San Juan   Singapore
Sydney   Tokyo   Toronto

To my mother, ROSEMARIE MOELLER,
who taught me so many valuable things

Contents

Foreword

Risk management is the "buzz phrase" in the financial world at the moment. This is not surprising in the light of the many well published losses in the market. The loss by Barring is perhaps the most notable because it brought down the bank. There are many in the industry who would like to know more about ways of avoiding such a catastrophe.

Value at risk (VAR) is just one risk management technique which has attracted a good deal of interest. It is new and promises control in a world that can seem chaotic and full of pitfalls. The authorities would like to see the VAR model used well. Therefore, it behooves one to understand the concept.

The publication of Heinz Riehl's book does the world a favor by explaining VAR in a way that most of us can understand. This book has not been written for the rocket scientist who wants to learn about VAR. It is for the rest of us.

Mr. Riehl also discusses credit risk in trading with equal clarity. He dissects the different elements of settlement risk and shows how to convert meaningless volume and notional amounts into loan equivalents in presettlement credit risk.

Liquidity risk, planning for funding in contingency scenarios, and balance sheet management are discussed in as straightforward a manner as state of the art internal controls to protect against errors and fraud. Heinz Riehl meets his self-declared standard for clarity in explanations: Eliminate the need to think!

At the heart of the book is a structure so clear that anyone in the industry with a little determination will be able to get a "bird's-eye" view of the subject. This understanding of the structure is essential and is further aided by copious cross references from chapter to chapter.

Eugène Prim, President
The Financial Markets Association*

---

*The Financial Markets Association was formerly known as the A.C.I. or Association Cambiste Internationale, which is the head organization of the International Forex Club.

Preface

Wonderful Company announces $850 million loss resulting from unauthorized Treasury and derivatives activities. Rogue trader had been hiding large risk positions and huge losses. Management was unaware of activities.

Headlines and media stories relating to losses suffered by financial institutions and international industrial companies have become quite common. What has happened is exactly what Federal Reserve Chairman Alan Greenspan warned about in a 1992 speech:

> We must all guard against a situation in which the designers of financial strategies [traders] lack the experience to evaluate the attendant risks, and their experienced senior managers are too embarrassed to admit that they do not understand these new strategies.

The reality today is that traders at banks and nonbanking institutions are motivated, through their eligibility for substantial bonuses, to take substantial risk positions to generate large trading profits. Their supervisors often accept high earnings without understanding how these earnings are generated.

One has to go back to the 1970s to see how the banking profession got into this situation. It all began when the Bretton Woods system collapsed in 1971 and exchange rates floated freely. Then, in 1979, the Federal Reserve discount rate was increased by 3 percent over the weekend, causing huge swings in U.S. dollar interest rates. In fact, twice over a 3-year period they moved from single digits to above 20 percent.

Against this background of volatility in interest rates and exchange rates, banks developed foreign exchange and interest rate hedge instruments (derivatives), allowing customers to protect their base business against gyrations in the financial markets. Obviously, the same instruments that could be used to *protect against* risk could also be used to *assume* risk, and that is precisely what happened on a grand scale. The business volume of foreign exchange and interest-rate-related trading activities skyrocketed. Banks and their customers engaged in trading to protect against risk and also to speculate for profit. This increased volume of trading was supported and facilitated by rapid progress in technology and computer systems that could instantly provide market participants with complex information.

At the same time, banks decided to have more equity capital on their balance sheets partially because they realized this was necessary and partially because regulators were demanding higher capitalization. This resulted in less leverage of banks' balance sheets and larger profit margin requirements in their deposit and loan businesses. To protect targeted returns on equity, it was no longer possible to lend money to creditworthy borrowers and retain those loans on the balance sheet. Bank managers realized that risk versus return was important and that "just making money was not good enough anymore." Banks needed to reduce the amount of loans on the balance sheet, and the solution—loan securitization—led to even more trading activity, which resulted in a need to review the techniques used to manage market risk and develop new methodologies in that area.

This book provides an easy-to-understand, down-to-earth guide that can help transactors and their supervisors fully understand all aspects of the business they are in and recognize how to make money in this new trading environment without engaging in unacceptable risks.

In price risk, which covers activities in foreign exchange, equities, and debt instruments, the focus is on the size of the *risk* instead of the size of *positions*. Volatility discovery is the key term. A good example is life insurance, which on the surface seems to be the most risky of all insurance businesses because a negative outcome always occurs. However, life insurers have a good idea of when people will die (estimate the size of the risk) and charge monthly premiums that allow them to pay out the value of the life insurance policy upon the policyholder's death and still make a profit. If the insurance company misjudges the length of the life of the insured people, i.e., people die earlier than expected, the insurance company would still take in premiums every month (make money) as long as people live, but it would not be enough to pay out the insured amount at the time of death and still have enough left to show a profit. This example highlights that just making money is not good enough any more; therefore, in this book the major emphasis is placed on analyzing return on price risk.

> *Risk management is not risk avoidance; instead, it means to the best of our*
> *ability, estimate the size of the risk and then assure adequate returns.*

The subject of constantly weighing risk versus return and assuring that there is enough return to justify the magnitude of the risk taken is so important to me and so pivotal in this book that I want the reader to take special notice of the only exhibit in this preface.

Just making money is not good enough anymore.

It is clear in any business that there are risks and we must always labor to recognize and quantify the size of those risks. Once the risks have been dimensioned, we must make sure that the returns outweigh those risks. If this positive result of our analysis cannot be assured, it is better not to do the business, because I am sure you guessed it, "Just making money is not good enough anymore!"

The substantial trading in long-term forward contracts (derivatives) also causes counterparty credit risk in addition to price risk. Here again, this book converts meaningless volume and transaction amounts into meaningful loan equivalent amounts. Once we have established these loan equivalents, we can determine minimum profit margins for individual transactions and portfolios to justify the creation of the loan equivalent amounts.

Another important and often underrated type of risk is funding liquidity: the ability to pay when contractual obligations are due. This book shows the latest techniques for managing liquidity on the asset and liability side and highlights the need for contingency funding plans to cope with different adverse scenarios. A discussion of liquidity management blends into balance sheet management for both liquidity and capital ratio purposes.

Finally, the risks involved in all aspects of processing the various transactions are discussed and state-of-the-art control techniques are explained. The focus here is on protecting against fraud and human error.

The frequency and magnitude of mishaps at many of the finest financial institutions have alerted regulators around the world to the need for education in this area throughout these organizations. The following analogy illustrates the point. At the end of the nineteenth century the first automobiles rolled through the streets, killing unsuspecting children at play. The world demanded an end to the building of automobiles. Instead, the driver's license was introduced to ensure that only people who knew how to handle a car would drive. Exactly the same is true for the financial markets business today. When people do not know what they are doing, substantial losses can occur, whereas for skilled participants, there are great opportunities. Against this background, many countries are now requiring that at least some people at the board level understand this business. As in street traffic, a greater depth of understanding will not eliminate accidents but will reduce them substantially.

> *The overall goal of risk management education as described in this book is to convert opportunistic transactors into risk-return-conscious people who behave as if they owned the business.*

It is important that traders and their supervisors understand the conceptual change recommended in this book, i.e., that they become entrepreneurs and behave like owners, instead of "just making money." The people who resist change will soon find that the world moved on without them, and that they are left behind. They will face the unpleasant reality that TIME WITHOUT CHANGE PRODUCES ONLY AGE. There is nothing we can do about it. In terms of calendar age, we know that with every year that passes we are one year older. In terms of physical age, some of us try to fool nature, but it does not work. Just look at the family album to see what you and your family and friends looked like twenty years ago. It is clear we cannot stop our physical aging.

However, there is one notable exception, and that is our professional age. If we keep up with change in our professional area, we can remain young professionally. This is important to understand. We should therefore not resist change in this area. For a trader in financial markets this means to stop "just making money." Instead, she should behave like an owner who assesses the risk and relates earnings to these risks. In this sense this book hopes to facilitate a change in traders' attitudes and make a contribution to the reader's eternal professional youth.

Acknowledgments

I would like to thank Citibank for having provided an environment in which I was able to develop and apply many of the ideas expressed in this book. The bank's treasurers and risk managers, especially in South America, provided invaluable feedback. In particular, I would like to thank my good friend Fernando Botargues, Vice President of Citibank in New York, for his contributions to this book.

I would also like to thank Beatriz Rincon Young of BankBoston in Boston for her input and suggestions, as well as Barbara Robinson, Senior Consultant with Childs Consulting Associates in Southfield, Michigan, for her assistance in structuring my material and her linguistic polishing of the text.

Last but not least I would like to thank my wife, Jill, for valuable suggestions, particularly in the chapter on options, and for her overall support and encouragement for this project.

Heinz Riehl

Managing Risk in the Foreign Exchange, Money, and Derivative Markets

1
Strategy of a Modern Bank

Management Objective: Increase Shareholder Value

Downsizing, rightsizing, mission statements, target marketing, customer focus, risk management. These are all buzzwords in an increasingly sophisticated global marketplace, and in fact, you probably are applying these concepts right now in order to increase . . . well, to increase what? What *is* the primary focus of corporate management? Certainly you want to improve cash flows, enhance the company's image and creditworthiness, and produce better products and/or services for your customers. But what is the ultimate reason for all these important goals? The management of a bank or any other corporation has only one objective that interests the owners of the business—i.e., the stockholders—and that is to increase shareholder value, which in most cases means increasing the price of the stock. Shareholders are happy when their equity in the company continually increases in value, and investors are attracted to companies with the potential for growth.

Of course, management cannot directly influence the market price for a company's shares, which is controlled by and depends on the overall trend in the market. In other words, only the market, influenced by the political and economic environment, can change the price of a stock. The only way in which a company can influence its market value is to improve its performance continually by increasing the amount of earnings per share (EPS). This figure is derived by dividing the earnings of a corporation by the number of outstanding shares of stock.

EPS increases when a corporation earns more revenue, but only if it earns that revenue through its business activities and not by issuing more shares of stock. Infusing revenue into a company by issuing additional shares of stock only dilutes the EPS figure. By contrast, if a company continues to make more money *without* issuing additional shares, the EPS increases and the price of the stock eventually should increase as well (Exhibit 1-1).

The "true price" of an investment is reflected in the relationship between the market value of the stock (price) and the company's income (earnings per share), commonly referred to as the price/earnings ratio (P/E ratio). An example can illustrate why this ratio is referred to as the true price. Suppose you call your broker to ask for the price of Wonderful Company shares and she tells you that the market price of the stock is 40. To decide whether to buy the stock, you need to know whether 40 is a high price or a low price for Wonderful Company stock. Obviously, you need more information to answer that question. Specifically, you want to know how much money the company makes and how many shares of stock are outstanding. It could be that the company issued 1 million shares of stock and earned $1 million. This translates into an EPS of 1 or a P/E ratio of 40 (40/1)—an indication that the price of the stock is high. However, if the EPS is 10, resulting in a P/E ratio of 4 (40/10), it is an indication that the price is low. This example illustrates the fact that the observed market price of a company's stock is meaningless without information about the company's income as represented by the P/E ratio.

Exhibit 1-2 shows how the P/E ratios of three rental properties reflect the relationship between the market price and the amount of income each property generates.

Even though the market price of apartment house C is higher than that of apartment house A, the true price is lower for apartment house C because the relationship between the income ($500,000) and the observed market price ($3 million) indicates a more favorable P/E ratio

	EPS	STOCK PRICE
Year 1	$6	60
Year 2	$7	70
Year 3	$8	80
Year 4	$9	99

Exhibit 1-1. Effect of EPS on stock price.

APARTMENT HOUSES			
	A	**B**	**C**
Market Price (Observed Price)	800,000	4,000,000	3,000,000
Income (Rent)	100,000	400,000	500,000
Price/Earnings Ratio (True Price)	8	10	6

Exhibit 1-2. True price of a real estate investment.

STOCK			
	A	**B**	**C**
Market Price (Observed Price)	100	30	40
Income (Dividend)	20	3	5
Price/Earnings Ratio (True Price)	5	10	8

Exhibit 1-3. True price of a stock investment that pays dividends.

(6) for the buyer. In the stock example in Exhibit 1-3, company A has the lowest P/E ratio because it has the highest return on investment.

The observed price of a stock represents the present value of all market-expected future cash flows for a company. The P/E ratio relates the market's perception of a company's future performance to its current performance. A comparatively high P/E ratio means that the price is high for the amount of earnings the company currently is generating per share. An "overvalued stock" reflects a shared belief among market participants that a company's earnings will be higher in the future. A comparatively low P/E ratio reflects the opposite belief.

Exhibit 1-4 shows that if a company has consistent increases in earnings, the market's expectations of future cash flows will be higher, and therefore the market will value the company at a higher price. This higher price is reflected through an increase in the P/E ratio from 10 to 11, which gives a double boost to the stock price, increasing it to 99 instead of 90.

	EPS	STOCK PRICE	P/E RATIO
Year 1	$6	60	10
Year 2	$7	70	10
Year 3	$8	80	10
Year 4	$9	99	11

Exhibit 1-4. Effect of a rising EPS and stock price on the P/E ratio.

If a company demonstrates to investors an ability *to consistently increase earnings per share rather than just make more money,* the P/E ratio eventually will improve. Remember, the objective is to make more money by increasing EPS without issuing more shares of stock.

Sources of Earnings

So far this discussion has focused on management's attempt to increase the price of a stock by increasing earnings per share. At this point it is appropriate to ask, where do these new revenues come from? Banks have two sources of revenue to increase their earnings. The largest part of earnings (far more than half) usually comes from the differential between interest earned on loans and interest paid on deposits. This difference is referred to as the *net revenue from funds,* which implies the use of money. A smaller part of a bank's earnings comes from *nonfunds revenue*—service-based fees and/or commissions and trading profits—which does not require the use of money. Management uses these two income streams to increase EPS within the context of a minimum capital/asset ratio that is mandated by the regulators.

In the past, an individual bank often could decide how much equity—capital owned by the stockholders—it needed to maintain capital adequacy. Since the early 1990s (see Chap. 13) regulators have determined the minimum percentage of assets that must be retained as equity capital. The deposit and loan business (net revenue from funds) generates risk assets on the balance sheet. Whenever the "holy cow"—the balance sheet—is touched, the incremental capital needed to support the incremental risk assets must be generated through retained earnings. In other words, capital must grow at the same rate as assets and liabilities to maintain the capital/asset ratio mandated by regulators or targeted by management.

For example, assume that regulators mandate a minimum capital/asset ratio of 5 percent for ABC Bank. Exhibit 1-5, shows that a 10 percent

ASSETS			LIABILITIES		
		10% Growth			**10% Growth**
Misc. Assets	1,000	1,100	Misc. Liab.	950	1,045
			Capital	50	55
Total Assets	1,000	1,100	Total Assets	1,000	1,100

Exhibit 1-5. Maintaining capital adequacy.

increase in loans, from 1000 to 1100, requires a corresponding 10 percent increase in capital from 50 to 55 to maintain the required capital/asset ratio of 5 percent.

This incremental $5 in required capital should not come from the issuance of new shares because, as was said above, management's main objective is to increase the price of the stock by increasing EPS. The issuing of new shares makes it necessary to earn even more money to increase the earnings for each one of the now-enlarged number of shares outstanding. Instead, the incremental capital must come from retained earnings, specifically earnings retained from the transactions which created the need for more capital in the first place. In other words, incremental assets and liabilities on the balance sheet must be priced so that after expenses, taxes, and a possibly growing dividend, there is enough profit left in the form of retained earnings to support the incremental assets from the viewpoint of capital adequacy.

What can happen if ABC Bank's capital/asset ratio drops below its mandated percentage, for example, from 5 percent to 4 percent? In the first place, the regulator will demand a rapid reduction in assets (sell loans) and/or an increase in equity capital (issue new shares). The regulator will prohibit any new business expansion and may demand partial or complete replacement of the management. The bank may be forced to sign a memorandum of understanding (MOU) in which it agrees to take these steps and consult with the regulator before making any significant decisions. In addition, investment advisers will recognize that ABC Bank is undercapitalized and will advise its shareholders to sell their stock. For the same reason, depositors will withdraw their savings from the bank. All this is highly undesirable, and therefore the minimum capital ratio must be maintained.

Banks require enough capital to maintain capital adequacy, and as was said previously, any *incremental capital must come from retained earnings.* If most of the bank's business is the traditional deposit and loan business on the balance sheet, the interest differential spread on all new loans and deposits has to be so large that even after allowing for all expenses, taxes, and possibly an annually growing dividend, there is enough left as retained earnings for capital to grow at the same rate that applies to assets. In the illustration in Exhibit 1-4, that means 10 percent of capital ($5) in retained earnings.

From this discussion, it can be seen that just making money is not good enough any more. The word *anymore* is important here because there was a time when you were a hero if you made $10 million, but this no longer is true. Today the boss will first ask you to what extent you touched the holy cow and how much capital you are tying up in the transactions with which you made the $10 million, in other words, how many incremental assets requiring capital coverage you added to the balance sheet.

Equity Capital and Leverage

The capital/asset ratio is also known as the leverage ratio. The following example illustrates this concept. Suppose you want to make an investment that will provide a 25 percent return on your money (return on equity target) and decide to purchase an apartment priced at $100,000 with the intention of renting it out. You pay $20,000 of your own money in cash and take a mortgage for the remaining $80,000. After 1 year the price of the apartment rises to $105,000. Was this a good investment? Did you achieve your return on equity (ROE) target? Assuming that your rental income equals all mortgage interest payments and costs and the cash flows equal zero, the answer is yes to both questions. The increase in the market price from $100,000 to $105,000 is only 5 percent, but if you decide to sell the apartment after 1 year for $105,000, you will earn $5,000 on your $20,000 cash investment, giving you a 25 percent ROE.

To continue, assume you have the same ROE target of 25 percent, but instead of paying $20,000 in cash, you pay the entire $100,000 out of your own pocket. To earn a 25 percent return, you need a much larger spread; the market has to go from $100,000 to $125,000. If you borrow $90,000 and invest only $10,000 in cash, a spread from $100,000 to $102,500 is enough for a 25 percent return. You can see that *the more leverage there is (the smaller the investment), the smaller the spread has to be to achieve a satisfactory return.*

Is a 20 percent ROE an unrealistic goal for a bank? In purchasing a $100,000 apartment, if the investment is 5 percent ($5000 down payment), the price of the apartment has to increase to only $101,000 for you to make 20 percent on the $5000 investment. You can see that in a *highly leveraged situation,* the *spread does not have to be very large* to achieve a 20 percent return.

Return on equity is a profitability ratio that expresses earnings as a percentage of net worth on the balance sheet. Return on assets (ROA), sometimes referred to as the spread, is a profitability ratio that expresses earnings as a percentage of the total assets on the balance sheet. The size of the minimum spread (ROA) required to achieve the bank's objective of maintaining capital adequacy while increasing EPS results from the capital asset/ratio mandated by the regulator and the return on equity capital (ROE) target set by management.

Exhibit 1-6 illustrates how different leverage scenarios affect the minimum spread. If leverage remains unchanged and the ROE objective is increased, a larger spread (ROA) is needed to maintain the regulator-mandated capital/asset ratio. If the ROE objective is decreased, the spread can be smaller.

For example, with a capital/asset ratio (leverage) target of 5 percent[1] and a goal of earning 20 percent on that 5 percent of capital, the minimum spread has to be 1 percent (20 percent of 5 percent) *after* tax (assuming a tax rate of 50 percent). You can see that lower leverage (6 percent in Exhibit 1-6) and/or higher ROE expectations (24 percent) require a larger minimum spread (1.2 percent). Likewise, higher leverage (4 percent) and/or lower ROE expectations (16 percent) require a smaller minimum spread (0.8 percent) to maintain the minimum required capital/asset ratio.

When a bank has a small amount of capital compared with assets, it is

CORPORATE RETURN TARGETS					
	Unchanged Leverage			Higher Leverage	Lower Leverage
	%	%	%	%	%
Capital/Asset Ratio (Leverage)	5	5	5	4	6
Return on Equity Capital (ROE)	20	24	16	20	20
Return on Assets Before 50% Tax	2	2.4	1.6	1.6	2.4
Return on Assets After Tax (ROA) (Minimum spread)	1	1.2	0.8	0.8	1.2

Exhibit 1-6. Correlation of leverage and ROE with required minimum spread.

highly leveraged and a small profit is enough to yield an attractive return on equity capital. However, when a bank has a large amount of capital relative to assets, it has less leverage and requires a large profit margin to earn an equally attractive return on its equity.

Higher leverage allows a smaller return on assets without reducing ROE.

It seems obvious that banks want to be highly leveraged to earn sufficient profits to meet their return targets and maintain capital adequacy. However, there is a catch, and the following story illustrates the dilemma. A group of people get together and invest in a lottery ticket; they win a very large prize and decide to use the winnings to open a new bank. Subsequently, the partners have a meeting to determine the capital ratio they will maintain for the bank. The first partner says, "Let's have a small amount of capital, just the bare minimum. Then we will need only a small profit on our assets to have a high return on the little equity we have." The second partner says, "Oh, no, I want to have a very strong bank with lots of capital. When I slip my business card to someone at the country club, I want everybody to say, 'What a strong bank! AAA.'"

Which partner is correct? The problem with the first partner's solution is that with low capitalization, no matter how brilliant they are at leveraging their capital, other people, including banks, will refuse to do business with them. Also, the bank will not be creditworthy, and therefore rating agencies will downgrade it, preventing it from getting credit lines. The problem with the second partner's solution is that the bank must make an enormous amount of money to gain a reasonable return on the very large equity. Therefore, the dilemma is between low capital and poor credit ratings on one side and high capital and a large ROA requirement on the other side.

Sweet Spot Capital/Asset Ratio

The correct solution for banks is to have just enough capital so that the counterparties with which they want to do business will accept them without question. If a bank has less than this, it has an insufficient amount and may get into counterparty and credit rating trouble; if it has more, it has too much capital and may not be optimizing it. A bank aims for the "sweet spot," which means having just enough capital so that it is accepted without question by all counterparties with which it wants to do business.

Desirable equity capital: enough but not too much (sweet spot).

All tennis players and golfers know what the sweet spot is, particularly if they are not very good at these sports. When you hit the ball incorrectly, your hand hurts and you make a terrible shot. But every now and then, when you hit the sweet spot, it feels like butter. You have hit the ball "just right" and the ball does just what you want.

Banks have more capital today than they had in the 1980s. This increased capitalization has resulted in part because there has been a regulatory push for it and in part because banks want to have more capital. From the above example of the lottery winners, it is clear that with less leverage and more capital, banks require bigger spreads whenever they touch the holy cow, that is, put something on the balance sheet.

If banks relied on the deposit and loan business to maintain the capital/asset ratio and increase earnings per share, they would have to make a minimum spread on those assets. For example, assume for the purpose of discussion that banks need a minimum spread of 2 percent. This requirement leads to what some people call a strategic dilemma:

- More earnings are needed for higher earnings per share.
- More assets are required for more earnings.
- More capital is required to support more assets.
- More capital cannot come from new shares.
- More capital must come from retained earnings.
- The minimum spread for retaining earnings must be 2 percent.
- Borrowers paying a 2 percent spread are not creditworthy.
- Creditworthy customers do not pay a 2 percent spread.
- But more earnings are needed for higher earnings per share.
- More assets are required for more earnings, and so on.

In other words, if a bank tries to make its minimum spread solely from loans, creditworthy borrowers will be unhappy because the spread and the resulting lending rate are too high. On the other side, if a bank increases the balance sheet by taking deposits which are not needed to fund already-existing assets—i.e., becomes a liability-driven bank—it must pay below the market interest rate to make the minimum spread and the depositors will be unhappy.

In recent years banks have solved this dilemma by going into the type of business that requires little or no capital investment and generates nonfunds revenue, such as fees and trading profits. For example, if an investor buys a car for $20,000 in cash and sells it the same day for $24,000,[2] only the profit of $4000 goes on the balance sheet. This type of yield-enriching product generates nonfunds revenues, which implies that there is no use of money. The simple objective of this solution is to enrich the substandard spreads in the interest differential business to such an extent that the combined earnings from fees and trading profits on one side and whatever spread a bank can get as an interest differential on the other side add up to the targeted ROA.

Here is one more example to illustrate this point. Suppose MegaBank makes a $100 million loan at a 0.5 percent per annum (p.a.) spread when the bank requires a 2 percent p.a. spread to maintain capital adequacy. In other words, it makes only $500,000 on the loan when it needs to make $2 million. To supplement the yield of the substandardly priced loan, the bank needs fee income and trading profits of $1.5 million.

Spread on loan of $100MM at 0.5 percent p.a.	$ 500,000
Fees and trading profits from the same customer	$1,500,000
Total earnings	$2,000,000, or 2 percent ROA

When the income streams of the two types of business are combined—interest differential enriched by fees and trading profits from the same customer—MegaBank earns the required spread of $2 million, which equals the ROA target of 2 percent p.a.

Account/Product Profitability

Note in the preceding example that MegaBank's fees and trading profits and the spread on the loan were generated from the same customer. This example focuses on the necessity of monitoring and measuring earnings by customer and using that information as the basis for future account planning and performance reviews. For instance, the dollar earnings on a customer account may appear to be profitable, but in fact the earnings are not sufficient to meet the ROA target. In this situation corrective action is required to increase the profitability of the account; if it cannot be improved sufficiently to meet the corporate return targets, it may be necessary to terminate the relationship.

This is another example of why just making money is not good enough.

As in any multiproduct company, the wide range of bank products requires an aggressive product management program. This process begins with the development of a detailed product description and risk analysis *before* the product is introduced to the market and continues with the tracking of earnings by product and by customer. Another story can illustrate the necessity of measuring product profitability. Advanced Bicycle Company (ABC) successfully produces an excellent hybrid bicycle for adults. Earnings rose from $10 million 2 years ago to $12 million last year, and everything is wonderful. In fact, things are so good that ABC introduced a second type of bicycle for children, and the company's earnings continue to grow to $15 million. ABC seems to be enjoying success with the new bicycle, and management considers increasing production. However, if ABC follows through with this plan without analyzing where the earnings are coming from, it may experience a disaster. It is possible that the company made $18 million on the adult bicycle and lost $3 million on the children's bicycle for a total profit of $15 million. Without a product profitability analysis, the company may commit resources—money and people—to producing the new product without realizing that the more children's bikes it sells, the more money it is going to lose.

To summarize, earnings are measured in two ways—by customer and by product—but the earnings total is the same with either measurement. Account profitability reports and product profitability reports provide management with the information needed to make decisions affecting relationships with customers and develop product plans with the goal of increasing earnings per share.

Changes in Banking

The point here is that an evolution has taken place in the banking industry. Traditionally, banks served as intermediaries between borrowers and lenders by making loans and accepting deposits. All this business was on the balance sheet, the focus was on credit/loan risk, and profit was derived from the interest rate differential. Banks still serve as intermediaries between customers who have money and those who need it, but the business no longer is on the balance sheet. The people who once were depositors have become investors in the debt instruments issued by those who need money. To continue to be intermediaries between customers who have money and those who need money and to increase nonfunds revenue, banks are *securitizing* their assets and liabilities for trading purposes.

For example, suppose Wonderful Company needs $100 million. Instead of directly borrowing that amount, it calls ABC Bank and asks for the price the bank would pay to purchase a 1-year promissory note with a face value of $100 million. Instead of debiting the bank's loan account and lending the money on the balance sheet, ABC Bank purchases an "IOU" from Wonderful Company and sells this security to other people who have money to invest. For this intermediation service, the bank charges a fee.

The same thing happens when the bank grants a mortgage to a home buyer. The bank originates the mortgage, charges a 1 or 2 percent flat fee up front, gives the money to the home buyer, bundles the mortgage with a thousand other mortgages into one mortgage-backed security, and sells the security to a big investor. The bank services the individual mortgages for the investor and charges fees accordingly; the home buyer, instead of being a borrower, is the issuer of a debt instrument.

This securitization of instruments, which also is known as asset trading, has several advantages over the traditional deposit and loan business. Asset trading does not affect the capital/asset ratio. If the bank buys and sells without recourse (see Chap. 13) on the same day, the mandated minimum ratio is irrelevant because the transactions are never on the balance sheet. Instead of unhappy borrowers and depositors, there now are three happy participants: Borrowers (issuers) have lower borrowing costs, depositors (investors) enjoy a higher yield, and the bank has the right kind of earnings.

Previously, when the main business was deposits and loans, earnings came from accrued interest differentials and credit risk was the dominant risk. Now the main business is asset trading, the earnings are trading profits, and price risk is the dominant risk. Securitization originally was developed to avoid touching the holy cow; now it also is used to manage liquidity (see Chap. 12) and manage the balance sheet (see Chap. 13).

After the bank buys a debt instrument from a customer who needs money, the bank may not immediately sell this instrument. In such a situation, the market interest rate may rise, causing a reduction of the security's price, and the bank loses money without anybody going bankrupt—this is price risk. When the bank trades foreign exchange or securities with customers, the bank's profit is either built into the transaction price as a spread or charged separately as a commission. If the bank immediately lays off the transaction in the market, this customer-related profit will be locked in. However, if the bank holds on to the acquired asset even for only a short period, the market rate may change and either enlarge the already existing customer-related profit or produce a loss. In other words, the bank has assumed price risk.

Change in Banking

Old Bank

- Lend to borrowers.
- Accept deposits.

New Bank

- Previous borrowers are issuers.
- Previous depositors are investors.

Asset Trading

- Price risk is dominant.

This analysis of the evolution of banking highlights the emphasis banks place on managing risk in traded instruments—including financial derivatives such as forwards, swaps, futures, and options, in addition to instruments relating to loan securitization—and shows that this business has become far more complex. For this reason, it is necessary to take a closer look at the management of all trading-related risks and at the new and improved methods of risk management that have been developed to help banks understand the business, recognize and assess the size of the risks, and then limit and/or control those risks.

Notes

1. In Exhibit 1-5, a capital/asset ratio of 5 percent is used as an example. In reality, the capital/asset ratio is made up of two tiers. Tier 1 consists of stockholders' equity and retained earnings; tier 2 consists of supplementary capital consisting of perpetual debt, preferred stock, and a negotiated percentage of reserves for loan losses. Also, the capital ratio is based on risk-adjusted assets as defined in Chap. 13.
2. Forward trade contracts involve counterparty credit risk, which also requires a small percentage of capital coverage (see Chap. 9).

2
Understanding the Business, Recognizing Price Risk

Changes in the banking business that are driven by the need to maintain capital adequacy while increasing earnings per share have altered the focus of risk management. In asset trading, the spread between what the issuer pays and what the investor earns is much narrower than it is in the interest differential business. Banks can trade at a very fine spread, say, $\frac{1}{8}$ percent or $\frac{1}{4}$ percent, because these transactions are not kept on the balance sheet and therefore do not affect the capital/asset ratio. However, for the short time the bank holds a security before selling it to an investor, there is the risk that the price of the security will drop if interest rates rise.

For example, XYZ Corporation issues a 1-year promissory note with a face value of $100 million and a coupon of 10 percent. On the first day of the transaction, at 9 in the morning, NBC Bank buys the security at a price of 100; that is, the bank pays XYZ Corporation $100 million and the company agrees to redeem the security after 1 year in exchange for the $100 million principal plus $10 million in interest, which is equal to the 10 percent coupon. Ten minutes after XYZ Corporation and NBC Bank agree to the deal, the Federal Reserve Bank increases interest rates by 1 percent; interest rates, which were 10 percent, are now 11 percent. To persuade an investor to buy the security, NBC Bank will have to offer the market rate of 11 percent even though it will receive only 10 percent from the issuer. The bank sells the debt instrument, which it bought at 100, for a lower price, in this case 99.1, and suffers a loss of 0.9. In the opposite scenario, interest rates can drop. If they fall, say, from 10 percent to 9 percent, the price of the security will increase to 100.9. The investor buys at 100.9, and NBC Bank makes 0.9 percent on the sale.

This example shows that as security trading increases as a banking activity, the focus on price risk also increases. For a bank, price risk is the risk that an adverse change in the market price will occur while the bank holds a speculative or customer-related net position in commodities, interest rates, or option-implied volatility.

Net Positions In Commodities

Changes in commodity prices affect the value of net positions in equities and foreign currencies. A net position includes what is on the balance sheet (assets and liabilities) plus what is not yet on the balance sheet but is irrevocably committed (unliquidated purchases and sales). In calculating a net position, assets and unliquidated purchases are positive values and liabilities and unliquidated sales are negative values (Exhibit 2-1).

A net long position means that the total of assets and unliquidated purchases is greater than the total of liabilities and unliquidated sales. A net short position is just the opposite.

Unliquidated purchases represent assets a bank is committed to purchase but does not yet have in its possession. For example, on Tuesday, June 10, BigBank negotiates the price of 100 shares of ABC stock at $42.50 and makes a commitment to purchase the shares on Friday. Three days later, on June 13, BigBank gets the shares and has to pay $4250. BigBank makes a deal on June 10 for value date June 13 (3 business days) and has a net long position in ABC shares beginning on June 10.

Net Position

+	-
Assets	Liabilities
Unliquidated purchases	Unliquidated sales

Exhibit 2-1. Four items make up net position.

Net positions carry a certain amount of risk. For example, suppose the deal to purchase shares of ABC stock at $42.50 is made at 11:05 a.m. on June 10 and at 11:06 the price of ABC stock drops from $42.50 to $41.50. Is this good for the bank? The answer is no. BigBank has a net long position of 100 shares and loses $1 per share, or $100, even though the net position is an unliquidated purchase. On June 13 the bank takes delivery of the shares and pays $4250 even though the market value may still be $4150.

With a net long position, an investor makes money if the price goes up and loses money if the price goes down; with a net short position, an investor loses money if the price goes up and makes money if the price goes down.

A net exchange position is a long or short position in a foreign currency. Although the above statement about making or losing money with net positions generally is true, it is possible to have a net exchange position that is net long in a currency and not lose money when the exchange rate goes down. Two examples illustrate this point.

The first example involves a bank outside the United States that needs to acquire dollars for 1 year. The market is quoting the following interest and exchange rates:

1-year local currency	3 percent p.a.
1-year Eurodollars	7 percent p.a.
Interest rate differential	4 percent p.a.
Spot rate	1.8000
1-year forward rate	1.7280

There are two ways in which the bank can acquire the dollars. The first alternative is straightforward: borrow the dollars directly at 7 percent. The second alternative is to borrow the local currency at 3 percent, sell the local currency, and buy dollars at the spot rate of 1.8000 *without* forward cover. If the bank chooses the second solution, it will have a net long position in dollars and a net short position in the local currency, which may result in an exchange loss if the exchange rate for dollars declines. In that case, the bank still will be ahead as long as the dollar does not depreciate more than the interest saving of 4 percent. The breakeven foreign exchange (FX) rate is the same as the forward rate of 1.7280 (1.80 minus the 4 percent interest differential). Suppose the dollar drops to 1.74. The bank has an exchange loss, but it is still ahead because the size of the interest saving (4 percent) exceeds the amount of the exchange loss (3.33 percent).[1]

The risk of the net long dollar position resulting from borrowing local currency and exchanging it for dollars is that the dollar will depreciate, causing an exchange loss. However, as the example illustrates, if the interest saving is larger than the exchange loss, it is possible to have an exchange loss and still make an overall profit.

One more example can demonstrate the management of a net exchange position. Assume the same market rates as those in the previous example, but for a shorter period. Mega Company needs to borrow dollars for 3 months. The treasurer sees that the company can borrow the local currency for 3 percent and thinks, "Why should I borrow dollars at 7 percent when money is also available at 3 percent?" The problem is that he will have to borrow in another currency. The bank assures the treasurer that the dollar is stable, and so the treasurer borrows the local currency at 3 percent and converts it into dollars at a rate of US$1/1.80. Now Mega Company is long in dollars and short in the local currency.

Three months later the dollar drops from 1.8000 to 1.7800, and Mega Company has an exchange loss of 0.0200. The treasurer loses 200 points on the exchange and saves 4 percent in interest. Is there any way of telling whether he has sustained a loss?

To compare the exchange loss with the interest saving, we convert the 200 exchange points for 3 months into an annual percentage of 4.44 percent p.a. The exchange loss expressed as a percentage is added to the 3 percent cost of borrowing the local currency for a total cost of 7.44 percent p.a., which is higher than the cost of borrowing dollars at 7 percent:

Spot LCY/$	1.8000
Spot 3 months	1.7800
FX loss	0.0200 = 4.44 percent p.a.
Cost of LCY (Local Currency)	+3.00 percent
Cost of created $	7.44 percent
Cost of actual $	7.00 percent
Net loss	0.44 percent

The breakeven exchange rate would have been 1.7820. If you compare this rate with the breakeven rate for 1 year in the first example (1.7280), you can see that when the time period is shorter, the discount is smaller and the breakeven point therefore is higher.

At the end of 3 months the treasurer says the company has a choice. It can buy back local currency, sell the dollars, and realize the loss (0.44

percent), or, because it still needs dollars, it can roll over the transaction and do it again. In this case the company borrows the local currency for another 3 months and extends the length of the net exchange position.

The treasurer is sure the dollar will not drop further, but he is wrong. It goes down to 1.77. Now Mega Company has an exchange loss of 300 points over 6 months. Does the treasurer have a profit or a loss? The exchange loss converted into an annual interest percentage is 3.33 percent p.a. The 300 points is a larger exchange loss, but 3.33 percent is good news, because when it is added to the 3 percent borrowing cost, the total cost of the dollars is 6.33 percent. Since the total cost is less than the 7 percent dollar interest rate, the company has made a *profit* of 67 basis points. The breakeven exchange rate would have been 1.7640.

Spot LCY/$	1.8000
Spot 6 months	1.7700
FX loss	0.0300 = 3.33 percent p.a.
Cost of LCY	+3.00 percent
Cost of created $	6.33 percent
Cost of actual $	7.00 percent
Net profit	0.67 percent

It seems that the more money the company loses, the better off it is. Why? When Mega Company spreads the 300-point loss over 6 months, it continues to gain from interest savings over the same period and therefore shows a profit. The interest differential is an accumulation of interest, and the longer it accumulates, the more there is.

The longer the time period, the greater the discount and the lower the breakeven point. Exhibit 2-2 illustrates this point.

Interest Difference	Time Period	Spot FX Swap Rate	Forward Breakeven Rate
		LCY 1.8000	
4% p.a.	12 Mo.	.0720	LCY 1.7280
	6 Mo.	.0360	1.7640
	3 Mo.	.0180	1.7820
	1 Mo.	.0060	1.7940
	1 Day	.0002	1.7998
	2 Days	.0004	1.7996
	3 Days	.0006	1.7994
	17 Days	.0034	1.7966

Exhibit 2-2. The effect of time on breakeven rates.

Net Exchange Positions on and off the Balance Sheet

Net foreign exchange positions can be either on or off the balance sheet. To illustrate, assume the same rates that were used in the previous examples:

1-year Eurodollars	7 percent
1-year local currency	3 percent
Interest rate differential	4 percent
Spot rate	1.8000
Swap rate	0.0720
1-year forward rate	1.7280

The following transaction illustrates how an exchange position can be on the balance sheet:

Borrow local currency at 3 percent.

Sell local currency and buy dollars spot at 1.80.

Invest dollars for 1 year at 7 percent.

One year later, reverse the transaction:

Collect dollars plus 7 percent interest.

Buy LCY and sell dollars spot at 1.80.

Repay the local currency plus 3 percent.

There is no exchange profit or loss; the interest gain is 4 percent.

The balance sheet reflects the liability created by borrowing the local currency and the asset created by purchasing dollars. These two transactions result in a short position in local currency and a long position in dollars. Even though the profit appears in the interest differential account, the nature of the risk is foreign exchange.

In this situation customers are well advised to accrue in a subsidiary account the interest costs they would have incurred if they had borrowed the currency they really need. In so doing, they build a reserve for the exchange losses that can occur. For example, if they borrow for a year, there may be no exchange losses in the first 5 months but exchange losses will occur in the remaining 7 months. If no such reserve is set up, they will show very large earnings in the marked-to-market position because of the low interest rate cost during the first 5 months of the 1-year period and then very high financing costs because of the exchange losses that could occur in the remaining 7 months.

In structuring on-balance-sheet FX transactions, the exact total cost of the borrowing is not known until the foreign exchange position is closed. Up to that point customers should accrue at the interest rate they would have paid if they had borrowed the currency they really need—or maybe at a slightly lower interest rate. For example, if the currency needed is dollars at 7 percent and the currency actually borrowed is at 3 percent, the customer may accrue a 6 percent cost, which is 1 percent cheaper than borrowing the dollars. If there are no exchange losses initially, the difference between 3 percent and 6 percent will be a reserve that can serve as a buffer if exchange losses occur later.

In high-interest-rate countries, companies frequently borrow low-interest-rate currencies, convert them into the high-interest-rate local currency without forward cover and have very good business results, sometimes over years. Then, at the end of the transaction periods, there is a devaluation which not only substantially distorts the profit and loss (P & L) of the companies but can lead to bankruptcy or financial difficulties because of all the years during which they overstated their earnings. These companies also were taking very big risks, and when those risks suddenly hit, they already had disposed of the earnings and sometimes found it very difficult to deal with the higher cost involved in repaying the low-interest currency.

An off-balance-sheet net position transaction can be structured using the same rates:

Buy dollars and sell the local currency 1 year forward at 1.7280.

One year later, reverse the transaction.

Buy the local currency and sell dollars spot at 1.8000.

The FX gain is 0.0720.

Since this is a forward transaction, it does not appear on the balance sheet. The profit appears on the income statement after the reversing transaction occurs or as the company periodically marks-to-market.

Net Foreign Exchange Positions and Personal Investments

When you buy securities which have been issued in countries other than your own, you also have a net exchange position. This is true even if that security trades at your local exchange and the price is quoted in the local currency.

Take the case of a German individual whose broker advised him to buy the above-mentioned ABC stock at $50. Assuming an exchange rate of DM 2.00 = $1, our German friend will first have to pay DM 100 to purchase $50, creating a net FX position that is long in dollars and short in marks. The just-acquired dollars are now used to purchase ABC stock at the current price of $50.

Scenario I in Exhibit 2-3 shows that the broker gave good advice: The stock rose 10 percent from 50 to 55. The dollar/mark exchange rate has not moved. In scenario II, however, there is still the 10 percent gain on the stock price, but the exchange rate has moved: The dollar has dropped against the mark by 20 percent from DM 2.00 to DM 1.60. The combination of a gain on the stock price and a loss on the FX rate produces an overall loss of 12 percent. If our German friend liquidated his position in ABC stock, he would get $55, or $5 more than he originally paid. But because of the drop in the value of the dollar, the reconversion of $55 into marks at the new lower exchange rate of DM 1.60 produces only DM 88, which is 12 percent less than the DM 100 originally invested.

The same applies to Americans investing in securities issued outside the United States. The danger is that there is a profit on that security calculated in the respective foreign currency but the foreign exchange losses exceed the profit on the security and lead overall to a loss. A doctor would say that the operation was successful but the patient died.

Investing in foreign securities is therefore a double play: one play in the security and another in the foreign currency. This is not always bad. Scenario III shows a case in which the stock loses 10 percent and the currency appreciates for an overall gain of 8 percent. Finally, the markets may both move in our favor (scenario IV) or against us (scenario V), and we are either very happy or very sad.

If we like a foreign security and do not want the simultaneous risk of a net exchange position, we should avoid this risk and either borrow the foreign currency needed for the investment or hedge with a forward/futures exchange contract.

Scenario	Stock Price in Dollars	Percent Change	$/DM FX Rate	Percent Change	Stock Price in Marks	Percent Change
	50		2.00		100	
I	55	10%	2.00		110	10%
II	55	10%	1.60	-20%	88	-12%
III	45	-10%	2.40	20%	108	8%
IV	55	10%	2.40	20%	132	32%
V	45	-10%	1.60	-20%	72	-28%

Exhibit 2-3. Double risk with the purchase of foreign securities.

Do not be fooled by a foreign security trading at a local currency price at your local exchange. The local currency price results from the foreign security's foreign-currency-denominated price at that country's exchange and the exchange rate for the two currencies. For example, some U.S. stocks trade as American depository receipts (ADRs) at foreign exchanges. If ABC stock was traded at an exchange in Germany, its DM-denominated price would equal the "Stock Price in Marks" in Exhibit 2-3.

For U.S. investors in foreign securities who are trading in dollars at U.S. exchanges, this means that they are not only buying the foreign security. In addition, they have a net long exchange position in the foreign currency even though they pay in dollars to purchase the investment.

Interest Rates

You probably have dealt with a wide variety of interest rate instruments. However, if you analyze the different types of interest rate *transactions,* you will see that there are only two types of interest rate *positions:* interest-rate-*level*-sensitive positions and interest-rate-*differential*-sensitive positions.

Interest-Rate-Level-Sensitive Positions

An interest-rate-level-sensitive position is a speculation on the movement of interest rates. Traders try to anticipate when interest rates will rise or fall and try to make a profit by speculating on those movements. The yield curve is a useful indicator of the future interest rate movements expected by market participants. Depending on these expectations, the curve may be normal, steep, or flat/inverted.

This discussion of yield curves is limited to the short-term yield curves prevailing in the money markets, typically up to 1 year. For example, the normal yield curve in Exhibit 2-4 indicates that no specific trend in the market is expected for short-term rates.

However, in a trendless market, long-term interest rates tend to be higher than shorter-term interest rates for three reasons. First, investors forgo the opportunity to compound interest. Second, the longer the tenor is, the more credit risk there is. Third, there is more of a liquidity risk.

A steep yield curve (see Exhibit 2-5) indicates an upward trend. It indicates that near-term supply exceeds demand and long-term demand exceeds supply.

When *investors* expect interest rates to go up, they prefer to invest their money for only a short period with the expectation that at matu-

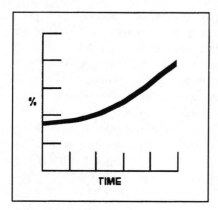

Exhibit 2-4. Normal yield curve.

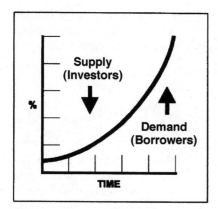

Exhibit 2-5. Steep yield curve.

rity they will invest it again at the then-prevailing higher rate. When *borrowers* expect interest rates to go up, they prefer to borrow today for a longer period to avoid borrowing again later at a higher rate. In an upward trend, investors want to invest for a *shorter* period and borrowers want to borrow for a *longer* period, creating an imbalance in demand and supply. Short-term supply creates a downward pressure on interest rates, and long-term demand creates an upward pressure on interest rates. These two pressures create a steep yield curve. Conversely, when short-term demand creates an upward pressure on interest rates and long-term supply creates a downward pressure, the yield curve is flat or inverted (Exhibit 2-6).

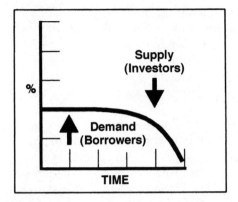

Exhibit 2-6. Flat/inverted yield curve.

As was said above, traders establish interest-rate-level-sensitive positions in order to speculate on the movement of interest rates. These positions are based on the traders' view of future rates, and the risk is that the rates may move in the opposite direction from what the traders expect.

To understand the price risk in an interest-rate-level-sensitive position, let us look at risk in three different types of business:

- *Nonnegotiable Assets/Liabilities*—gaps or mismatches between deposits/borrowings and loans/placements

- *Negotiable Assets/Liabilities*—purchase of fixed-rate securities without matched funding

- *Derivatives*—futures, forward contracts, and interest rate conversion agreements (interest rate swaps)

Nonnegotiable Assets/Liabilities. The first type of business is associated with the deposit/borrowing and loan/placement business. A bank has an interest-rate-level-sensitive position when the tenors for these instruments are mismatched, creating a gap. For example, assume that the interest rate is 10 percent and is expected to decrease in the future. One thing that can be done to prepare for a decline in interest rates is to place money with another bank for 13 months and fund that transaction with a 1-month borrowing, both at 10 percent. This is an interest-rate-level-sensitive position; in this case, the position is a negative gap because when we place long and borrow short, we are positioning ourselves for declining interest rates.

If interest rates drop at the end of 1 month as we expect, perhaps from

10 percent to 9 percent, we pay back what we borrowed and replace it with a borrowing for 12 months at the prevailing interest rate of 9 percent. At the end of the 12-month period we have a profit of 1 percent. However, if interest rates rise from 10 percent to 11 percent and we have to replace the borrowing at the higher interest rate, we will lose 1 percent for 12 months. The sensitivity of a negative gap position is shown in Exhibit 2-7.

Negative gaps built through mismatched assets and liabilities create price risk, and they also create liquidity risk. For example, interest rates may decline as expected, but for some reason the money market is very tight. In this situation, we have a profit on the price risk position but may face significant liquidity problems. If we think that interest rates are going up, we use the opposite strategy by borrowing for 13 months and placing for 1 month. If interest rates go up as expected, after 1 month we can place again for 12 months at the higher interest rate. This is called a positive gap because when we borrow long and place short, we are positioning for rising rates.

The risk in a gapped position is that rates can move in a direction opposite to what we expect. For example, if rates are expected to decrease, we may place for 13 months and borrow for 1 month at 10 percent. Then, if the rates go up, we have to replace the borrowing at the higher rate, say 11 percent or 12 percent. In this scenario we lose. It is important to recognize the price risk in gapped positions.

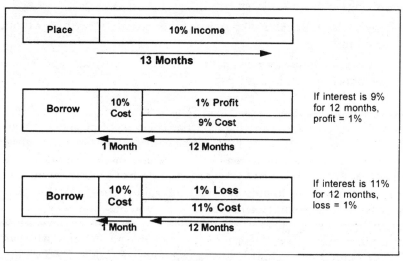

Exhibit 2-7. Negative gap: gapping with a bank placement.

Negotiable Assets/Liabilities. The second type of business—negotiable assets and liabilities—is associated with a different transaction technique but carries the same kind of interest-rate-level risk that characterizes gapping against nonnegotiable assets. This business is different because instead of borrowing and lending money, we are buying and selling securities, and the amount of liquidity risk is reduced because of the trading characteristics of the instruments.

For example, suppose we buy a fixed-coupon bond today at 100 with a 10 percent coupon and a remaining life of 13 months. Anticipating a decline in interest rates, we fund the asset with a 1-month borrowing. As a result, we are exposed to interest rate risk for 12 months, beginning 1 month from now. Assume that the same interest rate move occurs: The rate falls from 10 percent to 9 percent. When this happens, the price of the bond rises to approximately 101. At the end of the 1-month period we sell the bond at 101 and use the cash to pay back the money we borrowed. Our profit is 1 percent flat. The risk is that if the interest rate moves to 11 percent instead of 9 percent, the price of the bond will drop to approximately 99 and we will lose 1 percent flat on the sale of the bond. Exhibit 2-8 illustrates the risk of gapping with bond purchases.

Although this transaction technique is very different from the negative gap, the two transactions represent the same type of price risk.

There are many more products and instruments with which one can assume price risk than there are types of price risk. Each type of price risk is measured consistently, regardless of the instrument with which price risk is assumed.

Date	Action	Tenor Remaining Life	Coupon	Price	Market rate / Yield	P & L
Today	Buy bond/sell money Borrow money	13 months 1 month	10%	$100	10% p.a. 10% p.a.	
One month later: Rate decreases or Rate increases	Sell bond/purchase money Repay borrowed money or Sell bond/purchase money Repay borrowed money	12 months 12 months	10% 10%	$101 $99	9% p.a. 11% p.a.	1% (1%)

Exhibit 2-8. Gapping with bond purchases.

In comparing money market gapping and gapping with negotiable securities, we note a substantial difference in the impact on the balance sheet. Both approaches involve the same type of interest-rate-level risk and, given the same change in interest rates, produce the same earnings. However, the money market gapping affects the balance sheet for 13 months while the gapping with negotiable securities affects it for only 1 month.

Derivatives. Although derivatives originally were developed to protect against interest rate risk, they also are used to *assume* price risk. The value of a derivative instrument depends on the value of underlying cash products such as commodities and debt securities. Typically, derivatives are nondeliverable forward contracts which are periodically and/or at maturity settled for cash on the basis of the price development of the underlying product. They allow a bank to continue its interest spread business off the balance sheet.

A forward interest rate agreement (FRA) is an example of a derivative that works as a hedge instrument for borrowers and investors. For example, the treasurer at Mega Corporation knows that in 3 months he will need $100 million and worries that interest rates will be higher at that time. The customer asks BigBank, "What is 6-month money beginning 3 months from now?" The bank quotes 11 percent. If they come to terms, the bank and the customer make a deal for a notional amount of $100 million. BigBank is not lending $100 million; it is giving the customer a guarantee that 3 months from now, for a notional amount of $100 million, 6-month money will cost 11 percent. There is no commitment from the bank to lend the money at 11 percent.

In 3 months the customer looks at the market and sees that the interest rate for 6-month money has moved to 12 percent. He borrows from XYZ Bank at the prevailing rate of 12 percent, but he comes to BigBank and says, "You told me that interest rates would be 11 percent." BigBank says, "Yes, that's right. We will pay you the 1 percent difference." The borrower subtracts the hedge profit of 1 percent from the 12 percent interest rate XYZ Bank charges, and his net borrowing cost is 11 percent:

FRA	11 percent
Actual rate	12 percent
Hedge profit	−1 percent
Net borrowing cost	11 percent

Conversely, if the rates go down to 10 percent, the customer borrows from XYZ Bank at 10 percent and pays BigBank 1 percent. The net borrowing cost for the customer is 11 percent—the actual borrowing cost of 10 percent plus the hedge loss:

FRA	11 percent
Actual rate	10 percent
Hedge loss	+1 percent
Net borrowing cost	11 percent

Why doesn't BigBank just lend the money to the customer at 11 percent? The answer is that BigBank is not in the lending business. In this example, the FRA is not on the balance sheet for BigBank but the loan is on the balance sheet for XYZ Bank.

Let us examine how an FRA works for investors. Insurance companies never worry about higher rates because they always have premiums to invest; instead, they worry about lower rates. Their fear is that rates will go down and they will not be able to invest at the higher rate. Thus, an insurance company may come to BigBank and say, "What is 6-month money for $100 million, beginning 3 months from now? We don't want to invest with you. We only want an interest rate contract."

BigBank may quote $10\frac{3}{4}$ percent, which is less than the 11 percent the bank quoted to the borrower. If the actual rate after 3 months is 12 percent, the insurance company can invest at the prevailing rate of 12 percent. However, the company still has a $10\frac{3}{4}$ percent contract with the bank and therefore has an obligation to pay $1\frac{1}{4}$ percent. The bank collects $1\frac{1}{4}$ percent, keeps $\frac{1}{4}$ percent profit, and pays 1 percent to the borrowing customer:

FRA	$10\frac{3}{4}$ percent
Actual rate	12 percent
Hedge cost	$-1\frac{1}{14}$ percent
Net yield for investor	$10\frac{3}{4}$ percent

Bank Profit

Collect from investor	$1\frac{1}{4}$ percent
Pay borrower	-1 percent
Profit	$\frac{1}{4}$ percent

If the rate decreases to 10 percent, the bank has to pay $\frac{3}{4}$ percent to the insurance company and collects 1 percent from the borrowing customer:

FRA	$10\frac{3}{4}$ percent
Actual rate	10 percent
Hedge gain	$\frac{3}{4}$ percent
Net yield for investor	$10\frac{3}{4}$ percent

Bank Profit

Collect from borrower	1 percent
Pay investor	$-\frac{3}{4}$ percent
Profit	$\frac{1}{4}$ percent

These examples illustrate how this type of business works. Of course, in the real world, since banks never have two customers on the opposite side of a deal at the same time, they manage all the deals together as a book. Also, in the real world, FRAs are paid present valued at the beginning of the hedge period rather than future valued at the end of the period.

Although derivatives have been developed to hedge against interest rate risk, they also may be used as speculation tools to assume interest rate risk. For example, suppose a bank is planning to position for lower interest rates and a borrowing customer calls and says she wants a hedge against rising interest rates. The bank gives her the hedge and does nothing else because by giving the hedge it has positioned itself for lower interest rates. If the rates go down as the bank expects, the customer pays the difference to the bank.

Derivatives also are used to reduce risk. For example, in the situation where a bank is gapped with a bank placement, instead of borrowing the money for 12 months, the bank could have done an FRA contract for 12 months and closed the gap in terms of interest rate risk. The bank actually will borrow 1-month's money for each of the 12 months at the prevailing interest rate and in addition will pay or receive the difference between the market rate for the 1-month borrowings and the FRA rate.

Remember, there are two types of interest rate positions. We have given examples of the first one: interest-rate-*level*-sensitive positions where hedging and gapping strategies are based on the trend of the interest rate *level* for one instrument and one maturity as indicated by the yield curve. The second type of interest rate position is sensitive to the *difference* between rates for different instruments and maturities.

Interest-Rate-Differential-Sensitive Positions

Interest-rate-differential-sensitive positions are sensitive to a change in the interest rate differential, or the "spread" between interest rates. Spread positions result from speculative spread trading or from giving perfect hedges to customers which cannot be completely counter-hedged. Spread trading, or "putting on a spread," may be accomplished with either an *instrument* spread or a *maturity* spread.

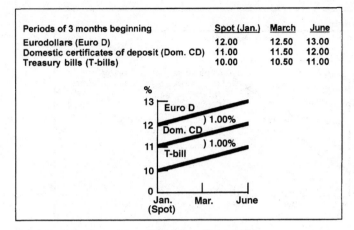

Periods of 3 months beginning	Spot (Jan.)	March	June
Eurodollars (Euro D)	12.00	12.50	13.00
Domestic certificates of deposit (Dom. CD)	11.00	11.50	12.00
Treasury bills (T-bills)	10.00	10.50	11.00

Exhibit 2-9. "Normal" yield relationships.

Instrument Spreads.   An instrument spread refers to a spread position between different instruments for the same maturity. Eurodollars, domestic certificates of deposit, and Treasury bills are three financial instruments that are traded in the futures market. These instruments are traded for March, June, September, and December. Exhibit 2-9 shows an example of a "normal" yield relationship. (This is shown only for presentation purposes; the "normal" yield relationship and the level of interest rates may be different in the real world.) Assume that January is spot and that March and June are the nearest active trading months. In this case there is a 1 percent difference between the interest rates for the three instruments for all the different tenors.

If you realize that this parallel yield relationship is normal, you will see that the yield relationship between the domestic CD and the T-bill in Exhibit 2-10a is not normal.

The difference between the domestic CD and the T-bill, which in our example is normally 1 percent, has narrowed to only 0.40 percent. The trader will see this and say, "This trend is not going to last. We are putting on a position that allows us to make money if the spread returns to normal." We do not know if the interest rate for the March delivery of domestic CDs is too low or if the rate for T-bills is too high—we are not interested in that. We only know that domestic CDs are low *relative* to T-bills and vice versa.

The expectation is that CD interest rates will rise and the price for the CD will fall, and we expect T-bill interest rates to fall and the price to rise. Thus we build a position by putting on a spread; we sell the domestic CD and buy the T-bill. A week later, assuming that the situation nor-

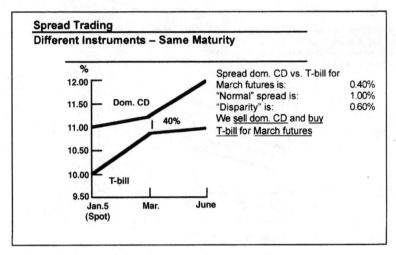

Exhibit 2-10a. Narrower-than-normal yield relationship.

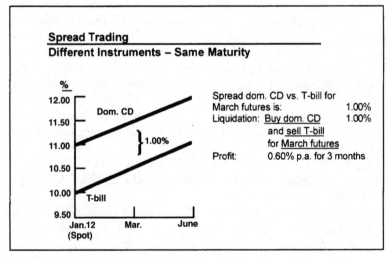

Exhibit 2-10b. Normalized yield relationship.

malizes again, we liquidate both positions. The profit is the difference between what the spread was a week ago and what it is now—0.60 percent p.a. (Exhibit 2-10b).

If the spread between two instruments with the same maturities is wider than normal, as in Exhibit 2-11a, we take an interest rate spread position by buying the Eurodollar contract and selling the domestic CD for March

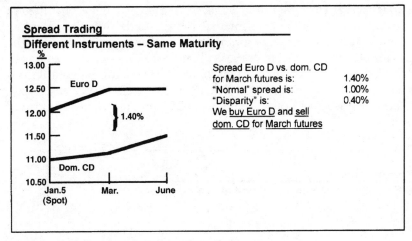

Exhibit 2-11a. Wider-than-normal yield relationship.

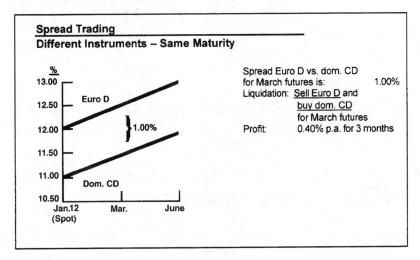

Exhibit 2-11b. Normalized yield relationship.

futures. When March futures normalize to 1 percent (Exhibit 2-11b), we liquidate the position (sell Eurodollar contracts and buy domestic CD contracts) and make a profit of 40 basis points.

This is an example of an instrument spread—different instruments, same maturity. The most widely used instrument spread is the TED spread (T-bills versus Eurodollars) and the Euro versus CP spread (Eurodollars versus commercial paper).

Maturity Spreads. A *maturity spread* is a spread between different maturities for the same instrument. In Exhibit 2-12a the difference between the March and June maturities for the same instrument is 0.50 percent. The expectation is that the yield curve will become more positive, as it is in Exhibit 2-12b, and we can speculate that March maturities will remain unchanged and June maturities will go up. If the June interest rate goes up, the contract price goes down. Therefore, in anticipation of the lower price,

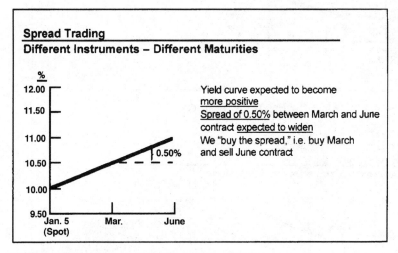

Exhibit 2-12a. Expectation of a positive yield curve.

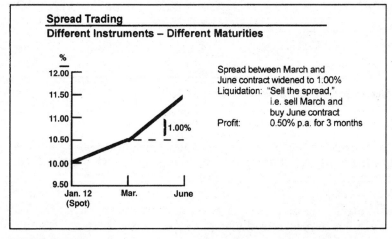

Exhibit 2-12b. Actual spread between March and June contracts.

in January we will sell the June contract and buy the March contract. When the spread between the March contract and the June contract widens to 1.00 percent, we liquidate the position by selling the March contract and buying the June contract.

As can be seen in Exhibits 2-13a and 2-13b, just as we can expect that the curve will become more positive than it already is, it can also become more negative than it already is.

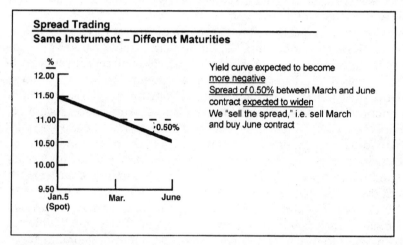

Exhibit 2-13a. Expectation of a negative yield curve.

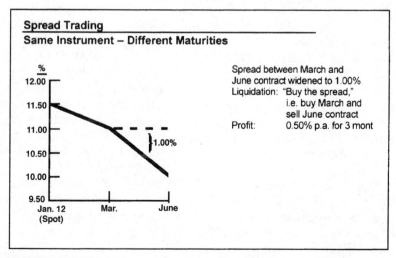

Exhibit 2-13b. Actual spread between March and June contracts.

Again, we are putting on a spread by buying and selling the same instrument. In the first case, to create an instrument spread, we buy and sell *different instruments* for the *same maturity*. In this example, to create a maturity spread, we buy and sell the *same instruments* for *different maturities*. The risk in a maturity spread is also known as yield-curve-risk.

The type of price risk inherent in interest-rate-differential-sensitive positions is basis risk. This type of risk can result from intended spreads that traders put on in the trading room. It also can occur when banks create basis spreads by giving perfect hedges to customers and then hedge with a different instrument.

Banks provide interest rate hedges to customers for different types of instruments, such as domestic CDs, Eurodollars, T-bills, banker's acceptances, and commercial paper. However, futures contracts are standardized (see Chap. 11) and are available only for domestic CDs, Eurodollars, and T-bills. Customers frequently want a hedge for a dollar interest rate instrument for which there is no futures contract, for example, commercial paper. Commercial paper is a very popular form of borrowing particularly for large, prominent companies with high credit standing.

To illustrate, suppose Wonderful Company needs $1 million for 3 years at a fixed interest rate and decides to borrow that money on a 1-month basis in the commercial paper market. It could simply borrow 1-month commercial paper 36 times, but borrowing 1 month at a time for 3 years has the same effect as borrowing at a floating rate. Therefore, Wonderful Company goes to its bank and says, "Quote an interest rate hedge for 3-year commercial paper dollars." The bank gives it the hedge, and Wonderful Company is perfectly hedged.

Then the bank protects itself by hedging in the futures market. Since there is no futures market for commercial paper, it may be necessary to hedge with Eurodollar futures. If the interest rates on commercial paper and Eurodollars both rise 3 percent, the bank makes a 3 percent hedge profit on Eurodollar futures and pays 3 percent to Wonderful Company.

However, the bank knows that rates do not always move exactly in parallel. If commercial paper goes up 3 percent, the bank has to pay Wonderful Company 3 percent, which is a loss on the hedge with Wonderful Company of 300 basis points (3 percent). If Eurodollars go up only 2.85 percent, the bank has a hedge profit on the Eurodollar hedge of only 285 basis points (2.85 percent) and an overall loss of 15 basis points. This is interest *differential* risk because the bank's risk is that commercial paper and Eurodollars will not experience a parallel shift in their yield curves. Specifically, it is an instrument spread.

The bank has another alternative. It can give Wonderful Company a $1 million hedge for 3 years and hedge with a $12 million FRA for 3 months, which is one-twelfth of the 3-year hedge period. If interest rates rise 3 percent, the bank loses 3 percent on $1 million for 3 years and makes 3 percent on $12 million for 3 months. The risk in this situation is that long-term interest rates can rise more than short-term rates do. If long-term rates rise 3.5 percent because the yield curve becomes more positive and short-term interest rates rise only 3 percent, the bank loses 3.5 percent on the long-term hedge to Wonderful Company but makes only 3 percent on its own short-term hedge.

This is still an interest-differential-sensitive position, but this time it is a maturity spread. The hedge the bank took was for 3 months (one-twelfth of the hedge period for 12 times the amount), and the hedge the bank gave was for 3 years.

Customer-related basis risk is the same type of risk as the differential risk that results when a trader intentionally puts on the spread. However, it has a different name because it is a different business technique with a different motivation behind it.

FX Swap Positions. Foreign exchange premiums are a reflection of the interest differential between the two currencies in an FX transaction. A change in the differential causes a change in the premium. For example, suppose we expect sterling interest rates to decline and want to make money without creating a money market gap, that is, without affecting the balance sheet. We know that when one interest rate changes, the differential changes and therefore the swap rate changes, and so we speculate on a change in interest rates by using foreign exchange contracts. The following example illustrates this strategy.

A trader sees the following rates quoted in the market:

1- to 6-months sterling interest rate	10 percent
1- to 6-month dollar interest rate	6 percent
Interest differential	4 percent
Spot exchange rate	$1.8000 per pound
Monthly swap rate (discount)	0.0060

The trader expects that sterling interest rates will drop from 10 percent to 9 percent and that the dollar interest rate will remain unchanged. If this happens, the interest differential will drop from 4 percent to 3 percent, and consequently the monthly discount will shrink from 0.0060 to 0.0045 (3 percent of 1.8000 is 0.0540 per year, or 0.0045 per month).

If the trader wanted to use the money market to position for a decline in the sterling interest rate, she would first place 6-month pounds and then borrow 1-month pounds, building a negative gap. Instead, she will build a foreign exchange swap position with two transactions. First, she will sell spot pounds at 1.8000 and buy 6-month pounds at 1.7640, which is .0360 (0.0060 × 6) less than 1.8000. Next, she will partially off-set this position. She will buy spot pounds at 1.80 and sell pounds 1 month forward at 0.0060 discount, resulting in a forward rate of 1.7940. She has now built a 5-month FX swap position, selling 1-month pounds at 1.7940 and buying 6-month pounds at 1.7640 (5 times 0.0060 per month discount, or 0.0300 discount for the 5-month period).

One month later the expected event occurs: The sterling interest rate drops from 10 percent to 9 percent, and the swap rate reflects the new interest differential of 3 percent. At a spot rate of 1.80, the new differential translates into an annual swap rate of 0.0540, or 0.0045 per month. This means that the 5-month foreign exchange swap position the trader built at 5 times 0.0060, or 300 points, for the period in her favor may be liquidated at 5 times 0.0045 per month, or 225 points, for the period against her; 300 points in favor of the trader versus 225 points against the trader equals 75 points in her favor for the 5-month period, which equals 1 percent p.a. for the 5-month period. This 1 percent is the same profit the trader would have made if she had built a 5-month negative gap in the money market. This positioning technique is preferred by FX traders who wish to speculate on changes on interest rates. It is also pre-ferred by traders who wish to assume interest rate risk without affect-ing the institution's balance sheet.

The construction of this position may be accomplished directly through a sale of 1-month pounds and a purchase of 6-month pounds. However, the trading liquidity for such a direct swap is limited, and the buildup of the position will occur at less attractive prices. By engaging in two swaps and going through spot, we find a substantially more liq-uid market. Also, if we are a market maker, we may be able to induce other market participants through the trending of our quotes to deal at our rates and as a result build the FX swap position at substantially more attractive rates.

There is one problem with this positioning technique. In the example it is assumed that the trader has an opinion about the downward trend in *sterling* interest rates but has no view on *dollar* interest rates. The trader may be correct in her expectation of a 1 percent decline in sterling interest rates. However, at the same time, the interest rate for U.S. dol-lars may decline from 6 percent to 4 percent, creating a widening of the interest differential from 4 percent to 5 percent:

1- to 6-month sterling interest rate	9 percent
1- to 6-month dollar interest rate	4 percent
Interest differential	5 percent
Annual discount	0.0900
Monthly discount	0.0075, or 0.0375 for the 5-month period

In this case, the trader would suffer a loss of 0.0075, representing the difference between the forward purchase at a discount of 0.0300 in her favor and a forward sale at a discount of 0.0375 against her. This loss would occur even though the basic speculation on lower sterling interest rates was correct. However, to avoid the balance sheet impact, the trader inadvertently introduced a second price risk in the form of speculating on the behavior of the interest rate for U.S. dollars. This speculation produced a loss in excess of the profit made on the primary speculation. A doctor might say again that the operation was successful but the patient died.

The position in the example is called an FX swap position because it is built entirely through the use of FX contracts and all prices are FX rates. However, as can be seen, the price risk of an FX swap position is interest rate risk. In fact, in terms of price risk, this FX swap position equals a 5-month negative money market gap in sterling and a 5-month positive money market gap in dollars, both for the 5-month period beginning 1 month from now. Therefore, this type of price risk is best captured and reported as two separate interest-level-sensitive positions, *not* as an interest-differential-sensitive position involving two different currencies.

For foreign exchange traders, the technique of anticipating the trend of interest rates with FX swap positions involves a special danger in terms of organizational structure (which traders are allowed to speculate on exchange rates and which are allowed to speculate on interest rates?) and also frequently in terms of primary skills. Obviously, FX traders must understand the movement of interest rates in order to make intelligent decisions about the movement of FX rates in the immediate future. However, understanding interest rates often is not their primary skill. Speculation on changes in FX rates usually covers a much shorter period, often hours or days at the most. Speculation on the movement of interest rates is typically of a longer nature, often several months.

As many emerging financial markets develop reasonably liquid forward exchange markets, it is inviting for FX traders to take FX swap positions in those currencies against dollars. We saw earlier in this chapter that gapping is most attractive with a steep yield curve, a situation in which one will make money if everything remains the way it currently is, that is, if no changes are anticipated. Just let time go by and we will be all right.

The danger is that FX traders may build up FX swap positions in exotic currencies in emerging markets without being familiar with the situation in those markets. The reason for higher-than-normal interest rates in a particular market may be that there is already a crisis in the making which an FX trader on another continent is not fully aware of.

While money market traders may not have counterparty credit lines to build up a money market gap in that country, FX traders may be able to trade those currencies with international banks which quote forward exchange rates and swaps for them. In the past the local currencies of emerging market countries were subjected to speculative attacks. The central bank usually responds to such an attack with extremely high interest rates to make it costly for speculators to maintain their net over-sold positions in those currencies. That is the environment in which an FX trader gets caught with an FX swap position which may become very expensive to roll over and may also pose a threat from a funding liquidity viewpoint.

Because of this danger, it is necessary not only to limit the currencies in which specific traders are allowed to trade but also to specify whether traders are limited to speculating on *exchange rates only* or also are allowed to speculate on *changes in interest rates*. (See the box on controlling price risk in Chap. 6, p. 118).

Summary: Interest Rates

There are three ways to assume interest-rate-level risk: with nonnegotiable instruments, such as bank placements and borrowings in the money market; with negotiable instruments, such as bonds; and with derivatives, such as FRAs, which are interest rate hedge instruments. Nonnegotiable and negotiable instruments are *on* the balance sheet; derivatives are *off* the balance sheet.

The nature of speculation is that we win if the trend moves in the direction we expect and lose if the opposite trend occurs. When we know the total amount we have at risk from interest-level-sensitive positions, we can determine a single sensitivity (a dollar amount) in the level of interest rates for all types of gapping because the risk is the same. This means that from a price risk point of view, the type of risk (not the type of product) is the important issue. This point is explored further in Chap. 4 in a discussion of the methodology for analyzing and assessing price risk in trading accounts.

Interest-rate-*level*-sensitive positions are sensitive to the movement of interest rates, for example, money market gaps, debt securities, and derivatives. When we speculate on the level of interest rates, we profit if the trend moves in the direction we expect and lose if the opposite trend occurs.

Interest-rate-*differential*-sensitive positions are sensitive to the difference in interest rates between two instruments for the same maturity or between two maturities for the same instrument. There are two ways to take interest-rate-differential-sensitive positions: (1) speculating by intentionally putting on a spread and (2) giving perfect hedges to a customer and then hedging ourselves with a different instrument or for a different period. Either way, the type of price risk is exactly the same, but it has a different name according to the intention: differential or spread risk (when speculating) and basis risk (when giving hedges to customers).

Many instruments, products, and situations may exist for all kinds of reasons, but when it comes to interest rate risk, short of options, we can distinguish whether the risk results from speculations on the movement of the *level* of interest rates or results from a change in the spread. Is it an interest-rate-*level*-sensitive position so that we worry about higher or lower interest rates, or is it an interest-rate-*differential*-sensitive position? That is the first question. Second, if it is an interest-rate-differential-sensitive position, is it an instrument spread—sensitive to the interest differential between two instruments—or a maturity spread—sensitive to a change in the shape of the yield curve?

Volatility in Options

In modern market risk management, volatility plays a key role in estimating value at risk in price risk positions (see Chap. 4) and estimating future loan equivalent amounts in presettlement counterparty risk (see Chap. 9). We will demonstrate that the implied volatility in options is a separate market price that is quoted as a percentage per annum. To enable the reader to understand this important concept, we will briefly describe the more traditional uses of options in which the focus of the option trade is either on commodity prices, including equities and foreign currencies, or on interest rates. Then we will provide an example which clearly shows that trading options is in fact trading volatility and that the expected future volatility is the most critical component among the factors needed to calculate an option premium, i.e., the price of an option.

An option is the right to buy or sell something (an underlying asset) on a given date (maturity) at a given price (the strike price). An option buyer pays a premium to the seller for the right granted by the option. Options are used for four purposes:

1. Buying options for protection (hedging)
2. Selling options for return enhancement (selling covered options)
3. Buying or selling options to speculate on changes in commodity prices or interest rates
4. Buying or selling options to speculate on option-implied volatility[2]

You may be more familiar with the first three traditional uses of options. The following examples illustrate the general concept of trading options when the focus is on the price of the underlying asset.

Buying Options for Protection (Hedging)

Assume an exporter to England has a receivable of 1 million pounds that is payable by the British customer 3 months from now. This net exchange position could be hedged by our customer through the sale of 1 million pounds in the foreign exchange market, using a spot contract, a forward contract, or a futures contract. While there are important differences between these three types of contracts, they all represent a firm commitment on behalf of the seller to deliver the pounds and on behalf of the buyer to buy those pounds at the agreed-on exchange rate of, for example, $1.50 per pound. As a result of the hedge, the customer reduces her net long position in pounds to zero. An alternative hedge mechanism would be for the customer to buy a pound put option with a strike price of $1.50. This gives the customer the *right* to sell the pounds at $1.50 without the *obligation* to sell them. Obviously, the customer will exercise her right to sell the pounds at $1.50 only if the market rate at the end of the option period is lower than $1.50. If the market rate is higher than $1.50, the customer will sell in the free market at the higher rate.

Selling Options for Return Enhancement (Selling Covered Options)

Assume that this customer is comfortable with her net long position in pounds and does not seek protection. In this case, the customer could sell a pound call option with a strike price of $1.53 at a premium of, say, 0.01. This transaction gives no rights to the customer. Instead, it is the buyer of this call option who has the right to buy the 1 million pounds at 1.53 but is not obliged to do so. Obviously, the buyer of the option will exercise at 1.53 only if, at the end of the option period, the market is higher than 1.53. Otherwise, the option buyer will buy the pounds in the open market at a lower rate. From the customer's viewpoint the situation is as follows: If the market price is higher than $1.54, the customer has an opportunity loss. She has sold the pound at 1.54 (1.53 plus 0.01 premium) and has given up the "opportunity" to sell the pound at the higher market rate. However, she should be happy because the pound was 1.50 when the call was sold. After 3 months, if the pound is below 1.53, the option will not be exercised. The customer still has a long position in pounds. The option premium of 0.01 can be used to offset any loss on this position. It should be clearly understood that *the strategy of selling covered calls is not a hedge*—the customer cannot be sure she will sell the pounds at a particular price (or better). All that is certain is that she will have $0.01 in her pocket and may or may not have sold the pounds.

Selling covered options is not hedging.

Buying or Selling Options to Speculate on Changes in Commodity Prices or Interest Rates

Assume that the exchange rate for the pound is expected to rise above the current market price of 1.50. We could buy pounds at 1.50 and run the risk of a decline in the sterling exchange rate, but the size of this risk is almost unlimited. Instead, we could buy a pound call option with a strike price of 1.50. This gives us the right to buy pounds at 1.50, but we are not obliged to do so. We have only the option premium at risk, which is considerably less than the size of the risk involved when we actually buy the pounds and incur a net position. The size of the risk is similar to a net position when we sell "naked" options, i.e., sell options without having an underlying price risk position. For example, if we expect the pound to drop below 1.50, we may sell a pound call option with a strike price of 1.50 for an option premium of 0.03. In this case, our breakeven rate would be 1.53 (strike price of 1.50 plus 0.03 option premium). If the market price at the end of the option period is higher than 1.53, we lose; if it is lower than 1.53, we make money.

In all three of these situations the focus of the option trade was the direction of the exchange rate of 1.50. We have not used the word *volatility*. When options are used for these more traditional purposes (directional trading), we will notice only that when volatility is expected to be higher in the future, otherwise comparable option trades have higher option premiums, and at times when future volatility is expected to be lower, otherwise comparable option trades will have lower option premiums. The next step is to discuss the actual volatility implied in options and show that this is a separate market price quoted in percent per annum and that it is therefore possible to buy volatility in expectation of appreciation or sell volatility when we expect that volatility will decline in the future. In this discussion of volatility, remember that this use of options is completely different from the three traditional option uses (in directional trading) described above, where the focus of the option trade was on commodity prices or interest rates.

Option premiums are calculated by entering four factors into a valuation model (e.g., the Black and Scholes formula) to come up with a fair market price:

- Relationship between strike price and market price
- Time to maturity
- Interest rate
- Volatility

As Exhibit 2-14 shows, five factors are plugged into the model. However, in this discussion we refer to the relationship between the strike price and the market price as a single factor even though these prices are identified and plugged into the formula separately.

Option dealers use many different models to price options. The choice of a model is dependent on a number of factors which are beyond the scope of this book. For our purposes it is important to become familiar with the basic theory behind option pricing models. We need an intuitive understanding of each individual factor and of how changes in each pricing component affect the size of the option price (premium).

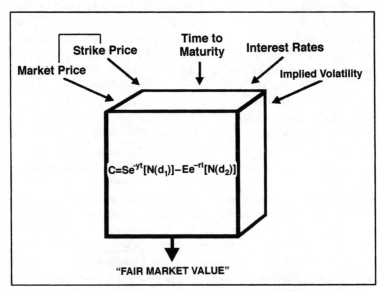

Exhibit 2-14. Calculating an option premium by using a valuation model (Black-Scholes formula).

The next several pages will discuss options through the use of simple examples. Options on foreign exchange rates will be used to illustrate the points we need to make. For instance, the buyer of a dollar call option against deutsche marks with a strike price of DM 1.70 has the right to buy dollars and sell marks at 1.70 at the maturity of the contract. The option premium is paid up front in cash. At the end of this section we will highlight the slight differences that exist in some other types of options, such as options on equities.

1. *Relationship Between Strike Price and Market Price.* The more out of the money, the lower the premium; the more in the money, the higher the premium. From the buyer's viewpoint, an option is in the money when the strike price is more attractive than the market price and is out of the money when the strike price is less attractive than the market price.

2. *Time to Maturity.* The shorter the time to maturity, the lower the premium; the longer the time to maturity, the higher the premium. There are American options and European options. American options can be exercised at any time. European options can only be exercised on the expiration date. While this is an important distinction in actual option trading, a further discussion of this distinction exceeds the scope of this book.

3. *Interest Rate (Risk-Free Rate of Return).* The lower the interest rate, the higher the premium; the higher the interest rate, the lower the premium. The seller of an option receives the premium in cash up front and can invest it in the market. When interest rates are very high, the seller can invest the option premium and earn a lot of interest; when interest rates are lower, he or she still gets an option premium, but the value of that premium is not as high in terms of the interest it can earn. In other words, the seller of the option views the interest that can be earned from investing the cash premium as part of the total compensation and therefore is satisfied with a lower option premium at times when interest rates are high and more interest can be earned from that premium.[3]

4. *Implied Volatility.* When expected volatility is higher, the option premium will be higher; when expected volatility is lower, the option premium will be lower. In other words, when the price of the underlying asset is expected to be stable, the option premium is lower than it is when the price is expected to fluctuate.

We can say that the first three factors in Exhibit 2-15—strike price versus market price, time to maturity, and interest rate—are "yes, sir" items in the option premium formula, meaning that there is no basis for negotiation between the buyer and seller. The buyer can say, "I want a strike price that is at the money, or way in the money, or way out of the

Options on Foreign Exchange Rates

Market Factor	_Option Premium_

1. Strike price vs. market price
    More out of the money
    More in the money
	↓ Lower
	↑ Higher

2. Time to maturity
    Shorter
    Longer
	↓ Lower
	↑ Higher

3. Interest rate
    Lower
    Higher
	↑ Higher
	↓ Lower

4. Volatility
    Lower
    Higher
	↓ Lower
	↑ Higher

Exhibit 2-15. Relationship of each component to the premium.

money"—no argument. He can say, "I want it for 84 days or for 3 years"—no argument. And the interest rate is a market rate—no argument.

Thus, when it comes to options trading, the entire action occurs in the fourth component: volatility. That is why *trading options is really trading volatility.*

Implied volatility is a separate market price that is quoted as a percentage per annum on a dealer screen and is used among professional option traders. The percentage figure represents a 50:50 probability that the spot price of the underlying asset will move up or down by that amount. For example, if the 12-month volatility of the dollar against the peso is quoted at 16 percent p.a., it means the market expects a 50 percent probability that the price will stay the same or *rise* by 16 percent or less and a 50 percent probability that the price will stay the same or *drop* by 16 percent or less (Exhibit 2-16).

To understand how professional options trading works, suppose a Morgan trader calls a Chase trader and asks if there is any interest in dollar/mark 12-month options. The Chase trader may say, "Yes, my market is 15.65 percent bid and 15.85 percent offer." If Chase is buying dollar/mark options, a volatility of 15.65 percent will be used to calculate the option premium; if Chase is selling dollar/mark options, implied

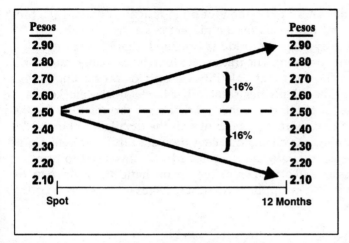

Exhibit 2-16. FX options—16 percent implied volatility for 12 months.

volatility of 15.85 percent will be plugged into the formula. Then the Morgan trader may say, "I would like to buy some options, but 15.85 percent is a little high. Can you make it 15.80?" The Chase trader will say, "No, I cannot," and they will bargain and agree on 15.83. Once they have agreed on volatility, there is a good chance they also will be able to agree on the actual option premium at which the transaction will be done.

Chase will simply say, "Give me the details." Why is Chase less sensitive to the other three factors? The way the pricing works, when the five factors[4] are plugged into the valuation model used to calculate the fair market value, the formula takes into account the fact that the more in the money, the higher the premium, and the more out of the money, the lower the premium. The same process is used for time and interest rates.

Another example will demonstrate that volatility in options is a separate market price. Assume the following market rates:

Amount	10,000,000 pounds versus dollars
Interest rate for dollar and pound	5 percent
Spot and forward exchange rate	$1.50
Strike price	$1.50 = 1 pound (at the money)
Maturity	2 months
Volatility	12.5 percent p.a.
Premium	2 percent flat

An options trader sells a put option for pounds against dollars at a premium of 2 percent flat based on the market price for volatility of 12.5 percent p.a. Shortly after the trade is executed, there is a rumor of a political or economic event. The trader sees that the exchange rate is still $1.50; however, she feels that volatility for options on sterling/dollar could be rising. She telephones some other banks in the market for a quote. They are all quoting a higher market price for volatility for the option she sold that morning. She plugs all the details into her model once more (nothing has changed except the volatility) and gets a premium of 2.5 percent flat. When the implied volatility used to price an option increases and all other factors remain unchanged, the price of the option is higher. When implied volatility decreases, the price of the option is lower.

Hedging Options

As we saw with the other FX products we discussed, we have to protect our net positions. When it comes to trading FX options, in addition to worrying about volatility as a separate market price, we also have to protect our net positions. For example, let us look at another transaction with the same market rates:

Amount	10,000,000 pounds versus dollars
Interest rate for dollar and pound	5 percent p.a.
Spot and forward exchange rate	$1.50
Strike price	$1.50 = 1 pound (at the money)
Maturity	2 months
Volatility	12.5 percent p.a.
Premium	2 percent flat

Assume the trader is selling a put option on 10 million pounds to a customer for 2 months at a premium of $2\frac{1}{4}$ percent flat, which means the customer is paying $\frac{1}{4}$ percent above the prevailing market rate. The trader could buy back the identical option at the prevailing professional market price of 2 percent. This gives the bank a $\frac{1}{4}$ percent customer-related profit margin, which will be recorded in that customer's account profitability report. The trader may not want to buy the option back because he expects volatility to decrease and thinks he can manage the risk and make more money than the $\frac{1}{4}$ percent profit margin. However, he cannot just sell the option, collect the $2\frac{1}{4}$ percent, and wait to see if the option buyer exercises the option; he needs to protect his position. Here is the trader's position after he sells the put option:

- The trader has sold a 2-month put option on 10 million pounds versus dollars.
- The strike price is $1.50.
- The market price at the time of the option sale is $1.50—an at-the-money option.
- The put option buyer has the right to sell 10 million pounds in 2 months at $1.50.

To hedge the foreign exchange rate risk in this position, the trader has to figure out the percentage of probability that the customer will exercise the option to sell the 10 million pounds. When he knows that probability, he hedges the same percentage. For example, if he is 100 percent certain that at the end of 2 months the pound will be $1.40, he knows the customer will sell to him at $1.50. In that case, he will hedge 100 percent by selling 10 million pounds at $1.50 and then waiting 2 months until the pound is at $1.40 and the customer sells pounds to him at $1.50. He is hedged because he presold the pounds at $1.50. If he is 100 percent certain that the pound will be $1.60 in 2 months, he will do nothing. He knows that if the market rate is $1.60, the put buyer will not exercise the option to sell pounds to him at $1.50. Instead, the customer will sell pounds in the market at $1.60.

Of course, it is not possible to be 100 percent certain about changes in market rates, and so the trader takes a *delta-neutral hedge position* to protect himself against a change in the FX rate of the pound. Delta implies change; a delta hedge makes the trader neutral toward change. Let's continue with the example and see how this works.

The trader assumes there is a 50 percent probability that the pound exchange rate will increase to a level above $1.50 and a 50 percent probability that it will decrease to a level below $1.50. This understanding of the 50:50 probability is the anchor point for intuitively understanding a delta-neutral hedge. Since the customer will sell pounds to the trader only if the spot price in two months is lower than $1.50, the probability that the customer will exercise the option is also 50 percent.

1. When the option is at the money, the trader hedges 50 percent, which means he squares his position by selling 5 million pounds.

   How can he be square if he is short 5 million pounds and has sold a put option for 10 million pounds? The 50 percent chance that the customer will sell him 10 million pounds is considered to be equal to an actual purchase of 5 million pounds. That is why he sells 5 million pounds to square the position.

   Some time passes, and the pound moves up to 1.52. The probability that at the end of 2 months it will be lower than 1.50 is now less than 50 percent. When the market rate is 1.52, the option is out of the money and there is only a 43 percent[5] chance that the customer will sell pounds to the trader.

2. Now the trader should be hedged 43 percent, and so he buys back 700,000 pounds at 1.52.

   Since the perfect hedge ratio is 43 percent, the trader should be short 43 percent, or 4.3 million, of the 10 million. Since he already has sold 5 million, he has to buy back 700,000 at 1.52 to be perfectly hedged. These 700,000 pounds are part of the 5 million sold at 1.50. However, even though he sold the 700,000 pounds at 1.50 and bought them back at 1.52, this is not a *loss*. Instead, it is a *cost* because he has the 2 percent option premium to finance the hedging cost. In other words, selling at 1.50 and buying back at 1.52 usually creates a loss. However, in this case, it is not a loss but only a cost. The trader received an option premium of 2 percent flat and decided not to spend that premium to buy back the entire option. Instead, he used bits and pieces of the 2 percent option premium to adjust the delta position whenever the underlying market rate moved and did this in such a way that he stayed (close to) delta neutral. It is for this reason that the cumulative negative foreign exchange rate differentials are costs and not losses up to an amount equal to the 2 percent premium the trader has in his pocket. Only if the aggregate rehedging expense resulting from higher volatility exceeds the option premium of 2 percent will the increment over 2 percent constitute a loss.

   Now the pound rises to 1.56. The probability that it will fall below 1.50 is now only 27 percent. The more out of the money, the lower the probability of exercise and consequently the lower the hedge ratio.

3. The trader should now be hedged 27 percent, and so he buys back 1.6 million pounds at 1.56 to reduce his delta hedge from 4.3 million to 2.7 million. Again, the buyback at 1.56 incurs a cost and not a loss because of the option premium in his pocket.

The higher the pound/dollar rate goes, the less likely it is that at the end of 2 months it will be below 1.50. The customer probably will not sell pounds to the trader at 1.50, and the trader will have bought back most of the original hedge of 5 million pounds at higher and higher prices.

When the trader buys an option and pays a premium based on a specific volatility assumption, the aggregate hedging income will equal the option premium paid. That means that if he buys or sells volatility at 12.5 percent, for example, and volatility does not change throughout the option period, the hedging cost/income will equal the premium that is paid or received, which was calculated using 12.5 percent implied volatility.

Exhibit 2-17 shows the seller's delta-neutral hedge positions previously described for

- The probability that the buyer will exercise the put option while the pound is *rising*
- The 50:50 probability that the pound will remain *unchanged* at $1.50
- The probability that the buyer will exercise the put option while the pound is *falling*

The percentage probabilities of exercise and hedge ratios were chosen to illustrate the concept. They do not necessarily correspond to the assumed market rates.

Market Rates

Spot and forward exchange rate	$1.50 = 1 pound
Strike price	$1.50 = 1 pound
Interest rate for dollar and pound	5 percent p.a.
Volatility	12.5 percent p.a.
Premium	2 percent flat

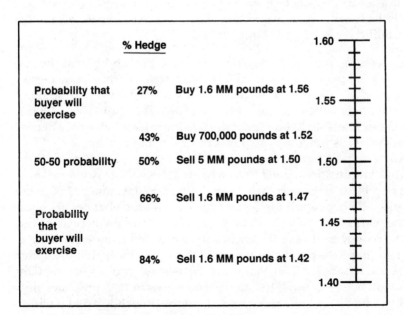

Exhibit 2-17. Delta-neutral hedge positions.

Sale of 10MM pounds put option versus $

Remaining life   2 months

Premiums received and paid versus costs and revenues can be summarized as follows:

Sell Options	*Buy Options*
Collect premiums.	Pay premiums.
All hedges are costs.	All hedges are revenues.

Continuing with Exhibit 2-17, let us start again with the first hedge, where we sold 5 million pounds at $1.50, and see what happens if the pound/dollar rate decreases.

If the pound moves to 1.47, the probability is 34 percent that it will rise so much that at the end of 2 months it will pass 1.50. That means there is a 66 percent probability that it will remain below 1.50 and that at the end of 2 months the customer will sell pounds to us at 1.50. To hedge this position perfectly, we should be short 6.6 million pounds.

1. We are already short 5 million pounds from the first hedge, and we therefore have to sell an additional 1.6 million at 1.47 to be short 6.6 million.

2. If it goes to 1.42, there is an 84 percent chance that at the end of 2 months it will not rise above 1.50. Therefore, we have to sell another 1.8 million to be short 8.4 million pounds.

The lower the pound moves, the greater the probability that the customer will sell pounds to us at 1.50. On the last day of the option period, if the pound is still below 1.50, we must sell the last few of the second 5 million pounds which have not yet been sold. The entire second 5 million pounds was sold below 1.50, which is the price at which we have to buy from the customer. Again, this is not a loss but a cost.

We determine what type of hedge adjustment is needed by comparing what our position *should be* to what it *actually is*. It is important to understand that at the point where an option is at the money (1.50 in our example), the hedge ratio is 50 percent because the chances are equal that the market rate will go up or go down. The point where an option is at the money is always the anchor for an intuitive understanding of delta hedging. This point also represents the probability that the option will be exercised—at 1.50 there is a 50 percent probability that the option will be exercised. If the market price goes to 1.52, the probability that it will go up or down is 50 percent but the probability that it will go so far down that it falls below 1.50 is less than 50 percent.

This description of dynamic delta hedging is reminiscent of the interaction between the person who is preparing to serve in a tennis match and the opponent who is preparing to return the serve. Exhibit 2-18 shows that the server stands (from his viewpoint) to the far left of the right side of the tennis court (S1), where servers often stand in singles matches. Assuming the returner is equally comfortable returning forehand or backhand, he will position himself so that the service field (area A) is equally covered on his right and left sides (R1). In other words, the returner is positioned in a "neutral" way so that he is not more vulnerable on one side than on the other. Now assume, instead of proceeding

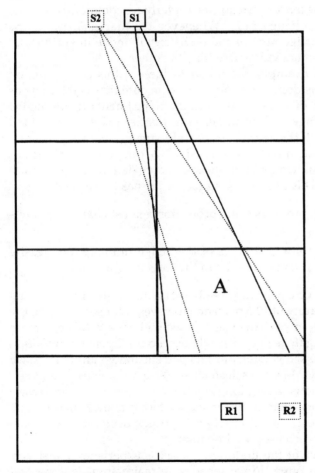

Exhibit 2-18. Analogy between a tennis serve and the return of serve to dynamic delta hedging.

with the serve, the server moves to his right, away from the middle of the court and toward the outside of the court (S2). If the returner stays in the R1 position, he will be vulnerable on his right side toward the sideline of area A. To avoid this vulnerability, the returner responds to the move of the server from the S1 position to the S2 position by moving a little farther to his right side so that he is again indifferent about which side the ball is coming from (R2). He is once again positioned in a "neutral" way. If the server still does not serve but instead moves back slightly to his left, the returner will react by moving back slightly to *his* left. Theoretically, this could go on until the returner requests that the server make up his mind.

In the analogy between the tennis serve and dynamic delta hedging, the server equals the market rate for the underlying commodity and the returner is the delta-hedge ratio. Whenever the market price or the server moves, the hedge ratio or the returner will move in such a way that one side is not more vulnerable than the other.

Returning to our example, the initial hedge—in this case 5 million pounds—typically is done for a forward value date that is the same as the expiration date of the option. Periodic adjustments of the hedge ratio reflecting changes in the underlying market price are executed with spot contracts. If the aggregate spot adjustments amount to a noteworthy portion of the initial forward hedge, we can swap the net result of the aggregate spot hedges from the spot value date to the expiration date of the option. This delta hedging technique has two advantages:

1. A forward hedge provides some protection against changes in interest rates.

2. The periodic minor adjustments of the hedge ratio are more easily executed in the spot market than in the forward market.

The hedging cost of 2 percent we anticipated in the example is based on an assumed volatility of 12.5 percent. However, if for some reason the market moves much more than expected, we will have to rehedge more often, and the aggregate hedge costs will exceed the 2 percent premium. In other words, if we sell volatility at 12.5 percent and volatility rises, we lose money just as we do if we sell stock at 100 and it moves to 102.

When we buy options, we are long volatility; when volatility increases, we make money, and when it decreases, we lose money. When we sell options, we are short volatility; when volatility decreases, we make money, and when it increases, we lose money.

If the market price of the underlying asset is experiencing a steady rise or decline, how often do we rehedge to maintain a delta-neutral hedge position? Each time the market price moves, we can plug it into a model, get the delta-neutral hedge ratio, and update the size of the hedge. In the example, the price probably did not just jump from 1.50 to 1.52; it first moved to 1.51. We could have bought 350,000 at 1.51 and then bought another 350,000 at 1.52, which would have been cheaper than buying 700,000 at 1.52. The more often we rehedge, the lower the cost of each hedge. However, there is a limitation to this hedging strategy. There could be a transaction cost of as much as $30 or $40 for each contract, and the amount of change in the market price may be too small to justify this expense per transaction.

Net Positions
(Departing from Delta Neutral)

It can be seen that it is not practical to be perfectly delta-neutral hedged at all times, and therefore management establishes departure limits from delta neutral. Exhibit 2-17 showed that at the market price of 1.50 (the point where the option is at the money), the hedge ratio is 50 percent. At 1.52, the hedge ratio is 43 percent, and if the option is for 10 million pounds, this means the trader should be short 4.3 million pounds.

If the trader's hedge is to be short 4.3 million but he is actually short 6.3 million, his position is 2 million shorter than it should be for a perfectly hedged position. Of the total 6.3 million, 4.3 million represents the delta hedge and 2 million is a net short position in pounds.[6] Let's say the market rate changes so that the trader should be 5 million short and he is short 6.3 million. Of the 6.3 million, we now have a situation where 5 million is the delta hedge and only 1.3 million is the net short position.

From the management viewpoint, there are two things to consider. First, management must have the ability to determine independently what these delta-hedge-related short positions should be to give traders limits for departing from delta neutral. For example, if management gives the trader a departure limit of 3 million pounds, this means that when the trader should be short 4.3 million, he may be short as much as 7.3 million or as little as 1.3 million. Obviously, that provides flexibility for the trader, who does not have to jump each time there is a slight change in the underlying spot rate.

Limits provide a benchmark for a judging whether the trader's actual position size after adjusting for delta hedge is within the established net position limits (the departure limit from delta neutral). Thus, from a limit and control viewpoint, it is important that management know what the delta-neutral position should be and then compare it with the trader's actual position; the difference cannot exceed the established departure limit.

The second managerial consideration is to track the earnings from general options trading (which we will define later as volatility trading) separately from the earnings derived from departing from delta neutral, which really means having a net FX position. To illustrate that point, assume that the trader has a budget of $10 million for the year and that at the end of the year it turns out that he made $13 million. It appears that the trader did very well. However, in scrutinizing the source of these earnings, we see that he made $12 million of the $13 million by successfully departing from delta neutral and only $1 million from volatility trading.

If that is the case, the trader is still a good trader but not necessarily a good volatility trader. A management decision in such a case would be to move him out of the options area and make him a spot exchange trader, because that is his proven area of expertise. The trader has a very successful spot exchange business under the umbrella of an option and volatility business. This situation is not very cost-effective because operationally the options business is much more intense then a simple spot exchange business. An option book is more expensive to administer, more computers are required, and traders require different skills. Management wants to avoid having a situation where it thinks it is making money in options volatility but in fact is making the money in spot exchange. For this reason, management must be able to track the earnings separately to determine which earnings come from departing from delta neutral and which come from volatility trading.

It is important to highlight the point that trading options means trading volatility and that we can speculate and position volatility. When one believes volatility will rise, one will buy options and keep them delta neutral. When one buys an option, one pays out the premium and performs the initial hedge, and every rehedge generates hedge income. If there is no change in the expected volatility, the aggregate hedge revenues will equal the premium paid.

Volatility Is a Separate Market Price

The profitability of a perfectly delta-hedged option depends on the relationship between the implied volatility assumed at the time the option was priced and the volatility actually occurring in the market (the magnitude of the underlying asset's price fluctuation) during the option period. If these two turn out to be the same, the aggregate hedging cost will be equal to the option premium received. If the actually occurring volatility is lower the hedging cost will be less, and the trader will make a profit. In this situation, actually occurring volatility in the market means less price fluctuation and less frequent rehedging. Because each rehedge costs money, less frequent rehedging means an aggregate rehedging cost that is lower than the option premium earned. The result is an overall profit.

In other words, if the volatility actually occurring in the market throughout the option period is the same as the implied volatility assumed at the time the option was priced, the aggregate hedging cost will equal the premium received. However, if actually occurring market volatility is lower, the trader wins, and if actually occurring market volatility is higher, the trader loses. The trader speculates on a change in the market price called implied volatility.

> *To understand the business and recognize the risk, it is important to understand that when we trade options, we trade implied volatility. To the extent that we are not exactly delta-neutral hedged, we also have a net position risk.*

Buying or Selling Options to Speculate on Changes in Volatility

In this story we are assuming that we bought the options and remained delta neutral because we think that volatility will go up. In other words, we bought volatility. If we are right and volatility does rise, there are two ways we can make money. The first way is to keep the option on the book until maturity or expiration and rehedge frequently, which we have to do because the volatility is higher. That means we have more opportunities to rehedge, and each time we rehedge, we have revenue. As a result, the aggregate rehedging revenues will exceed the option premium paid when we bought the option.

An alternative behavior would be to buy the option, remain delta neutral, and wait until the volatility goes up. At that time, we can call another market participant and ask him to tell us the value of this option. This third party will calculate the option premium by using the higher volatility (in addition to the three "yes, sirs") and will arrive at a higher option price. We can then sell the option at a price higher than the price we paid for it.

To continue the story, assume that we think volatility will go down and sell options—sell volatility—and collect the premium. We do the initial delta hedge and then keep rehedging to keep the delta-neutral position; every rehedge costs money. If we are right—if indeed the volatility goes down—there will be less need to rehedge and therefore we will have a lower rehedging cost. Remember, we sold the option and took in the premium. The initial hedge and every rehedge cost money, and as the volatility goes down, there is less need to hedge and therefore lower aggregate rehedging costs. That is one way to make money, because the aggregate rehedging cost will be lower than the premium collected.

As soon as volatility goes down significantly, we can call another market participant and ask what the value of this option is. The trader will calculate the option premium by using the now-prevailing lower volatility, which, combined with the three "yes, sirs," will lead to a lower option premium. We can buy back the option at a lower cost then the premium we earned when we sold the option.

Measuring Gamma

One also analyzes the sensitivity of the hedge ratio to changes in the market price of the underlying asset. This is known as measuring *gamma*. Gamma is the sensitivity of delta (hedge ratio) to a change in the underlying market price. For example, if we want to get a feel for how sensitive an option book is to changes in the underlying market rate, we can ask, If the underlying spot price changes by 1 percent, how much rehedging would we have to do? The answer might be, If there is a 1 percent change in the underlying spot price, we will have to rehedge 1.25 million pounds.

The greatest sensitivity is at the money; the farther the option is in or out of the money, the less sensitive we are to a change in the underlying market rate. To illustrate, when the pound moves from 1.50 to 1.52, the actual change is 1.33 percent. At 1.52, there is a 7 percent change in the probability that the customer will exercise the option (the difference between 50 percent and 43 percent). Suppose the customer has the right to sell pounds to us at 1.50 and the market price is 2.50—way, way out of the money. At that price, a 1.33 percent change moves the price to 2.535. Is there a 7 percent change in the probability of exercise every time there is a 1.33 percent change in the price? No, because the farther out of the money the price moves, the smaller is the change in the probability that the customer will exercise. This is an extreme example that demonstrates that the change in the percentage of probability is not *linear*. The same is true for deep in-the-money options. Changes in market prices do not affect the delta-hedge ratio on a linear basis. The sensitivity of the delta-hedge ratio is greatest when the option is at the money, and it becomes lower when the option is more in or out of the money.

The main purpose of measuring gamma is to assure that the size of the option book does not exceed an institution's capacity to trade in the market. In other words, if a 1 percent change in the price of the underlying commodity requires a hedge so large that it exceeds our ability to transact in the market, we have a problem and must take corrective action.

Summary: Volatility in Options

There are four components in the calculation of an options premium: the relationship between the strike price and the market price, the time to maturity, the interest rate, and volatility. The first three do not lend themselves to arguments for trading, but the fourth—the anticipated future volatility for the time period for which an option price is to be quoted—is the major factor in option pricing.

When we trade options, we trade volatility. Volatility often is quoted and agreed on between professional options traders before the price of an option is calculated. Lower volatility produces a smaller option premium, and higher volatility produces a higher option premium.

When it comes to options, we focus on the sensitivity to changes in the market rate and volatility. We can protect ourselves against a change in the market rate by maintaining a delta-neutral hedge position, but we cannot protect ourselves against an unexpected change in volatility.

The difference between the correct delta-neutral hedge ratio and the actual hedge ratio is the net position in commodity options or the interest-rate-level-sensitive position in options on interest rates. Management should monitor delta-neutral hedge positions and set limits on departure from delta neutral for traders.

Gamma is the sensitivity of the delta hedge ratio to changes in the underlying market price. The gamma limit protects one against a situation in which a modest change in the underlying market price requires a volume of rehedges that exceeds our capacity to execute these rehedges in the market.

Notes

1. This calculation ignores the income or expense from hedging interest receivables and payables.
2. For a discussion of implied volatility, see pages 45–48, 56–57, and 99.
3. This theory is reversed when one buys equity call options. The alternative to controlling the stock is to buy it spot. This requires one to pay cash which otherwise would have earned interest. When one buys a call option on the stock, one avoids tying up the cash, which can continue to earn interest. This is reflected in the cost of such a call option on equities. Therefore, in this case, the rule is that the higher the interest rate, the higher the option premium.

4. There are five components needed to calculate an option price. In the earlier count of four components, we treated the relationship between strike price and market price as one component. However, as is obvious to the reader, these are really two components, expanding the total count to five.

5. This and the subsequent percentages are only examples that illustrate dynamic delta hedging. The hedge ratio is not always 43 percent because it may be influenced by the level of volatility and other technical factors.

6. In options on interest rates, departure from delta neutral represents an interest-rate-level-sensitive position.

3

Measuring Price Risk Positions

In the last decade many changes have taken place in the financial world. The product line is broader, tenors are longer, risk is determined by more than just the size of a position, the market is more volatile, competition is greater, and global trading takes place 24 hours a day. These changes have brought about an increased focus on price risk, causing banks to doubt the ability of their price risk management systems to cope with the new environment. In the past, banks managed risk by setting limits on the *size of positions,* but that system did not achieve the objective of limiting the *size of the risk.* Today, banks limit to certain percentages of budgeted earnings the amount that can be lost on price risk positions. These limits are known as the value at risk (VAR) limit for trading positions and the earnings at risk (EAR) limit for accrual positions. An effective price risk management system provides techniques for finding answers to the following key questions:

- What is our profit or loss at any point in time?
- How might our profit or loss change? (How much risk do we have?)
- How will price risk be monitored and limited?

Chapters 3 through 7 will answer these questions and in so doing describe a price risk management system that is responsive to the new needs in an environment of substantially increased trading in increasingly complex financial instruments. Before beginning, let us highlight some of the points that make up this discussion of price risk.

The question, What is our profit or loss at any point in time? is answered simply by creating the best possible mark-to-market process we can deliver. We will highlight the significance of segregating the mark-to-market responsibility from the dealing function and discuss how to deal with situations in which market prices are not readily available.

Finding the answer to the second question—How much risk do we have?—is the heart of modern price risk management. We are introducing a new price risk management system which focuses on the size of the risk instead of the size of the position. This value at risk is derived by converting volume and notional amounts of price risk positions into position sensitivity, which is the dollar equivalent of a 1-unit change in the market price. Then we multiply this dollar equivalent of a 1-unit change by volatility, which is the size of the price change that usually occurs overnight, i.e., not a disaster scenario. You will see how the different types of price risk discussed in Chap. 2 are affected by this process and become familiar with the new language. The critical aspect of valuing risk is the estimate of future overnight volatility. Different volatility discovery methodologies are discussed, and the pros and cons are analyzed. There is also a detailed discussion of different confidence levels so that the meaning of a certain amount of dollars at risk is understood. Trading liquidity and the resulting defeasance periods are discussed as part of volatility.

In the section on monitoring and limiting price risk, the most important point is to establish the overnight limits in terms of VAR and use volatility to back into the volume amounts. In other words, the amount of VAR remains unchanged and the amounts for volume limits rise and fall as volatility falls and rises. VAR limits are set to reflect expected trading revenues, and the importance of customer-related earnings is highlighted. Finally, different types of price risk are aggregated through covarying at the individual dealing room level and identifying as well as aggregating individual market factor sensitivities across product lines at the corporate level. At the end, we will be looking at the latest proposals for the allocation of equity to price risk.

What Is Our Profit or Loss at Any Point in Time?

For accounting purposes, any position in the balance sheet can be viewed either as a trading account or, by default, as an accrual account. The main difference between these positions is the holding intention and consequently the mark-to-market requirement. Trading positions are marked-to-market daily; accrual positions are not (see "Marking-to-Market the Trading Portfolio" and "Valuing the Accrual Portfolio," below).

Since it is assumed that positions held for trading purposes can be liquidated at any time, the accounting system values them on a daily basis at the current market price—the price at which traders can liquidate the position in the market. Any differences between these daily market values and the book values are reflected immediately as profits or losses in the income statement.

When a position is not intended to be held for trading purposes (accrual accounts), the accounting system assumes that the position will be held until maturity, and consequently, it is not necessary to mark-to-market the position. The only profits or losses that affect the income statement are the interest differentials between asset yields and liability yields, independent of current market prices.

Trading accounts usually are represented by marketable commodities or securities and the majority of the derivatives (such as FX, government bonds, securitizable loans, equities, swaps, and options). *Accrual accounts* are represented by all the other positions in the balance sheet (mainly deposits and loans). Since the main distinction between these two accounts is the holding intention, a bank may have two positions in the same marketable security: one a trading position and the other an accrual position. There is one exception to this dichotomy. A third type of account, *held for sale,* is an accrual account that is marked-to-market. We will describe this account later in this chapter and in the discussion of accrual positions in Chap. 4.

The difference in the accounting treatment between trading accounts and accrual accounts makes it necessary to differentiate between them for purposes of price risk measurement. It is necessary to understand not only how much price risk is involved in a position but also the point in time when the accounting system may recognize this risk. The following example will clarify this distinction.

Assume we bought at par two positions in the same government bond. Each bond has a nominal value of $1 million, a 10 percent coupon, and a remaining life of 12 months. Both bonds are funded with overnight money at 8.5 percent. One position is booked in the trading account; the other is intended to be held until maturity and is booked in the accrual account. Now assume that interest rates rise by 1 percent. Overnight money rises from 8.5 percent to 9.5 percent, and the increase in the 1-year interest rate reduces the market value of both positions from $1 million to $991,000.

For accounting purposes, the trading position may be liquidated at any time, and it therefore is marked-to-market at the new price of $991,000. Since the book value of this position is $1 million (purchase price), a $9000 loss is shown immediately in the income statement. The accrual position is intended to be held until maturity, and the accounting system continues to accrue the 10 percent coupon of the bond until it matures in 1 year. However, since the overnight funding cost has risen by 1 percent, the profit margin shrinks from the original 1.5 percent (10 percent coupon minus 8.5 percent funding cost) to 0.5 percent for the remainder of the year. In dollar terms, the 1 percent smaller spread on a $1 million position over 1 year represents $10,000 less revenue.

The same change in interest rates on exactly the same types of positions may have different accounting implications. In the trading account there is an immediate $9000 loss, while the accrual account will show $10,000 less in revenue spread over 1 year. The difference between the $9000 and the $10,000 is the effect of the *present value*. The $9000 happens today, while the $10,000 happens over 1 year.

Marking-to-Market the Trading Portfolio

Marking-to-market the value of actual and contingent assets and liabilities is accomplished by simulating the liquidation of a portfolio, which means looking at an entire portfolio and determining the price at which each position can be liquidated if it becomes necessary to do so. Daily marking-to-market of all price risk positions keeps us informed about current profits and losses. See also rate reasonability process on pages 282–285.

Sources of Market Rates

The process of daily marking-to-market of the active trading accounts is based on market prices from liquid markets provided by news vendors such as Reuters or from organized exchanges, banks, dealers, and brokers. For illiquid markets, we may get the prices used in recent transactions. Finally, we may conduct a reasonableness test by comparing the prices used in past and future transactions with those used in the mark-to-market process (see below).

Premiums/Discounts for Unusual Positions

It is not always possible to liquidate a price risk position at the market rate/screen rate. The size of the position, the length of the maturity, or the exoticness of the instrument or currency involved may force us to accept discounts on long positions and pay premiums on short positions. Prudent judgment is required in such cases to arrive at a market price at which the position can be liquidated realistically. For a related discussion, see "Defeasance Period" in Chap. 5.

Reasonableness Test

Sometimes there are situations in which no market price exists for a price risk position on the books. In such cases a bank has to rely on the prices attached to the institution's most recent trades in those instruments/commodities. In addition, it is conceivable that there are no such trades for several days, in which case one must reluctantly rely on estimates provided by the trader. Eventually, this exotic instrument will be traded again, and the price of this trade should be in close proximity to the estimates provided by the trader during the preceding days. If there is a substantial difference between the estimated rates provided by the trader on days without turnover and the price of the first transaction after this nontrade period, the trader must offer a very convincing explanation. Otherwise, the trader's estimates must be viewed in retrospect as being unreasonable. It is imperative to communicate clearly to traders that the intentional provision of unrealistic market prices to manage earnings leads to severest disciplinary action.

Present Value for Forward Results

Spot positions are valued by finding out the price at which they can be liquidated today; profit or loss is calculated as the difference between the book value and the market value. Forward positions are valued by finding the current value of a cash flow that will occur on a future date. The current value of a cash flow is lower than it will be on the future value date.

When we mark-to-market, we are interested only in the profit today. For example, if we have a 1-year forward position that will yield a profit of $1 million in 1 year, the million-dollar cash flow will occur in 1 year. If the interest rate is 10 percent, the present value of the anticipated profit of $1 million is approximately $910,000. Therefore, one important component in the mark-to-market process is that all results have to be brought to present value.

By marking-to-market and calculating present value, we are creating hypothetical positive and negative cash flows which represent the profits and losses that will occur if we liquidate these positions today. At the end of each day, when all risk positions have been identified, we know the worth of a trading portfolio valued at the appropriate market rates and discounted to present value, and at least once a month (typically at the end of the month) we also know the worth of an investment portfolio.

Independence from the Dealing Function

The mark-to-market process must be *independent* of the trading and marketing process. Traders should *not* calculate their own profit, since their compensation includes performance-based bonuses. In this context, it should be noted that traders may not overstate earnings only when there are losses. Traders also may attempt to understate earnings to move positive results into the following year or into a different performance evaluation period. This situation occurs when earnings substantially exceed the budget and traders perceive that their bonuses will not be notably higher than a certain level regardless of how much money they make in the current evaluation period.

In terms of protecting an institution against rogue traders, an independent mark-to-market process is a major, if not the most important, tool. Only rarely do traders attempt to cheat blatantly. More often, there is room for judgment in a somewhat gray zone of appropriate market prices. Take, for example, a large and perhaps longer-term interest differential or spread position in which a very few basis points can have a big impact on earnings. In such a situation it may be difficult for personnel outside the dealing room to capture the difference between a slightly excessive conservative valuation (we do not want to overstate our earnings) and an intended hiding of profits.

Insisting on segregation of responsibility in this and many other situations should not be interpreted as management not trusting the traders. Instead, it must be viewed as a good business practice. In addition, one should always remember that "the good ones can be just as bad as the bad ones if the good ones have a chance to be bad."

If we have less-liquid assets that are not so easily bought and sold, traders may say they cannot sell those assets at any price. If there is doubt that this is actually true or to provide an incentive to liquidate the portfolio, management can implement a penalty charge in the mark-to-market process.

For example, in March a high-risk bond is purchased at 90. The market is still 90 in April, and consequently, when the bond is marked-to-market, there is no profit or loss. Management can tell the traders that if they have this instrument in their portfolios for more than 3 months, there will be a 2-point charge for this position in the fourth month and every additional month until the position is liquidated. In other words, even though the market may be 90, in the fourth month (July) the position is valued as if the market were 88, and for each additional month the instrument is in the trader's portfolio the bank takes another 2-point charge. If that is done for 5 months, the loss will total 10 points and the book value of the bond will be written down from 90 to 80.

The more one does this, the greater the incentive is for the trader to sell this asset because he knows that he is going to be charged 2 points every month. Suppose that after the bond is written down to 80, it is sold at 90. What happens to the 10-point profit? The bank may not give the credit to the trader because if it does, this process will become a convenient way of establishing a reserve of deferred earnings. These earnings have to be credited to people at least two or three levels above the trader in the organization. In other words, these earnings have to go to people who are far enough away from the trader that those who have an influence on selling the position do not benefit from it. In this case, the farther removed the recipient is from the trader, the better.

Input from Outside Vendors

Most products can be independently marked-to-market quite easily using the closing prices in the daily newspaper, but this only works if all of the following are true:

- there are relatively few positions,
- the product is simple; and,
- the newspaper or other reliable source carries the price.

Unfortunately in practice this is often not the case. Many products require some kind of model or "advanced calculator" that uses market inputs to determine the current value. This means models must be independently verified, inputs have to be verified to outside sources, and the entire system must be kept secure. (We don't want to see a case where the traders provide the valuation model to the back office and tell them where to get the inputs.) In cases involving complicated products, end users may be tempted to get the fair-market value from the bank that originally sold them the deal. The hazards that this entails are well documented. It is critical to have a valuation by someone who is *not* a party to the transaction.

The alternative is to use an independent mark-to-market service operating over the Internet. This brings several benefits:

- a completely independent mark-to-market
- a reasonableness check where illiquid market data inputs are required (such as correlation or certain volatilities)
- confidentiality of the client's portfolio
- ease and convenience of use and a rapid turnaround.

One firm breaking ground in this area is Mutant Technology, based in London, England. They have devised a system that allows a firm's auditors, back office, middle office, traders, or salespeople to use their desktop computers and existing Internet or Intranet software to access a multitude of models with unbiased inputs. Each authorized user can obtain valuations of an existing deal, a portfolio of deals (for instance, all swaps done by a particular customer), a proposed deal, or the bank's entire value at risk. All the inputs and models are independent, provided by Mutant Technology. In my opinion, this is the best way to guard against mark-to-market funny business.

The basic process involves logging onto the site and requesting an independent mark-to-market for any portfolios that the user is authorized to see. These trades would typically be preloaded on the valuation server or, if there are only a few trades, they may be uploaded at the time. The valuation server responds with the current mark-to-market value of the portfolio and provides a query facility on a trade-by-trade basis if required.

It is not possible in this brief section to do more than provide an overview of what is going on in this area because it is still very much in the early stages of evolution; however, the use of Internet delivery mechanisms to provide an independent mark-to-market service is a product whose time has come.

Given the importance and complexity of certain price risk portfolios, banks should consider buying professional valuations of their price-risk positions and portfolios from firms that are highly specialized to perform exactly that function. Such additional outside input can be of great value for the risk management and audit functions of large market participants who appreciate the independence of the information. It can also be very useful for less active market participants whose risk management and audit functions are less focused on financial trading. Those companies may, so to speak, "outsource" the mark-to-market process to an outside professional firm or use it simply to verify their internal calculations.

Valuing the Accrual Portfolio

As was said earlier, accrual positions include all the positions held by a bank where the holding intention is *not* trading. In fact, the bulk of a bank's balance sheet, including almost all the loans and deposits, represents accrual positions. Since the bank does not intend to use these positions for trading, they are assumed to be in the bank's books until their maturity dates regardless of the marketability of such positions. This assumption is especially valid since the accounting system restricts their sale before maturity. Exceptions usually are limited to contingency situations or situations where management declares in advance its intention to retain some selling flexibility.

Since it is assumed that accrual positions will not be sold before maturity, these accounts are not marked-to-market. Instead, the accounting procedure accrues the spread between assets and liabilities until maturity. This adds a time factor to the price risk measurement in accrual positions (an exception applies to held-for-sale accounts). The risk measurement for accrual positions not only recognizes a potential impact on earnings but also recognizes the time frame for when this impact will be recognized by the accounting system.

To understand this accounting feature, let us look at an example. A $100,000, 2-year asset at 11 percent p.a. is funded with a 2-year liability at 9 percent p.a. The current market interest rate is 10 percent p.a. If these transactions are marked-to-market, the accounting system will recognize today a $3470 profit (present value of the 2 percent spread each year— $2000 at the end of year 1 and $2000 at the end of year 2—at a 10 percent interest rate). That represents the profit from the position if we sell these assets and liabilities today at current market rates. However, because we know the intention is not to sell these positions before maturity, we know we will not realize the $3470 today. Instead, we will accrue $2000 for each of the 2 years, i.e., 2 percent p.a. spread evenly over the 2-year period (drip income).

Accrual instruments may be recorded in two types of accounts: *held-to-maturity* and *held-for-sale* accounts. The *held-to-maturity* account includes all instruments which will not be sold before maturity; in fact, they *cannot* be sold before maturity. An example of a *held-for-maturity* instrument is a nontransferable certificate of deposit.

While it is an accrual account, the *held-for-sale* account includes instruments that may be sold at any time with no restriction, such as a short-term central bank note. The intention is to hold instruments in this account until maturity, but management retains the right to sell them before maturity if necessary. The accounting system treats these instruments as it does any other held-to-maturity instrument except that once a month they are marked-to-market. Any difference between the book value and the market value of these positions is reported as a reserve of the capital account, not in the P&L account. The reserve is reversed against the P&L account only if the instruments are sold. From a price risk viewpoint, held-for-sale accounts are considered accrual accounts and are monitored against accrual limits. However, the mark-to-market feature is controlled against separate VAR management action triggers (MATs), which are discussed in Chap. 6.

Summary

The major difference between a trading position and an accrual position is the holding intention and the requirement for a mark-to-market process. Trading positions are marked-to-market daily, while accrual positions are not.

In trading positions, the daily profit or loss is the daily change in the mark-to-market value of the portfolio. By marking-to-market, we are actually valuing present and future and positive and negative cash flows at the present date (present value). This marked-to-market value is determined by simulating the orderly liquidation of these positions at current market prices. At the end of each day, when all risk positions have been identified, we know the worth of a trading portfolio valued at the appropriate market rates and discounted to present value.

Accrual positions are not marked-to-market (with the exception of held-for-sale accounts). Instead, the accounting procedure accrues the spread between assets and liabilities until maturity. This procedure adds a time factor to the price risk measurement in accrual positions, since profit and loss are recognized only when an instrument reaches maturity.

4

Assessing the Size
of Price Risk

How Might Our Profit or
Loss Change?

The mark-to-market process provides information about the current status of profits and losses; that is, it indicates what profits or losses actually are at a particular time. For example, a trader buys a commodity at 95 in the morning, and the price rises to 100 at the end of the day. The trader wishes to keep the position overnight and reports a mark-to-market profit of 5, which is shown in the evening report to management.[1] The book value of this position is adjusted to 100, and the price risk position is carried overnight. The interesting question now is: How much risk does this position involve overnight? The answer to this question must be part of the evening report, and we are now ready to examine this subject.

Assessing the Size of Price
Risk in Trading Positions

Let us begin with a story about a Frenchman in the pioneering days of aviation who had a very small airplane that could accommodate only one person. One Sunday morning he decided to fly the plane from Paris to London. He successfully executed the distance but unfortunately missed the London airport by several miles. The plane landed in a rural area, where an Englishman happened by on his way to church. The Frenchman, still sitting in the plane, pulled down the window and

71

asked him, "Excuse me, sir, can you tell me where I am?" The Englishman replied, "You, sir, are sitting in the cockpit of that airplane." The Frenchman said, "Oh, merci, monsieur. May I ask you another question? Do you happen to be by profession an accountant?" The Englishman replied, "Indeed, I am an accountant, but I'm very surprised. How did you know?" The Frenchman said, "Well, it's very easy. All the information I have received from you so far is 100 percent correct, but for me it is also 100 percent useless."

Similarly, we can simulate a conversation on a Friday afternoon at BigBank between the boss and a trader in which the boss calls to ask, "How are we going into the weekend?" The trader reports the following: "In foreign exchange we are $85 million long against reserve currencies, we are $20 million short against regional exotics, we have money market gaps of $500 million 1 month against 6 months, and we are short 65,000 ounces of gold." This answer makes the boss unhappy because that is not why he called. The information he has received from the trader is 100 percent correct, but it is also 100 percent useless. The boss wants to know what could actually go wrong over the weekend— i.e., how much money can be lost if the market moves against BigBank in the normal way—not the consequences of an end-of-the-world catastrophe.

Value at Risk

The trader's answer to the boss's inquiry is characteristic of the old language in which positions are described in terms of volume. To illustrate a more accurate way of describing a position in terms of how much could potentially be lost, let us examine the Grandmother Story. It goes like this. A banker in his late fifties comes home from the office and finds to his great pleasure that his mother, the grandmother of his children, is visiting. Mothers always worry about their children, and the mother looks at her son and says: "You look pale and stressed out. Was it a difficult day at the office?" The son says: "Yes, Mother, it was a tough day, but to tell you the truth, in the afternoon I did not do any bank work at all. Instead, I reviewed the deferred income in my pension account, which can be invested in various ways. Until today I had all my money in short-term fixed income, something that you, Mother, might call a savings account. However, after several hours of agonizing analysis, I decided to switch all my money from savings into equities. Specifically, Mother, I bought 29,358 shares of the ABC stock at $13\frac{5}{8}$."

Mother is an 89-year-old lady who is still very sharp, but 29,358 shares at $13\frac{5}{8}$ does not mean anything to her. The son sees this and decides to try another way of explaining his position to his mother. He says, "Mother, you understand that I switched from savings into equities." His mother nods. The son continues: "Regarding the shares I bought, if the price of the shares changes overnight by 1 percent, the impact on me will be $4000." The mother's face lights up because she begins to understand. A 1 percent change in the price of the shares overnight equals $4000. The mother reflects for a moment and then asks, "And how much does it usually change?" The son says: "Mother, that is a very good question. Nobody knows. But since you say 'usually,' let's say it usually changes about 1.5 percent every night." The mother reflects for a second and then exclaims: "I see. That means that every night you have $6000 at risk." The son then says: "Mother, you got it."

You can see that the son's first statement is in volume terms (29,358 shares at 13⅝), which neither grandmothers nor bank presidents understand. The second approach uses *sensitivity* language—the dollar equivalent of a 1-unit change. This position sensitivity indicates the size of the position, but it does so in more comprehensible language. The resultant $4000 can easily be multiplied by the "usual change"—i.e., volatility—which leads to the size of the risk, the value at risk. Exhibit 4-1 illustrates the difference between the old language and the new language used to describe the size of a position and its risk.

The gist of the Grandmother Story is the distinction between the size of the *position* and the size of the *risk*. The old language of 29,358 shares at 13⅝ indicates the size of the position. If that is converted in terms of sensitivity—the dollar equivalent of a 1-unit change—we are still describing the size of the position. There is no difference in volume language—29,358 shares at 13⅝ and 1 percent sensitivity equals $4000. Both are indicators of the size of the position. The only difference is that the dollar equivalent of a 1-unit change—the sensitivity—is much more useful because we can multiply the *sensitivity* to the dollar equivalent of a 1-unit change by *volatility* to get the *value at risk*. It is very important to

Old Language:	**Bought**	**29,358 shares of ABC stock at 13 5/8**
	Invested	**$400,000**
New Language:	**1% position sensitivity in ABC stock**	**$4,000**
	Expected volatility overnight	**1.5%**
	Value at risk	**$6,000**

Exhibit 4-1. Old language versus new language.

recognize that sensitivity is an exact measure of the size of a position—computers can calculate precisely the dollar equivalent of a 1-unit change, which is 1 percent when it comes to commodities or 1 basis point (bp)^2 in terms of interest rate risk and volatility risk.

To summarize this important concept, sensitivity is the size of the position—$4000 in this story. When we multiply sensitivity by volatility—in this case, 1.5 percent—we get the size of the risk, which is the value at risk—$6000.

Let us look at one more example to make this point clear. The Bahamian dollar is pegged one to one against the U.S. dollar, just as the Brunei dollar is pegged against the Singapore dollar. In any one of these two foreign exchange pairs, if we have a $100 million equivalent foreign exchange position, the 1 percent position sensitivity in both cases will be $1 million. That tells us how big the position is—1 percent of $100 million is $1 million. We multiply $1 million by the volatility, which in all two cases is zero, and the value at risk is zero.

If we have the same $100 million position against the Euro, we again have a 1 percent position sensitivity of $1 million, exactly the same as in the previous example. The only difference is that in the dollar/Euro position, the volatility is assumed to be 1.5 percent and the value at risk therefore is $1.5 million. We can see that sensitivity tells us exactly how big the position is ($1 million) but tells us nothing about the size of the risk. Only when we multiply sensitivity by volatility do we get the value at risk.

Put yet another way, the only reason we are interested in sensitivity is that we want to multiply sensitivity by the volatility to find out how much is actually at risk. This objective requires explaining a couple of additional points. You may wonder why sensitivity is 1 percent or 1 bp, and the answer is that it has to be something with a 1 to facilitate the multiplication of the dollar equivalent of the sensitivity by volatility, which usually is an odd percentage. Suppose the banker had told his mother that if there is a $^7/_8$ percent change, the impact on him will be $3500. Then she says, "How much does it usually change?" and he says 1.5 percent. No one would be able to immediately state the value at risk. This makes it desirable to use the dollar equivalent of a number with 1 for sensitivity. Whether it is 1 basis point, 10 basis points, 100 basis points, or even 10 percent, it does not make any difference.

It is also useful to set the size of the number with 1 slightly below the actual volatility because it is easier for most people to multiply up than it is to divide down. For example, the man also could have told his mother that a 10 percent change in the price of the stock will mean a $40,000 impact, which is also correct. Then, when she asks how much it usually changes, he says 1.5 percent. It is possible, of course, to figure out that if 10 percent equals $40,000 then 1.5 percent is $6000, but most people will agree that it is easier to go from 1 percent equaling $4000 to 1.5 percent equaling $6000, which I call multiplying up, than to divide down from 10 percent equals $40,000 to calculate that 1.5 percent is $6000. For this reason, we find out the volatility number and then set the "oneness" for the sensitivity unit below that number.[3]

The Grandmother Story can be applied to all three families of financial market prices: commodities (including foreign exchange), interest rates, and implied volatility.

Position Sensitivity for Commodities

Exhibit 4-2 shows how value at risk is calculated for commodities. For example, assume we have a volume position of a $10 million foreign exchange position against 20 million marks. We are using 1 percent as the sensitivity indicator, which means that if we want to calculate 1 percent of the volume position, we take away two zeros from 10 million, resulting in a 1 percent position sensitivity of 100,000. If volatility is 1.5 percent, the value at risk (VAR) is $150,000. The second commodity is a $5 million position in equities. It has a 1 percent position sensitivity of 50,000, a volatility of 2 percent, and a resulting VAR of 100,000. The VARs of the positions in oil and metals are 450,000 and 32,000, respectively.

Volume Position	1% Position Sensitivity	Volatility	VAR
FX $10,000,000 vs. DM 20,000,000	100,000	1.5%	150,000
Equities 100,000 shares at 50 vs. $5,000,000	50,000	2.0%	100,000
Oil 1,000,000 Barrels at 15 vs. $15,000,000	150,000	3.0%	450,000
Metals 10,000 oz gold at 400 vs. $4,000,000	40,000	0.8%	32,000

Exhibit 4-2. Value at risk for commodities.

Position Sensitivity for Interest Rates

We can also apply the VAR formula to interest rates. Exhibit 4-3 shows that we have a $500 million money market gap for 1 year and that the sensitivity indicator is 1 basis point. The $500 million represents 100 percent; therefore, when we multiply by 1 basis point, we take off four zeros, resulting in a 1-basis-point sensitivity of $50,000.[4] If volatility is 7 basis points, the VAR is $350,000.

In other words, we put the entire gap position on the computer and assume a funding cost of, say, 6.00 percent p.a. We press the button, and the computer gives us the amount of our funding cost of $30 million at 6.00 percent (6.00 percent of $500 million in the example). Then we calculate the funding cost one more time, but this time we assume a funding cost of 6.01 percent, which of course is higher ($30,050,000). The difference between these two funding costs—$30 million at 6.00 percent and $30,050,000 at 6.01 percent—represents the 1-basis-point position sensitivity of $50,000. This difference multiplied by the volatility of 7 percent gives us the VAR of $350,000.

Similarly, with $800 million in Treasury bills, we take off four zeros and the sensitivity for 1 year is $80,000, whereas for 6 months it is $40,000. The volatility is 8 basis points for this position, and so the VAR is $320,000. When we have a fixed-income portfolio consisting of many different bonds with different maturities, amounts, and coupons, we proceed in a similar manner. We value the portfolio at the going market yield, say, 6.50 percent p.a. Then we assume a market yield of 6.51 percent, or 1 basis point higher, and value the portfolio again. This will result in a portfolio value slightly lower than the value calculated at 6.50 percent. The difference between the two portfolio values, one calculated at a yield of 6.50 percent and one calculated at a yield of 6.51 percent, is the 1-basis-point sensitivity of this portfolio. Again, we multiply this portfolio sensitivity by the volatility and obtain the VAR of the portfolio.

If we take off four zeros from the 300 million in FRAs and multiply by 2 for the contractual maturity of 2 years, we get a sensitivity of 60,000. The volatility is 6 basis points, and the resulting VAR is $360,000.

In Exhibit 4-3 examples have been chosen to help the reader follow the logic of the system without using a calculator. For instance, a $500 million money market gap for 1 year is an extremely rare occurrence, since gaps usually build up gradually, reach a peak, and then come down again. However, in the unlikely event that a trader had no gap at all yesterday and today builds up a gap of $500 million for exactly 1 year, then for 1 day a situation will prevail that can easily be calculated as we have shown. However, the following day this calculation is incorrect because the life of the gap is no longer 1 year. Even if the volume

Volume Position	One Basis Point Position Sensitivity	Volatility	VAR
Money Market Gap $500,000,000 1 Year	50,000	7 Basis Points	350,000
T-Bills $800,000,000 6 Months	40,000	8 B.P.	320,000
FRAs $300,000,000 2 Years	60,000	6 B.P.	360,000
Spreads $1 Billion T/ED 3 Months	25,000	2 B.P.	50,000
Bonds $10,000,000 30 years 9 3/8%	10,000	5 B.P.	50,000

Exhibit 4-3. Value at risk for interest rates.

remains exactly $500 million, the sensitivity will be slightly less than $50,000 because the gap period is now less than 1 year. People who have seen how the gapping business works know that a gapped position is never a round sum for an even amount of time (e.g., 3, 6, or 12 months). Again, the examples in the exhibit were chosen so that the reader can follow the logic of the system.

When we move on to the last example in Exhibit 4-3, a $10 million bond for 30 years with a coupon of $9\frac{3}{8}$ percent, we see that the 1-basis-point sensitivity is $10,000. This is another example that illustrates how the system becomes more powerful when the instruments become more complex. As we initially look at this and try to use the method of knocking off four zeros, it seems that the sensitivity should be 30,000 instead of 10,000 because the period is 30 years. The reason why this 1-basis-point sensitivity is $10,000 is that the *duration* of the 30-year bond with a coupon of $9\frac{3}{8}$ is exactly 10 years, and therefore we treat this like a 10-year position; the true economic life is 10 years, and the sensitivity therefore is $10,000.

Duration is a measurement of the true economic life of a bond. To understand the position, we have to distinguish between the contractual maturity and the duration of the bond. When we have a 30-year *zero-coupon bond*, the duration of that bond and the contractual maturity are both 30 years because there will be no cash flow before the contractual maturity of the bond. However, if we have a *coupon* bond with a very small coupon, such as 1 percent, the contractual maturity remains 30 years. However, since we get some cash flow every year from that 1 percent coupon, the duration—the true economic life—will be shorter than 30 years. When there is cash flow before maturity—i.e., when there is a coupon—the duration is shorter than the contractual maturity. It follows that the higher the coupon is, the more cash flow there is every year and therefore the shorter the duration is. It so happens that at $9\frac{3}{8}$ percent the duration is exactly 10 years.

One can say that sensitivity accounts for tenor and duration. If we want to know the size of the position and the sensitivity of the position to a 1-unit change, we do not need duration anymore. Chapter 5 discusses the creation of time buckets on the volatility curve. This discussion complements the statement made above to the effect that sensitivity supersedes duration. It points out that the way to cope with different tenors is to break up the volatility curve into "maturity buckets" and that the size of each bucket is determined by the commonality in the volatility of market prices for different maturities. Then the same volatility percentage is applied to all the tenors in that bucket.

The reader may wonder what is so fancy about this system. Under commodities, we knock off two zeros; for interest rates, we knock off four zeros. Who needs this? If we know the volatility, we can go directly to VAR. That may be true for commodities. When we have a $10 million position against marks and know the volatility is 1.5 percent, many of us probably can figure out directly that 1.5 percent of $10 million is $150,000 VAR. However, as positions and instruments become more complex, the true power of this system becomes more evident.

Position Sensitivity for Implied Volatility

The third family of financial market prices is implied volatility. Exhibit 4-4 shows a position similar to the ones we looked at before. We have an at-the-money option position of 10 million pounds, the same market price and strike price of 1.50, 1 year to maturity, a 6 percent interest rate for both sterling and dollars, and 13 percent assumed implied volatility. This option has a value, but it is not important to know that value. What we are interested in knowing is the risk of this perfectly delta-hedged position.

We remember from the discussion in Chap. 2, "*Understanding the Business, Recognizing Price Risk,*" that the only risk in a perfectly delta-hedged option position is that the implied volatility changes—this is an implied volatility position. If implied volatility is now 13 percent, we can

Volume Position	One Basis Point Position Sensitivity of Volatility	Volatility of Volatility	VAR
Option in FX £10,000,000 vs. dollars Spot and strike price 1.50 One year to maturity Interest rates both 6% Volatility 13%	140	30 B.P.	4200

Exhibit 4-4. Value at risk of an implied volatility position.

ask, What happens if the volatility changes from 13.00 percent to 13.01 percent? The first thing we intuitively know is that the value of this option position will increase, because when implied volatility goes up, the value of the option goes up. We know it will be higher, but we do not know how much higher. Therefore, we have to find out the 1-basis-point sensitivity of this option position to a change in implied volatility.

How much will the value of this option change if the implied volatility changes from 13.00 percent to 13.01 percent? We calculate the option value (premium) one time using an implied volatility of 13.00 percent and again using an implied volatility of 13.01 percent and note that the difference between the two options values is $140. This means that we have a 1-basis-point sensitivity in our implied volatility position of $140.

This is the ultimate example of the power of this price risk management system. Earlier we said that when it comes to commodity positions, we sometimes can apply the volatility directly to the position size without going through sensitivity to determine the VAR. Also, when we have exceptionally easy and nearly never-occurring types of interest rate risk positions, we also can easily calculate the VAR (although we pointed out that in real life these positions are never that even).

However, if the reader does not look at the chart in Exhibit 4-4, he or she will have no idea of how many dollars equivalent is a 1-basis-point change in implied volatility. The reader does not know whether this is a one-digit, two-digit, three-digit, or four-digit number. A computer model is required to calculate the dollar equivalent of a 1-basis-point change in implied volatility and conclude that the position sensitivity of the implied volatility is 140. This cannot be verified by an easy calculation; we simply have to believe what the model tells us.

Remember that the position sensitivity of 140 does not tell us anything about the riskiness of this option position. It only tells us the size of the option position or, better, the size of the implied volatility position. This is not a position in a commodity, and it is not a position in an interest rate—it is an implied volatility position. The size of the implied volatility position is such that if there is a 1-basis-point change in implied volatility, the value of the option will change by 140. Just as the mother asked, "How much does it usually change?" we have to ask that question now. How much does the implied volatility usually change overnight, or, more professionally, what is the volatility of the implied volatility? As we see in Exhibit 4-4, if we assume that the overnight volatility is 30 basis points, we can then multiply volatility by the dollar equivalent of a 1-basis-point change (140), as we have done with commodities and interest rates, and obtain a VAR of $4200.

The reader will have difficulty accepting this just because the model says it is so. This is one reason why these and other financial models have to be validated from time to time (see "Model Validation" in Chap. 15). However, for most people the act of dialing 15 digits on the telephone, listening to three rings, and having a known voice halfway around the globe answer is still a mystery. It happens every day, and most people would not be able to explain how it actually works. The same is true of television and many other conveniences that surround us in day-to-day life. We therefore suggest that you simply accept that this is so because people who are familiar with the inside of the model confirm that it is in fact correct, just as there are people who understand and can explain why after we punch in 15 numbers, the phone rings halfway around the world, who understand why we get a television picture of a sporting event that is 1000 miles away, and who understand why a jumbo jet stays in the air.

The point of this discussion is that position sensitivity expressed in dollars is always correct because it is calculated on computers. However, position sensitivity is not a goal by itself; its value lies in the fact that we can multiply the dollar equivalent of position sensitivity by volatility to get what we really want—the value at risk. One caveat is that VAR is only an estimate because we are multiplying the sensitivity of the position by volatility, which is an estimate. In other words, position sensitivity is an indication of the *size* of a position. When we multiply position sensitivity by estimated volatility, we get an indication of the value that is potentially *at risk* in a position.

Multiple Market Factor Sensitivity

For instruments that involve more than one market factor, calculating the VAR is not as straightforward as the method described earlier in this chapter. To understand what multiple market factor sensitivity means, let us consider a simple example of a forward exchange contract. A forward exchange rate is sensitive to three market factors: the spot exchange rate and two interest rates. We could analyze the sensitivity of the spot exchange rate and the sensitivities of the two interest rates to a 1-unit change, multiply each of the three sensitivities by the appropriate volatility, and add them together to derive the total VAR for this net forward exchange position. However, that would definitely represent an overstatement of the risk because of the covariance, or degree of similarity, in the way the three factors move. It is extremely unlikely that all three market factors will move against us at the same time.

A better approach is to determine the sensitivity of the net forward position to a 1-unit change and then multiply the sensitivity by the volatility of the forward exchange rate to derive the VAR. When we estimate the volatility of the forward exchange rate, we focus on the volatility of the dominant market factor, which might be the spot exchange rate in the case of a short-term forward and might be the two interest rates in the case of a longer-term forward. This approach reduces the possibility of overstating the VAR of the forward exchange position.

Price Sensitivity in Options

One notable exception to the use of multiple market factor sensitivity involves option books, where the sensitivity and volatility of the implied volatility should never be combined with the sensitivity and volatility of the underlying market price. The reason why these two sensitivities should not be combined into one position sensitivity is that both implied volatility and the underlying market price are dominant market factors in options.

There are two gauges for measuring the price sensitivity of an option portfolio: the sensitivity of (1) the option price to a 1-unit change in implied volatility and (2) the price risk position in foreign exchange or interest rates resulting from an imperfect delta hedge. In addition, we measure gamma, which is the sensitivity of the delta-hedge ratio to a 1-unit change in the underlying market price. Gamma, however, is not directly a price risk. Instead, we would like to know the size of gamma to see whether the size of rehedging required from a change in the underlying market price is within our capacity to execute these trades. We therefore can say that gamma relates to price risk only indirectly via trading liquidity, not directly as is the case with risk positions in implied volatility, FX, and interest rate risk.

Both gamma and implied volatility are not 100 percent linear (see Chap. 2). Because of this phenomenon, volatility-based results should be calculated differently from the usual process in which we determine the dollar equivalent of a 1-unit change and then multiply by the usual change, the volatility. Let us say that the volatility of the underlying market price is 2 percent and that for gamma purposes we wish to find out how much rehedging would be required if such a 2 percent change occurred. In such a case we simply assume directly a 2 percent change and find out what the impact is. This may produce a result different from what we would get if we simply doubled the impact of a 1-unit change. The same technique will be used in calculating the VAR of implied volatility positions. If the level of the implied volatility is 13 percent and the usual change in this implied volatility is 30 basis points, we calculate the option value once at 13 percent and once at 13.30 percent. The difference in the results will be the VAR of this particular implied volatility position.

When it comes to options, we do *not* want to combine the sensitivity to changes in *implied volatility* and the change in the VAR of the portfolio on one side with the sensitivity to changes in the *underlying market price* and the change in the VAR of the portfolio on the other side. They should remain separate because they are both dominant factors in most options. The value of an option can change when the underlying market price changes and also when implied volatility changes. We want to know separately how sensitive our options portfolio is to a 1 percent change in the underlying market rate. Then we want to know how sensitive the option book is to a 10-basis-point change in implied volatility. That is, we want two separate VARs. However, when we mark-to-market, we have a loss or profit month to date for the whole option book because the valuation model often takes both factors into account in calculating the option price.

For example, suppose we sell a put that gives the option buyer the right to sell pounds to us at $1.50 and we do not perform a delta hedge. As a result, we are short implied volatility. We do not hedge this transaction, and a new war in the Middle East causes the price of oil to double, a situation which would be good for the pound but also would create a high level of uncertainty. Two things will happen: (1) implied volatility will go up, which will hurt this option because we have sold it, and (2) the price of the pound will go up, which means it is extremely unlikely that the customer will exercise the option to sell pounds to us.

These two forces will affect the price of the option. That price will be driven up because of the higher volatility and will be pushed down because the market price moves farther away from the strike price and therefore more out of the money. The dominant force determines what happens to the premium, and in this case time is an important factor. When there is only a short period of time left until the exercise date, the fact that the spot price moves farther out of the money is very important. If the option has 5 years to go, implied volatility is much more important.

It is necessary to track implied volatility and market price independently because combining them leads to inconclusive results. Theoretically, the value of the option could remain unchanged and we could think that nothing is changing in the market when in fact there are two substantial movements which by coincidence happen to be offsetting.

Value at Risk System and Country Risk

High-risk bonds (sometimes referred to as junk bonds) sometimes are issued by entities which are considered by market participants to be particularly risky for economic and/or political reasons. Assume that a sovereign country issues fixed-rate debt yielding 9 percent—2 percent above the interbank Eurodollar interest rate curve of 7 percent (Exhibit 4-5). If we track sensitivity, volatility, and the resulting VAR at the 9 percent level, we will be aggregating the volatility of the 7 percent Eurodollar interest rate with the volatility of the country-specific risk premium of 2 percent. In such cases, it is better to disaggregate the 9 percent yield and determine sensitivities, volatilities, and VARs separately for the 7 percent Eurodollar interbank yield and the country-specific 2 percent risk premium of this bond. Many institutions hedge the Eurodollar interest rate risk in their high-risk bond portfolios so that the only remaining price risk is the VAR that reflects the political and economic risk of the issuing country.

This approach has several advantages. First, the traders of these kinds

	Eurodollar Interest Rate	Country-specific Risk Premium
High-risk Bond @ 9% total yield	7%	2%
Track separately	Sensitivity Volatility VAR	Sensitivity Volatility VAR
Hedge	7% Eurodollar interest rate	
Result		2% remaining price risk

Exhibit 4-5. The disaggregated yield of a high-risk bond.

of portfolios often are recruited from the emerging market countries issuing these bonds because they are familiar with those countries; they usually do not have expertise in trading Eurodollar instruments. Second, hedging away the VAR resulting from Eurodollar interest volatility reduces the total VAR of the portfolio and allows the traders to use their entire VAR limits to assume more risk in an area where they have expertise—speculating on rising or falling country-specific risk premiums.

Summary

Traditional approaches to managing price risk focused on nominal positions. Managers described risks in terms of the face value of positions outstanding in various currencies and financial instruments. The modern approach to price risk centers on the idea that any position exposes a position taker to potential dollar losses which can be estimated and expressed in dollar terms.

The potential dollar loss amount for foreign exchange and interest rate positions results from multiplying the sensitivity of the position to a 1-unit change in the market price of the instrument by the expected overnight volatility percentage of the same market price. The VAR for options positions is calculated by finding the volatility of the implied volatility and the volatility of the underlying asset.

Assessing Price Risk in Accrual Positions

Earlier in this chapter you were introduced to the concept of assessing the risk of a position in terms of the amount by which the profit or loss may change. The interest risk inherent in trading positions is measured on a daily basis by marking-to-market the instruments in the trading portfolio and then calculating the value at risk of those positions. The interest rate risk in accrual positions is assessed through earnings at risk (EAR).[5] The EAR process is a forward-looking management tool that evaluates risk against planned earnings to avoid earnings surprises.

A bank's net interest income can be affected significantly by the impact on the balance sheet of changes in the interest rate. Interest rate risk exists when assets and liabilities mature or reprice at different times. For example, if more liabilities than assets reprice in a given period (similar to a negative gap) and market interest rates are declining, the bank's repriced liabilities (funding costs) will decrease. A lower funding cost increases the asset/liability interest rate spread and improves net interest income. Conversely, if more assets than liabilities reprice in a given period (similar to a positive gap), declining market interest rates will reduce the asset/liability interest rate spread, which will reduce net interest income.

These fluctuations in net interest income are effectively "neutralized" when assets are funded by identically matching liabilities. In other words, to eliminate interest rate repricing risk, all assets and liabilities must have the same maturity and amortization profiles. Although matched funding eliminates interest rate risk, it does not maximize profits. To increase earnings, many banks *selectively* mismatch asset and liability repricing to take advantage of forecast interest rate movements and the shape of the yield curve. Of course, rates do not always move as expected, and when banks create mismatches between the maturity and repricing of assets and liabilities, they also create interest rate risk.

For example, assume that a bank's $100 million balance sheet is composed of personal loans with an average maturity of 13 months that are funded by customer deposits with an average maturity of 1 month. In this situation the bank is running a 12-month negative gap (lending long and borrowing short). This negative gap position is shown in Exhibit 4-6.

The bank knows that the spread is fixed for the first month (in this case at 0 percent) and that after the first month the liabilities will have to be repriced. This can happen at lower or higher rates in an amount equal to the expected volatility, say, 1 percent. If the bank feels that in 1 month the funding cost may decrease by 1 percent while the return on

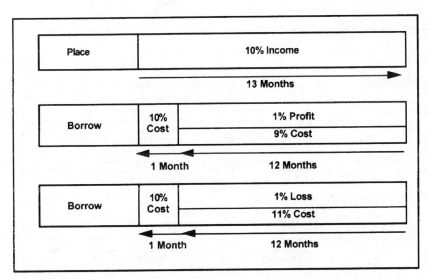

Exhibit 4-6. Twelve-month negative gap position—lending long and borrowing short.

assets remains the same, the expectation is that the spread may increase by 1 percent for the remaining 12 months. Conversely, if rates are higher, the funding cost will be higher and the spread will be lower.

Assume that the bank's $100 million balance sheet is composed of the same personal loans but that the average maturity is now 2 months. These loans are funded with the same customer deposits, but the average maturity is 12 months. In this situation, the bank is running a 10-month positive gap (lending short and borrowing long). This positive gap position is illustrated in Exhibit 4-7.

The bank knows that the spread is fixed for the first 2 months and that after the first 2 months the assets must be repriced. This can happen at lower or higher rates in an amount equal to the expected volatility, say, 1 percent. If the bank feels that in 2 months earnings may decline by 1 percent for the loans while the funding cost remains the same, the expectation is that the spread may decrease by 1 percent for the remaining 10 months. Conversely, if rates are higher, the return on assets will be higher and the spread also will be higher.

Earnings at Risk

You can see that interest rate risk in accrual portfolios is embedded in positive and negative gap positions. To find out the size of the risk, banks follow four basic steps to measure the amount of interest earnings that may be lost (earnings at risk) when these positions are closed.

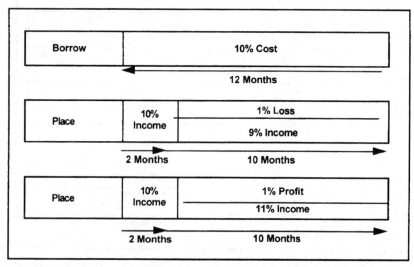

Exhibit 4-7. Ten-month positive gap position—lending short and borrowing long.

The first step in measuring EAR is to define how long it will take to return to an interest-rate-neutral position, in other words, the time required to close all interest rate gaps in the balance sheet. The faster a neutral position can be reestablished, the lower the potential risk is. This period is referred to as the *defeasance period*. The defeasing (hedging) is done with derivatives much the same way derivatives are used to close money market gaps (see Chap. 2). The defeasance period is determined by the characteristics of the instruments involved, the degree of a particular bank's participation in the market, and the bank's overall sophistication. This period may range from a few days for instruments in very liquid markets to several months for a hedging structure that is implemented by a business that is not actively involved in hedging transactions. In the latter case, the time required to develop a hedging strategy and get the corresponding approvals must be included in the defeasance period (for a discussion of the defeasance period, see Chap. 5).

The second step is to identify the combined interest rate gaps per tenor for each of the portfolios in which the bank wants to assess EAR. This step is done by projecting a repricing schedule for all accounts in the balance sheet clustered in predefined tenor brackets.

The third step is to assume a parallel movement in the general level of interest rates in the market over the corresponding defeasance period in an amount equal to the 2-standard-deviation (2SD) volatility. This means that all market rates are assumed to move at the same time and the same pace. This parallel movement is analyzed separately for increasing rates and decreasing rates because both have the potential to reduce net income. Normally, however, liabilities reprice more frequently than do assets, which makes banks more vulnerable to rising interest rates. Note that the effect of rising interest rates and the effect of decreasing interest rates may not be symmetrical if, for example, a particular position includes embedded options.

The fourth and final step is to convert the potential impact on earnings generated by this parallel movement of interest rates into a dollar amount. The conversion process takes into consideration the size, the tenor, and the type of interest rate gap. This dollar figure is known as earnings at risk.

Let us return to the example in Exhibit 4-6—the $100 million 12-month negative gap—to see how EAR is identified in a negative gap position.

- *First step.* Assume that the gap may be closed in 1 week.
- *Second step.* A $100 million negative gap is observed from the end of the first month to the end of the thirteenth month (12-month gap).

- *Third step.* A 2SD interest rate movement during a 1-week defeasance period is estimated to be 1 percent p.a.

- *Fourth step.* A 1 percent p.a. *increase* in rates applied to a 12-month $100 million negative gap represents an EAR amount of $1 million.

Similarly, refer to the example in Exhibit 4-7—the $100 million 10-month positive gap—to see how EAR is identified in a positive gap position.

- *First step.* Assume that the gap may be closed in 1 week.

- *Second step.* A $100 million positive gap is observed from the end of the second month to the end of the twelfth month (10-month positive gap).

- *Third step.* A 2SD interest rate movement during a 1-week defeasance period is estimated to be 1 percent p.a.

- *Fourth step.* A 1 percent p.a. *decrease* in rates applied to a 10-month $100 million positive gap represents an EAR amount of $833,000.

Note that both the $1 million EAR and the $833,000 EAR represent potential *future* losses, and EAR therefore should always include the related time frame. It is not the same to have $1 million EAR during the next year and to have it during the next 5 years. Even though the amount of risk is the same, the management of most banks will be much more concerned about the $1 million EAR for the next year.

This exercise is done irrespective of the current level of interest rates and the current spreads that a bank is generating. In fact, in the example it is not necessary to know in advance if the current market interest rate is 10 percent, 11 percent, or 30 percent p.a. or if current earnings generated by the portfolio are $3000 or $3 million. The reason for this is that EAR assesses the *change* in the spread independently from the *size* of the spread. This is one of the main features of the EAR process—its simplicity. In building interest rate gaps, only the *repricing* of the principals is considered.

Cost to Close

Cost to close is the calculation used to mark-to-market the accrual portfolio for risk management purposes. The cost-to-close figure represents the future or undiscounted value of the portfolio if all interest rate gaps are closed at *current* market interest rates. The cost-to-close figure changes when market interest rates change.

Because of this feature, EAR can be calculated through the cost-to-close calculation. EAR represents the difference between the cost to close of a portfolio at current market interest rates and the cost to close of the same portfolio at current market interest rates plus or minus a 2SD movement in interest rates.

Although this approach to estimating EAR is not as straightforward as the process described in the last section, it does not require additional work. Let us see how the cost to close is calculated and how EAR is calculated through the cost to close.

Refer again to Exhibit 4-6, a $100 million 12-month negative gap. For this example, assume that the 13-month loan is given at 11 percent p.a., the 1-month deposit is taken at 9 percent p.a., and the current market interest rate is 10 percent p.a. If we had to close that gap today, we would need a contract to borrow beginning in 1 month for a 12-month period at 10 percent p.a. For the first month there is no repricing, and therefore our spread will remain fixed at 2 percent p.a. For the remaining 12 months, the spread will decrease to only 1 percent p.a. because the funding cost will increase from 9 percent to 10 percent p.a. As a consequence, the cost to close (or future portfolio value) will be $1.167 million (a 2 percent spread for the first month and a 1 percent spread for the remaining 12 months on a $100 million balance sheet).

If a 1 percent p.a. 2SD volatility in interest rates occurs, the market interest rate will increase from 10 percent p.a. to 11 percent p.a. To close the gap, 1 month from now we would have to borrow for 12 months at 11 percent p.a. The cost to close under this assumption therefore would be only $0.167 million (a 2 percent spread for the first month and a 0 percent spread for the remaining 12 months on a $100 million balance sheet).

As can be seen from the example, the value of the portfolio decreases when interest rates increase because we are running a negative gap; an increase in rates represents an increase in the funding cost. Additionally, it can be seen that the variation in the cost to close resulting from a 2SD movement in current market interest rates equals the EAR of $1 million calculated using the original methodology.

Repricing Schedule

One of the most important steps in the EAR measurement is to correctly estimate the repricing of all accounts in the balance sheet. This can be very easy with instruments in which there is a contractual repricing date and a *single* cash flow; for example, the repricing date of a 90-day certificate of deposit is 90 days. It may be somewhat more complicated with instruments in which there is a contractual repricing date and *multiple* cash flows. In this case, the repricing profile should follow the corresponding cash flows; for example, in a fixed-rate $1 million 2-year bond with two annual principal payments of 50 percent each, $500,000 will reprice in the first year and $500,000 will reprice in the second year.

In both cases, repricing schedules always should consider the remaining life of the contracts, not the original tenors. The difficult task is to determine the repricing dates of instruments that *do not have a contractual repricing date*, such as checking accounts and saving deposits. In this case the repricing is estimated with an *actuarial* analysis or a *replicating* analysis.

Actuarial analysis is done when the repricing date is associated with the estimated runoff of the instrument. For example, checking accounts pay no interest, and so we can say that while they are in the bank's book, they carry a fixed rate of 0 percent. However, if from a liquidity point of view we determine that 90 percent are core deposits that we will not lose—they will not run off—in less than 5 years and the remaining 10 percent may be withdrawn at any time, we may assume that 90 percent of the checking accounts reprice after 5 years and the remaining 10 percent reprice on an overnight basis. This assumption includes the idea that at the runoff date we will be forced to replace this instrument with another one that may carry an interest rate above 0 percent.

Replicating analysis is done when it is possible to relate the repricing of a particular instrument to the repricing of a portfolio that that instrument indirectly mimics or closely follows. For example, the money market demand account rate may vary infrequently and may be set according to a formula that is not directly related to market rates. However, an analysis may indicate that the behavior of this rate is similar to the behavior of a combination of other market rates at different maturities. In this case we assume that the repricing of the money market demand account rate is the same as the repricing of the replicated portfolio rates.

Basis Risk

A large risk may exist in an accrual portfolio that EAR does not capture. The best example is basis risk, as will be explained in the following scenario. Suppose a bank maintains a large portfolio with an average maturity of 5 years for both assets and liabilities. In this portfolio, assets are based on floating prime rate and liabilities are based on floating London Inter-Bank Offered Rate (LIBOR). If the EAR methodology, which assumes a parallel movement in interest rates, is used, the bank shows no risk; the spread remains exactly the same if LIBOR and prime move in parallel. However, the two rates may not move in parallel, causing the spread to change. The risk of a nonparallel movement in interest rates is called *basis risk*. In this case the bank has basis risk for 5 years.[6]

EAR captures the risk of a change in the *level* of interest rates because it assumes that this change will occur in parallel. Basis risk captures the risk of a change in interest rate *differentials*. An accurate measurement of the full accrual risk should include both EAR and basis risk. Both risks are important, and both may cause earnings to decline over time.

Market Value Sensitivity

Market value sensitivity (MVS) is an alternative approach to estimating the interest rate risk embedded in the balance sheet. MVS resembles the VAR approach adapted to accrual accounts. This methodology assumes that the whole balance sheet can be marked-to-market on the basis of current interest rates. It also assumes that any sensitivity to changes in interest rates of this marked-to-market value can be described as the interest rate risk embedded in the balance sheet. MVS is used to estimate how much the market value of the equity (MVE)—the marked-to-market value of the balance sheet—may vary when a 2SD interest rate movement occurs in the market.

Theoretically, MVE should equal the amount any investor is willing to pay in exchange for all fixed-rate cash flows in the balance sheet, assuming that interest rates are the only factors considered in determining that value.[7] Under this assumption, the marked-to-market value will be the present value of every future cash flow in the balance sheet at current market interest rates. The MVS approach assumes that a potential movement in interest rates (2SD volatility) occurs, resulting in a recalculation of the MVE at the new rate. The difference between the size of the MVE before and after the movement in interest rates is known as the market value sensitivity.

MVS = actual MVE − potential MVE

MVS = MVE at current interest rates − MVE at current interest rates ± 2SD movement

---

MVS may be calculated by using the following steps:

1. Estimate all future fixed-rate cash flows (repricings) embedded in the balance sheet, including future interest payments/receivables, and separate them by tenor.
2. Estimate the net cash flow for each tenor by netting assets from liabilities that reprice in each tenor.

3. Calculate the actual MVE by discounting each cash flow at current interest rates.

4. Calculate the potential MVE by discounting each cash flow at current interest rates ± a potential 2SD volatility movement (+2SD for a negative gap, −2SD for a positive gap).

5. Estimate the MVS by calculating the difference between the actual MVE and the potential MVE.

Let us look at a very simple example to clarify this process. Assume that ABC Bank's balance sheet is composed of $100 million in 3-year loans yielding 12 percent p.a. that are funded with 1-year deposits costing 9 percent p.a. Also assume that the current market interest rate during the entire 3 years is 11 percent (flat yield curve) and that the 2SD volatility is estimated at 50 bp. From a cash flow point of view, repricings will occur as follows. From the loans, ABC Bank will receive $12 million in years 1 and 2 as interest and $112 million in year 3 as interest plus the principal repayment. From the deposits, the bank will pay $109 million in year 1 as interest plus principal repayment. Net cash flows therefore will be a negative $97 million in year 1, a positive $12 million in year 2, and a positive $112 million in year 3 (Exhibit 4-8).

What is the marked-to-market value (MVE) of this balance sheet?

- The actual MVE (at current interest rates) is positive $4.25 million because that is the present value of the three net cash flows at 11 percent.

- The potential MVE (if rates *increase* by 2SD) is positive $3.45 million because that is the present value of the three net cash flows at 11.5 percent.

- The potential MVE (if rates *decrease* by 2SD) is positive $5.06 million because that is the present value of the three net cash flows at 10.5 percent.

In all cases the market value of the balance sheet is positive even if market rates potentially move by 2SD, because spreads are always expected

	Year 1	Year 2	Year 3
Loans	$ 12 MM	$12 MM	$112 MM
Deposits	$109 MM		
Net cash flow (assets − liabilities)	- $ 97 MM	$12 MM	$112 MM

Exhibit 4-8. Net cash flows for ABC Bank.

to be positive. The spread is fixed at 3 percent for the first year (the difference between the 12 percent yield on assets and the 9 percent cost of liabilities). For the second and third year the spread may be 1 percent (if the funding repricing occurs at current interest rates of 11 percent), 0.5 percent (if market rates move up by 2SD, funding is repriced at 11.5 percent), or 1.5 percent (if market rates move down by 2SD, funding is repriced at 10.5 percent).

As you can see in this example, the market value of the balance sheet (MVE) decreases when interest rates increase; in this case, it will decrease from $4.25 million to $3.45 million. Since ABC Bank is running a negative gap, it is exposed to funding repricings at higher interest rates. The $800 thousand difference between the actual MVE value and the potential MVE value is the MVS.

The MVS process allows us to calculate sensitivity at any expected change in market rates. It is not necessary to assume that a parallel movement of interest rates will occur. We may say, for example, that interest rates for 1 year are expected to move 50 bp and interest rates for 2 years are expected to move 70 bp. This means that we may analyze our portfolio against changes in the interest rate level and also against changes in the shape of the interest rate yield curve. In a world that is much more sophisticated than it was in the past, this analysis is more accurate and therefore essential.

In the real world, MVS is not this simple. An important part of the balance sheet does not have well-defined repricing dates, e.g., demand deposit accounts (DDA) accounts. Consequently, it is difficult to build correct cash flows to calculate a reasonably accurate mark-to-market value. We can solve this problem by developing some repricing assumptions, but the validity of the results is questionable when MVS is based mainly on assumptions.

An important additional assumption that is needed when market value sensitivity is analyzed is the volume of assets and liabilities involved. This is particularly true for the assets and liabilities in the balance sheet that are not influenced by the dealing room: the customer-related deposit and loan business. These volumes may rise or fall depending on assumed higher or lower interest rate levels and also depending on the economic outlook for a boom or recession.

Let us look at one more simple example to clarify the MVS concept. Market value sensitivity could be the sensitivity of a bank's stock price to changes in interest rates. As we know from the discussion in Chap. 1, the true price of the stock is the price/earnings (P/E) ratio. Assume that a bank has a P/E ratio of 10 (a stock price of $100/earnings per share of $10) and 100 million shares outstanding. Further assume that a 1 percent rise in interest rates would create a loss of $100 million, or

	Stock Value	Impact of a 1% change in interest rates	MVS
Outstanding shares	100 million	100 million	
Earnings	$1 billion ($10 per share)	$900 million ($9 per share)	$100 million ($1 per share)
Stock price	$100	$90	$10
P/E ratio	10	10	

Exhibit 4-9. MVS of bank stock to a 1 percent change in interest rates.

$1 per share. At a price/earnings ratio of 10, the impact of a change in earnings per share of $1 means that the price of the stock will change and decrease by $10. In other words, if the bank makes $1 billion and these earnings fall by $100 million because of a 1 percent adverse change in interest rates, the reduced earnings of $900 million ($9 per share) will depress the stock price from $100 to $90, assuming that the P/E ratio remains unchanged. As can be seen in Exhibit 4-9, the market value sensitivity of the bank's stock price is the difference between $100 and $90.

MVS versus EAR

The main difference between EAR and MVS is that MVS is based on a theoretical marked-to-market value of the portfolio while EAR is not. MVS is a management tool that is used to analyze the balance sheet as a single price risk position. In other words, it assumes that there is a market value for the balance sheet and that the risk resides in any change of that value caused by interest rate movements. EAR, by comparison, is not concerned with the present value of the portfolio. In fact, it is not concerned even with the current spread the portfolio carries. It evaluates only the potential decrease in earnings and the time periods when the accounting system will recognize it.

In the first MVS example we assume that if interest rates rise by 2SD, $800,000 is currently at risk for the full portfolio. This $800,000 will not be reported by the accounting system today because accrual accounts are not marked-to-market. EAR is concerned with the time frame when differences in earnings may occur. Therefore, EAR will reflect the impact of the 50-bp decrease in the spread on $100 million gap in years 2 and 3 (in this case, equal to a $500,000 risk in each year). The table in Exhibit 4-10 illustrates the difference between MVS and EAR.

It can be seen that MVS does not indicate *when* earnings may be affected

Today	Year 1	Year 2	Year 3
MVS	$800,000		
EAR		$500,000	$500,000

Exhibit 4-10. Comparison of MVS and EAR.

but only the total *size* of the risk. By analyzing only MVS, we do not know if the $800,000 represents the present value of a big risk that will occur in the distant future or the present value of a smaller risk that will occur in the near future.

You also can see that EAR shows the risks on an undiscounted basis, which is why the sum of the EAR risk ($1 million) is higher than the MVS risk ($800 thousand). However, if we discount both EAR risks at present value, we will obtain a number very close to MVS.

Summary

A large percentage of the balance sheet is represented by accrual positions, which are positions that are assumed to be on a bank's books until their maturity dates. The accounting procedure for these positions is to accrue the spread between the assets and the liabilities until maturity.

There are two types of accrual accounts: held-to-maturity and held-for-sale accounts. Instruments that will not be sold before maturity are included in the first account; instruments that are intended to be maintained in the balance sheet but can be sold before maturity if required (usually represented by marketable instruments) are included in the second account.

EAR measures and controls the potential impact of parallel interest rate movements on planned accrual earnings. Interest rate risk results from a mismatch in the maturities of assets and liabilities.

The cost to close is the undiscounted value of the accrual portfolio assuming the closing of all open gaps. EAR also can be defined as the increase in the cost to close of the portfolio if current interest rates move by a 2SD volatility.

Because EAR measures only the risk of a parallel change in the level of interest rates, a calculation of basis risk should complement EAR to cover the risk of changes in interest rate differentials.

Market value sensitivity is an alternative approach to estimating the interest rate risk of the balance sheet. It resembles the VAR approach used for trading accounts. It assumes that the balance sheet can be marked-to-market (market value of equity) and that any sensitivity in this value resulting from 2SD interest rate movements represents the interest rate risk embedded in the balance sheet.

Notes

1. Refer to the Sample Price Risk Report in Chap. 6.

2. A 1-basis-point change is the equivalent of 0.01 percent p.a. (e.g., the difference between 6.50 percent p.a. and 6.51 percent p.a.). Notice that it represents a per annum amount. One basis point irrespective of a time period such as a day, a week, or a month would be 0.01 percent "flat." For example, if we were talking about 10 basis points flat on a six-month transaction, it is equivalent to approximately 0.20 percent p.a.

3. In some countries at some times in the past, the volatility for local currency interest rates was between 20 percent and 30 percent p.a. for overnight risk. In such a case, the dollar equivalent of a 1-unit change might be set at 10 percent. For example, when I know volatility is 25 percent, it makes sense to say, Well, my 10 percent sensitivity is such and such because it is easy to go from 10 percent to 25 percent. It is almost like driving a car. If one can shift gears, one can drive the car in several different gears, but for every speed there is one gear that is particularly suitable.

4. Today's present value is actually a little less than $50,000. We accept this inaccuracy to facilitate an understanding of how the system works.

5. The EAR measurement should include *all* the accounts in the balance sheet, including trading positions. Trading accounts are included in the EAR computation with overnight repricing and therefore do not generate any accrual (interest rate) risk. Usually, all the accounts included in the EAR computation must reconcile with the balance sheet.

6. Basis risk is very similar to the instrument spreads described in Chap. 2. These instrument spreads, such as Treasury bills against Eurodollars (TED spread), are intentionally taken in the dealing room, whereas basis risk is the unintended residual of customer-related interest rate hedging.

7. Of course, in the real world this is not the case because a business can be described as a sum of many factors, including franchise advantages, the position of the business in the market, and image.

5
Volatility Discovery

Discovery Methodology

In the Grandmother Story, when the man tells his mother that a 1 percent change will produce an effect of $4000, the mother immediately asks, "And how much does it usually change?" This is the grandmother's way of asking what the overnight volatility of the stock price is. The question here is: How do we know what percentage figure to use for volatility when we calculate value at risk? This is a fascinating question because, after all, we are calculating the size of the risk. However, the volatility discovery process also is important for another reason. We will see in Chap. 6 that the official limits for price risk are expressed and set in terms of value at risk. Once the VAR limit has been determined, it remains unchanged, *but the position limits for the traders are derived through volatility.*

Exhibit 5-1 demonstrates how volatility affects a trader's position limit. The VAR limit of $100,000 never changes. Instead, the position

---

Controlling FX Rate Risk

- Limit for value at risk $ 100,000

- Daily volatility assumptions
  - — 1%   ➔   Derived position limit $10,000,000
  - — 2%   ➔   Derived position limit $ 5,000,000
  - — 1/2%   ➔   Derived position limit $20,000,000

Exhibit 5-1. Deriving the position limit from the VAR limit.

- **I**mplied in actively traded options
  Only for reserve currencies
- **Reasoned management judgment**
  Based on historical data analysis
- 1 standard deviation equals 84% confidence
- 2 standard deviation equals 97.7% confidence

Exhibit 5-2. Discovery of volatility.

limit changes whenever there is a change in volatility. At 1 percent overnight volatility, the derived position limit is $10 million. If volatility rises to 2 percent, the position limit will automatically be reduced to $5 million, and if volatility falls to ½ percent, the derived position limit may be increased to $20 million. As a result, the amount of dollars at risk remains constant at $100,000; only the position limits change. We will return to this subject in Chap. 6, but it is important that the reader be aware of this important additional role of volatility.

Future volatility cannot be predicted exactly, but it must be estimated to the best of one's ability. An estimation of volatility is based on the notion that events which have been observed in the past will prevail in the future. Exhibit 5-2 shows the sources and confidence levels for estimating future volatility.

Volatility Implied in Options

One source for estimated future volatility consists of the implied volatilities derived from option prices. In the earlier discussion of options, we said that five components, including implied volatility, are used to calculate an option price (see Chap. 2). For actively traded currencies, we know the option prices quoted at official exchanges and in the over-the-counter market between banks. When the option price is known, we can conclude that the five components which were used to calculate the price are also known. We know the four "yes, sir" elements (the strike price, the market price, time, and interest rates) because they are a given or are quoted in the market. The fifth component needed to calculate the option price is indirectly given (implied) in all situations in which we actually have the market price; when we know five of the six, we can solve for the unknown. Why should we again estimate future volatility when we can use the volatility implied in actively traded options as the estimated future volatility for calculating value at risk?

The following is an example of how one market price can be implied in a set of other market prices. What is the local currency rate?

Spot FX rate   100 = $1
1-year forward outright rate   110 = $1 (10 percent premium for dollars)
1-year dollar interest rate   5 percent (lower interest rate)
Local currency rate?   Answer: 15 percent

This 15 percent interest rate is "implied" in the 10 percent premium for dollars. Given the 10 percent premium and the interest rate for dollars of 5 percent, the local currency interest rate has to be (is implied to be) 15 percent, that is, 10 percent higher than that for dollars. To make it easier, we can use simple arithmetic based on the assumption that if we know two of three, we can solve for the unknown ($5 + x = 15$, $x = 10$, $5 + 10 = 15$).

This same principle applies to volatility in options. Therefore, we can conclude that any premium/price for an option includes an implied opinion (price) about the volatility expected in the future.

That is the end of the volatility discovery story, provided that there is a deep, highly liquid option market. Although the option product is still somewhat exotic, there is an active market for the reserve currencies and increasingly for other currencies. When there is a liquid market where one can trade $50 million or $100 million worth of options without changing the market price, one certainly can use volatility implied in actively traded options to calculate the VAR of a position (Exhibit 5-3).

Calculation of an Option Price
- Strike price versus market price
- Time
- Interest rate level
- Volatility

Information Available from Exchanges that Trade Options
- Strike price and market price
- Time
- Interest rate level
- Option price

When we know four out of five values, we can solve for the unknown – VOLATILITY

Exhibit 5-3. Volatility implied in exchange-traded options.

Volatility Based on Historical Data and Reasoned Judgment

We still have to address the volatility discovery alternative for currencies that do not have an actively traded options market. Here we have to do what weather forecasters do: Look back at the past, interpret the past as intelligently as possible, and assume that in the future there will be similar conditions. In other words, the future will be extrapolated from the past.

To illustrate the methodology for estimating future volatility, there is an analysis of historical data in Exhibit 5-4. There are seven observed changes in the price of gold in this 8-day period. The net price change is $14, and the average change is $2. The average change ($2) is subtracted from each daily change to get the numbers in column A. Then, to eliminate any negative numbers, the numbers in column A are squared to get the numbers in column B. The square root of the average for column B is the 1 standard deviation of the daily change in gold prices, i.e., 3.7 dollars or about 0.9 percent per day. This daily 1SD of 0.9 percent is converted into an annual percentage change of 14.4 percent, which is the formal market definition of historical volatility ($0.9 \times 16 = 14.4$ percent; see page 103).

This example is designed to illustrate the process. In the real world, we need data for a considerably longer period, such as 6 to 9 months. If the sampling period is too short, events or the absence of events during that period will dramatically influence the volatility extracted from the limited data. In comparison, if the sampling period is too long (such as 2 to 5 years, as some people propose), even dramatically high price fluc-

Day	Gold Price	Daily Change	A	B
1	400			
2	405	5	3	9
3	411	6	4	16
4	408	(3)	(5)	25
5	411	3	1	1
6	407	(4)	(6)	36
7	412	5	3	9
8	414	2	0	0

$$96 / 7 = 13.71$$
$$\text{Standard deviation: } \sqrt{13.71} = 3.7$$

Exhibit 5-4. Discovery of volatility from a historical database.

tuations will not have a notable impact. I personally think that any-where between 6 and 9 months is a happy medium between sampling periods which are too short and those which are too long. A popular technique is to double weight the most recent 1-month data because the immediate past often provides a better forecast for the immediate future than do events that occurred a long time ago.

The other requirement to make this more of a "real-world" example is that the price changes should be expressed as a percentage, not in absolute numbers. For example, a change of 5 represents $1\frac{1}{4}$ percent at a price level of 400 in Exhibit 5-4, 1 percent at a price level of 500, and $1\frac{2}{3}$ percent at a price level of 300. It is clear that tracking daily changes in percentages produces more accurate results than does tracking absolute numbers.

The percentage of volatility derived from historical data should be determined by a group of people (volatility committee) knowledgeable about financial markets but not connected with the dealing function. There may be five qualified individuals identified in writing, with a minimum of three being required to judge on a weekly basis the appropriateness of the volatility results provided by the historical database. Obviously, this group should convene instantly when political or economic events occur which are likely to change future volatility dramatically. If they are satisfied with the results, they should state this in writing. If they are not satisfied, they must put in writing their reasons for the use of volatility that is higher or lower than the level of volatility suggested by the historical database.

Option Implied versus Historical Data

There are lively discussions among professionals about which method of volatility discovery should be used. The majority of market participants prefer to estimate future volatility on the basis of historical data rather than the implied volatility in options.

An exercise may resolve this dilemma. Assume we want to know the 6-month volatility for dollars against marks. We can look at a dollar/mark option and identify the implied volatility, or we can employ our favorite method for interpreting historical data to discover what the volatility should be for the next 6 months. We probably will get two different numbers. Then, if we observe the actual volatility over the next 6 months, we will have a third number: the volatility that actually occurred during this 6-month period. In the majority of cases we will see that the volatility implied in options is closer to reality than is the volatility suggested by the historical database. This result is not surprising because, after all, the historical database is a straightforward calculation of numbers. People who trade options (which means trading implied volatility) have first-hand knowledge of past volatility and can combine their experience with the historical data to derive the future volatility percentage that will be used to calculate the price of an option. In other words, the traders are adding their judgment to their awareness of the past. In the majority of cases this should produce more accurate results than will a cold, sober interpretation of historical data.

When the option market is liquid enough for a given currency, it is preferable to use the volatility implied in those options. When the option market is not liquid enough, we have to use judgment, and the interpretation of the historical database has to be the starting point for that judgment.

It is the responsibility of the risk management function—sometimes referred to as the middle office—to determine the appropriate volatility. While management may change position limits to reflect a change in volatility only when a cumulative volatility movement of, say, 15 percent occurs (buffer limit), the actual volatility must be tracked on a continuing basis or at least daily. This is relatively easy for market prices for which option-implied volatility is used, but the updating and interpretation of historical data require a more elaborate process. For example, daily samples must be taken at the same time of day, and the frequency of meetings of the volatility committee must be clearly determined. In addition to regularly scheduled meetings, the committee must convene immediately if unusual political and/or economic events occur, because analyzing historical data will not immediately reflect the new volatility scenario.

In addition to everything that has been said about the volatility discovery process in this chapter, it is important to recognize that this process must be a routine which is on automatic pilot. Judgmental adjustments may be made only by the volatility committee.

Daily and Multiday Volatility

All these methods for discovering future volatility—option-implied volatility, historical data, and reasoned management judgment—yield a percentage figure for *annual* volatility. However, as you saw in our VAR calculations, we need to know daily volatility, and we therefore have to convert the commonly available annual volatility. Statisticians and mathematicians agree that daily volatility should be calculated by dividing annual volatility by the square root of time. We now want to introduce the reader to this shortcut approach to converting annual volatility into daily volatility. If we assume that there are 256 business days in a year, which is approximately correct, we can calculate the square root of 256, which is 16. When we have annual volatility of, for example, 24, all we have to do is divide 24 by 16 (the square root of 256), and the result is a daily volatility of 1.5 percent. It is recommended that you make a mental note about this shortcut. It is extremely helpful to use this mechanism to convert annual volatility into daily volatility without employing a calculator.

In this example we calculate a daily volatility percentage which can be used for commodity prices such as foreign exchange and equities. For the calculation of VAR for interest rate risk positions, we need daily volatility expressed in basis points. We begin with the same process that was just described: Take annual volatility for the respective type of interest rate, divide by the square root of time, and obtain the overnight volatility percentage. This percentage—let us use 1.5 percent as an example—is applied to the general level of interest rates for the currency in question. If the interest rate is 8 percent p.a., 1.5 percent of 8 percent produces an overnight volatility of 0.12 percent p.a., or 12 basis points. The same 1.5 percent overnight volatility percentage applied to an interest rate level of 6 percent p.a. produces 9 basis points; at an interest rate level of 20 percent p.a., it produces 30 basis points; and so on.

Like interest rates, volatility percentages have a curve, which means that there are different volatility percentages for different maturities. When we are looking for daily volatility, it may not always be optimal to base the daily volatility calculation on annual volatility. Instead, we can use the implied volatility in the shortest maturity for actively traded options. If this happens to be 3 months, we will base the daily volatility calculation on the volatility implied in these 3-month options. The implied volatility in 1-month options is an even more desirable base for this calculation if these options are actively traded. In other words, if we are calculating volatility for VAR-related purposes, we should extract this volatility from actively traded options with a maturity that is as close as possible to the time period for which we are seeking the volatility percentage. For more regarding multiday volatility, see "Defeasance Period" later in this chapter.

Confidence Levels and Standard Deviation

Each technique for estimating volatility—option-implied volatility, historical data, and reasoned management judgment—yields a percentage figure for estimated future volatility. This percentage is quoted among professionals on an annual basis.

The percentage figure that is derived for future volatility represents 1 standard deviation (SD) of volatility. What does that mean? If we discover that 1SD daily volatility is, for example, ¾ percent, it means that 68 percent of the time the price change *will not* be more than ¾ percent. It follows that 32 percent of the time the price change *will* be more than ¾ percent. However, since there is a 50:50 chance that the price will go up or down, the loss will exceed ¾ percent only 16 percent of the time, because there is also a 16 percent chance that we are on the right side and will make a large profit (Exhibit 5-5).

If 1SD volatility is ¾ percent, then

- 68 percent of the time the price change *will not* exceed ¾ percent.

- 32 percent of the time the price change *will* exceed ¾ percent.

- 16 percent of the time the loss *will* exceed ¾ percent.

- 84 percent of the time the loss *will not* exceed ¾ percent.

To have a higher level of confidence in our estimate of future volatility, we apply 2SD volatility to position sensitivity to derive the value at risk (Exhibit 5-6).

If 2SD volatility is 1½ percent, then

- 95.4 percent of the time the price change *will not* exceed 1.5 percent.

- 4.6 percent of the time the price change *will* exceed 1.5 percent.

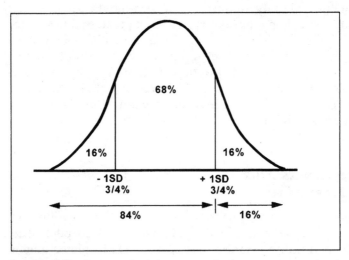

Exhibit 5-5. One standard deviation volatility.

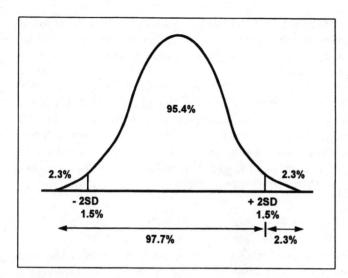

Exhibit 5-6. Two standard deviation volatility.

- 2.3 percent of the time the loss *will* exceed 1.5 percent.
- 97.7 percent of the time the loss *will not* exceed 1.5 percent.

Exhibits 5-5 and 5-6 represent bell-shaped curves and assume an equal distribution.

It is important to understand what it means when we look at the dollar sensitivity position of a 1-unit change and multiply that by 2SD volatility. For example, if we look at a $1 million VAR, we have to know how likely it is that we will actually lose that amount or that the loss will exceed that amount.

Actually, for this to occur, several things would have to happen at the same time, including taking a position on the wrong side of the price movement and being so surprised by rapid changes in the market that our traders do not have a chance to react. In fact, because of the possibility of timely trader interference, the probability that we could lose more than $1 million is less than 2.3 percent.

This point is illustrated by an incident that occurred some years ago in the former Soviet Union and had an effect on market movements. When the news hit the wire that the Soviet leader Gorbachev had been kidnapped by political rivals and taken away from Moscow, the U.S. dollar skyrocketed in the exchange market, producing a 6SD move. There was no chance to react. Everybody who was long in dollars made a lot of money, and those who were short lost a lot. Over the subsequent

2 to 3 days it transpired that Gorbachev was alive, had returned to Moscow, and had been reinstated in his job. In response to these events, the movement of the U.S. dollar in the exchange market was reversed. This time the change was predictable; traders had a chance to adjust their risk positions and avoid large losses. This example applies to perhaps half the situations in which a price change beyond 2SD occurs and traders "can see the dark clouds coming and open the umbrella." On that basis, one might be able to justify the fact that the 2.3 percent probability that losses may exceed reported VAR amounts calculated with 2SD volatility could be cut in half, which would put the confidence level equated to 2SD volatility near 99 percent.

Standard Deviations and Senior Management

Senior managers must understand the meaning of reported VAR. Most important, they must understand that the reported amount of VAR is not the maximum amount that can be lost. Once different confidence levels are properly understood, there will be a desire to have higher and higher confidence levels with smaller and smaller probabilities that the reported VAR amounts will be exceeded.

The problem with very high confidence levels is that the VAR also gets very high, and this point is important for senior managers to understand. The same volume position of, for example, $100 million has lower VAR if we use 1SD volatility than it does if we use 2SD volatility. As one can see in Exhibit 5-7, even if the basic 1SD volatility remains unchanged,

---

Reported value at risk amounts are not the maximum amount of money that can be lost. Theoretically, the worst possible scenarios are losses so large that the financial health of the institution can be endangered.

Volume Position	Standard Deviation	Volatility	Value at Risk
$100 million	1	3/4%	$750,000
$100 million	2	1.5%	$1,500,000
$100 million	3	2 1/4%	$2,250,000
$100 million	4	3%	$3,000,000

Exhibit 5-7. Correlation of standard deviation volatility and value at risk.

the same volume position combined with a higher standard deviation and therefore correspondingly higher volatility produces higher VAR.

The following story illustrates the point. Everyone knows that airplanes have crashed in the past and will continue to crash in the future, but people fly in spite of the certainty of future plane crashes. This does not seem to make sense except when we allow for the following analysis. We can predict the number of future plane crashes by extrapolating from the number of past crashes and making positive and negative adjustments for more planes in the air and better safety procedures resulting from past crashes. We can also calculate flying activity, which varies from person to person; some people are on a plane every week, and others fly once a year. We can make an allowance for our preferred airlines on the basis of the past safety record, age of the fleet, and so on. With all of this information, we can calculate the probability that we will be passengers on a crashing plane. This is the risk.

Now let us look at the return—the convenience of flying. Most people have determined that there is a risk of being on a crashing plane, but the size of that risk—i.e., the probability of occurrence—is so small and the return—i.e., the convenience—is so great that they consciously accept this risk in order to continue to benefit from the convenience. This is exactly what senior managers must do. To the best of their ability, they must assess the size of the risk, including the appropriate confidence level; compare this level of risk with the past return and expected future return; and then decide whether they want to continue doing this business. *Remember, just making money is not good enough anymore.* This also means that in case of a very substantial event-related loss, both management and traders will be sad, but nobody will feel guilty because everybody knows that the possibility of a large loss exists regardless of how unlikely it may be.

Senior managers must, to the best of their ability, assess the size of the risk, including the appropriate confidence level; compare this level of risk with the past return and expected future return; and then decide whether they want to continue doing this business.

Volatility for Different Tenors

A portfolio consists of securities with different tenors. We know that volatility is different for different tenors, but is it correct to calculate the VAR by multiplying the position sensitivity of all positions with the same volatility? To answer that question, let us look at an illustration of a securities portfolio funded with overnight repurchase agreements (Exhibit 5-8).

Portfolio	One Basis Point Position Sensitivity	2sd Volatility	VAR
$10MM 91-day T-bill	$250	10	$2,500
$ 5MM 1-year placement	$500	8	4,000
$ 1MM 9 3/8% 30-year bond	$1,000	6	6,000
Total 1 bp position sensitivity	$1,750		
Total potential loss amount			**$12,500**

Exhibit 5-8. Securities portfolio with varying tenors.

In the traditional bank, a position would be represented by the security description in the first column under "Portfolio." In the second column we see the 1-basis-point position sensitivity for each security. The purpose of knowing the dollar equivalent of a 1-basis-point change is to multiply it by volatility (third column) and get the value at risk (fourth column).

Can we aggregate the total position sensitivity for the portfolio ($1750) and multiply that total by one estimated future volatility percentage to get a realistic estimate of the VAR? In this example, the tenors on the yield curve range from 3 months to 30 years, and we know that volatilities are different at different points on the yield curve. Therefore, the answer is that we cannot multiply the total portfolio sensitivity by just one volatility.

We cope with different volatility levels by breaking up the yield curve into "maturity buckets." The size of a bucket is determined by a reasonable commonality in the volatility. As long as volatility is approximately the same, maturities can be in the same bucket, but when there is a substantial change in volatility, a new time bucket is started. In determining the number of buckets needed, a trade-off must be made between accuracy and convenience. The collective VAR amount for the portfolio is calculated by multiplying the position sensitivity of each bucket by the appropriate bucket-related volatility and then aggregating the resulting bucket VARs.

Defeasance Period

The value at risk of a particular price risk position is calculated by assuming that a risk position can be liquidated in 1 day, which is the reason why the position sensitivity is multiplied by daily volatility. However, a particular position may require more than 1 day for liquidation because of its size, the length of its tenor, or the exoticness of the currency of the instrument or the instrument itself. It is intuitively clear that a price risk position which takes several days to liquidate involves more VAR than does an identical position that can be liquidated within a day. The period required to liquidate a position—i.e., to "defease" a position—is called the defeasance period.

Earlier in this chapter we discussed the conversion of daily volatility into multiday volatility (multiply by the square root of time). Exhibit 5-9 illustrates how this applies to the defeasance period.

Assume that we have a $100 million position for which the defeasance period is 4 days. Since the square root of 4 is 2, we must double the applicable daily volatility, in this case 1.5 percent, and arrive at twice the volatility (3 percent) and therefore twice the value at risk amount than the size of the risk would have been if this same position could have been liquidated within a day. If this $100 million position happens to absorb the trader's entire VAR limit, doubling the VAR amount—because of the 4-day defeasance period and the doubling of volatility—will require the trader to cut the $100 million position in half and reduce it to $50 million. This example shows that the process of determining the defeasance period is as important as the volatility discovery process in converting approved "carved in stone" VAR limits into position limits for traders (Exhibit 5-10).

When we estimate the time it takes to liquidate a position, we want to keep in mind that liquidation must be done without attracting the atten-

Daily volatility	1.5%
Defeasance period	4 days
Square root of 4 = 2	
2 x 1.5% = 4 day volatility	3%

Exhibit 5-9. Calculating volatility for the defeasance period.

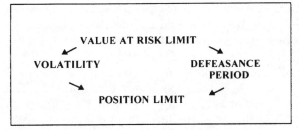

Exhibit 5-10. Volatility and defeasance period affect the position limit.

tion of other market participants, including central banks and regulators. The best approach is to equate a percentage of the daily turnover in a given commodity or instrument with our capacity for smooth daily position liquidation. The percentage of turnover is clearly a matter of judgment, but many people agree that something like 50 percent of daily turnover is a reasonable number. This means, for example, that a daily turnover of $100 million creates a liquidation capacity of $50 million per day, so that a $200 million position would command a defeasance period of 4 days.

As with volatility, documentation and management judgment are required to set the applicable percentage of daily turnover and the historical sampling period needed to determine the size of the daily turnover in a given risk-taking unit. Here again, I feel that anywhere between 6 and 9 months is a reasonable period and that incremental weight on the most recent past, such as 1 month, is appropriate.

Some institutions may take investment positions in commodities or instruments in which they do *not* trade on a daily basis. In such a case, one cannot apply the approach to determining the applicable "position liquidation capacity" that was just described. Instead, one might take a percentage of the estimated daily total market turnover to determine the defeasance period. Depending on the type of institution and its overall presence in financial markets trading, this percentage might range from 0.10 percent to 1 percent of daily activities in the market as a whole.

Changes in trading liquidity and therefore in defeasance periods must be tracked with great care because it is very dangerous to "sit on the tracks, see the train coming, and not be able to jump off." These changes are sometimes hidden or not immediately obvious. One trap for traders is one-sided trading liquidity, a situation in which it is very easy to build up a position but very difficult to liquidate it. Another danger occurs when reduced trading liquidity is institution-specific; that is, a reduction in trading liquidity is applicable only for a specific market participant, not for the market as a whole. This may occur if the credit rating of a market participant has deteriorated to such an extent that other counterparties do not have adequate lines for that participant. Such developments and other eventualities must be anticipated by the risk management function so that defeasance periods can be adjusted appropriately.

Given the importance of the volatility discovery process, institutions should develop a volatility memorandum that covers all aspects of the process and continually update it with the latest developments. The memorandum should be written in clear language which facilitates its use as a benchmark for auditing the volatility discovery process. Any changes in the volatility discovery methodology must be approved by the volatility committee.

Summary

The translation of value at risk limits into position limits occurs through both an appropriate assessment of the applicable volatility and realistic estimates of defeasance periods. Volatility and defeasance periods can move in the same direction, causing substantial increases or decreases in the resulting position limits. However, they also may move in opposite directions and completely or partially offset each other.

Institutions that trade on a daily basis will use a percentage of daily turnover to estimate the defeasance period, while institutions that do not take positions on a daily basis may use a percentage of the total market turnover to estimate the defeasance period. Volatility for the defeasance period is calculated by multiplying the square root of the number of days in the defeasance period by daily volatility.

Anticipated future volatility can be extracted from actively traded options or determined through the analysis of historical data. Volatility differs for various time periods in the future. Therefore, we have to establish time buckets in such a way that within each bucket there is approximately the same volatility. Value at risk numbers make sense only when the appropriate confidence level is fully understood. The volatility implied in options is 1SD annual volatility, which must be converted to 2SD daily volatility for the calculation of VAR. Many banks use 2SD volatility, which means that in 97.7 percent of cases the loss *will not* be larger and in 2.3 percent the loss *will* be larger. Lately, regulators have demanded a 99 percent confidence level. This equals 2.3 SD and produces even higher VAR amounts. It is critical for senior management to understand these confidence levels as part of their risk versus return evaluation and to make the ultimate decision about whether their institutions should be in a particular business.

6

Controlling
Price Risk

Understanding the business, recognizing the risk, and using meaningful language to describe position size and value at risk are the first steps in a process that makes it possible to set meaningful limits for managing and controlling price risk in trading portfolios. To control risk positions, management has the following objective:

> *Limit the size of price risk instead of limiting the size of the position.*

Controlling Price Risk in Trading Positions

In the traditional bank environment where the master limit was set for the size of the position, the tendency was simply to increase the position limit from year to year. For example, assume a scenario where the limit for traders was $40 million last year and the traders ask for $50 million this year. Management may say that since the traders made money last year, everything must be okay, and so they will approve the $50 million. Neither traders nor management really understand what $40 million or $50 million means in terms of risk.

Value at Risk Limits

The type of limit that is set now allows us to know the amount that actually can be lost on a position. For example, if we approve an overnight value at risk (VAR) limit of $100,000, we can visualize a thousand hundred-dollar bills stacked up in front of the trader and know that the trader has permission to take risk positions overnight that could result in losing the $100,000. Nobody wants a loss, but management has given its official approval for that situation to materialize. If we ask how it is possible to set limits on the amount of actual risk, we soon come to the conclusion that we must relate the size of these *risk* limits (not position limits) to the expected earnings resulting from risk positions (see Exhibit 6-9).

Country/Trading Center Limits

Therefore, in the process of controlling price risk in trading positions, management focuses on the amount of dollars actually at risk and sets VAR limits for each trading center and country on the basis of the budgeted annual trading profits. For example, suppose the combined annual budgeted trading profits resulting from proprietary trading (speculation)[1] and customer-related trading for a trading center are $12 million. The VAR limit may be established at $1 million—equal to 1 month's earnings.

When professional readers apply the risk/return analysis technique described later in this chapter, they find that their institutions probably have position limits equal to approximately 3 months' earnings, and so the proposed 1-month ratio in the example appears low. However, if you look again, you usually will find that only 30 to 40 percent of these large position limits are used. This suggests that the limits are too high and could easily be cut in half to equal $1\frac{1}{2}$ months' earnings. If we then allow for the impact of customer-related trading profits as described below, a VAR limit equal to 1 month's earnings appears quite reasonable.

There is yet another way of looking at the reasonableness of this type of limit. Assume that you convert your personal financial risk positions into a VAR based on 2SD volatility and relate that overnight risk to your monthly income. The definition of your monthly income would be your total income (annual salary and bonus plus income you might have from financial assets, support from other people, and any miscellaneous sources) divided by 12. Further, envision that you think about this just before dozing off at night and realize that when you regain consciousness after 6 to 8 hours, you may have lost the just-defined amount of monthly income. Would you consider that significant? It is hard to find a person who would not immediately say yes. The conclusion is that if risking 1 month of your income overnight is significant for you personally, it is also significant for your employer. The only difference is the number of zeros at the end of the figures.

Earlier, we mentioned the two sources from which financial institutions derive trading income: customer trading profits, which are more predictable and have less risk, and proprietary trading profits (speculation), which are less predictable and have higher risk. Traders prefer making money by speculating on future trends, but they also need customer business to add stability to the earnings; the two complement each other. The more customer-business traders have, the more likely they are to succeed in speculation. Conversely, the more involved traders are in the professional market, the easier it is to execute a customer's order competitively. To give traders an incentive for increasing customer-related profits, the managements of many banks allow customer-related profits to be included in the calculation of total trading profits and use the combined number as a basis to determine the VAR limit.

The importance of customer business in financial trading cannot be overemphasized. Without the benefits of customer-related trading, it is very difficult to make money at all; the earnings generated from strictly proprietary trading may not be enough to absorb the cost of an elaborate control system, charges for capital allocation against the assumption of price risk, and the risk/return expectations of management. The ideal goal for earnings is that half the trading profits be generated from proprietary trading and the other half from customer-related business. On that basis, a VAR limit set to equal 1 month of budgeted trading profits really equals 2 months of budgeted profits from proprietary trading, and this VAR limit seems high when one remembers one's personal situation before dozing off at night.

VAR Sublimits

In addition to the country/trading center limit, which may equal 1 month's earnings, management sets VAR sublimits for each risk-taking unit. As can be seen in Exhibit 6-1, the aggregate VAR sublimits may exceed the country VAR limit.

The extent to which aggregate sublimits exceed the country/trading center limit depends on the criteria shown in Exhibit 6-2. The scoring on these criteria is helpful to management in determining the extent to which aggregate sublimits may exceed the country/trading center VAR limit, i.e., to what extent the country/trading center limit is "leveraged."

Setting the country limit is a *science*; very little judgment is needed. The maximum country VAR limit is a percentage of budgeted earnings. Setting the maximum for aggregate sublimits is an *art*. It requires the evaluation of the criteria in Exhibit 6-2 to ascertain a reasonable overall

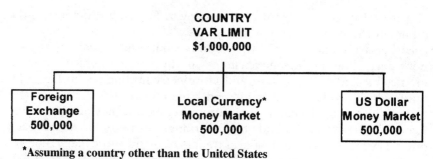

*Assuming a country other than the United States

Exhibit 6-1. Aggregate sublimits may exceed the VAR limit.

CRITERIA	SCORE (1=Low, 5=High)
Diversity of price risk and types of market factors (correlation)[1]	_____
Customer revenues as percentage of total revenues	_____
People skills	_____
Process / Treasury MIS[2] / Audit results	_____
Development, sophistication, complexity, and depth of market	_____

[1] See Exhibit 6.5 and related discussion.
[2] MIS stands for Management Information Systems.

Exhibit 6-2. Criteria for setting aggregate VAR sublimits versus the country VAR limit.

limit structure that assures protection of the VAR limit established for the country or trading center.

For each currency or product, 2SD volatility is identified and used to convert the VAR sublimits into sensitivity limits. These sensitivity limits are the only limits for which the traders are responsible and against which they are audited. Sensitivity limits for each desk of the US$ unit in country X are used to illustrate this process in Exhibit 6-3.

The head of this unit has four different desks and decides to allocate $120,000 of the $500,000 VAR sublimit to the 30-year-bond people. Assuming a 2SD volatility of 6 basis points, the one-basis-point sensitivity limit is $20,000. In other words, the size of the position is limited to an amount where a 1-basis-point change in the yield of the bonds will cause a maximum impact of $20,000; if the 2SD volatility of 6 basis points occurs, the bond desk may lose $120,000.

US Dollar Unit	1 Basis Point Sensitivity Limit	2SD Vol.	VAR Desk Limit
9 3/8% Bonds 30 Years	20,000	6bp	120,000
91-Day T-Bill	6,000	10 bp	60,000
Money Market Gaps – 1 year	30,000	8 bp	240,000
2-Year FRA	10,000	8bp	80,000
Total			500,000
Sensitivity limit = VAR desk sublimit ÷ Volatility			

Exhibit 6-3. Sensitivity limits for a U.S. dollar unit with a VAR sublimit of $500,000.

Desk	1 Basis Point Sensitivity Limit	2SD Vol.	VAR desk limit
9 3/8% Bonds 30 Years	10,000	12bp	120,000

Exhibit 6-4. Higher volatility and lower sensitivity limit.

The dollar amount of VAR remains unchanged irrespective of volatility. In other words, if the volatility for the long bond doubles from 6 to 12 basis points, management will not double the VAR sublimit of $120,000 but will leave it exactly the same. Instead, management will cut the position limit for the trader: The 1-basis-point sensitivity limit will be decreased from $20,000 to $10,000 (Exhibit 6-4).

Through this process, the size of the VAR remains unchanged irrespective of volatility.

Value at Risk Limit for a Senior Trader

We have described how the risk management function converts VAR limits into position limits for traders through volatility. An alternative to this process can be used in a situation where there is a senior trader who supervises several other traders who take on risk in a great variety of commodities and instruments. To facilitate the process, we can give a VAR limit to the senior trader, who will then convert parts of it into different position sensitivity limits as requested by his traders. This is acceptable as long as the risk management function provides the senior trader with the different volatilities needed to convert parts of the VAR limit into position sensitivity limits. It is critical, however, that the ownership of the volatility discovery process remains with the independent risk management function. Also, under this system it is the senior trader's responsibility to make sure that the aggregate VAR resulting from the miscellaneous positions taken by the traders does not exceed the VAR limit provided by the risk management function.

If the VAR limit is given to the senior trader, management also must identify the currencies in which the senior trader may take price risk positions under the VAR limit. This is done to ensure that the trading personnel under the senior trader's supervision assume price risk only in the currencies in which they have appropriate expertise. Finally, senior management may establish VAR sublimits that must be respected by the senior trader. Refer to the VAR sublimits that we've just discussed and the discussion of FX swap positions in Chap. 2.

---

*Management must identify each currency in which the senior trader may take price risk positions under the VAR limit. Additionally, management must specify whether traders are allowed to speculate on both **exchange rates and interest rates** or only on **exchange rates**.*

Overnight/Daylight Limits

In any situation in life, the sooner one addresses a problem, the smaller the damage is. That is also true for price risk positions in the financial markets. Traders, like most people, usually are either sleeping or playing during the night; they are not guarding the positions. For this reason, overnight limits are implemented for all price risk positions. Even though traders are on the job during the day, there are also daylight limits to assure that traders do not take excessive positions during the day. The daylight limits usually are a multiple, such as 200 or 300 percent, of the overnight limits.

Covaried versus Noncovaried VARs and VAR Limits

Exhibit 6-5 shows five units each reporting $1 million VAR for a total country VAR of $5 million. This noncovaried amount of $5 million VAR is almost certainly an overstatement of the total risk because it is very unlikely that in the same night the market prices for all five price risk positions will move by 2SD against us. It is therefore desirable to look back and analyze how these market prices moved relative to each other

Unit	VAR	Covaried VAR
Unit 1	1 million	
Unit 2	1 million	Covaried equals
Unit 3	1 million	possibly
Unit 4	1 million	3 MM VAR
Unit 5	1 million	
Total	5 million noncovaried	

Exhibit 6-5. Noncovaried versus covaried value at risk for five risk-taking units.

in the past (i.e., when market price 1 rose, what happened to the other four market prices at the same time?). Here again, the length of the sampling period for examining past movements of market prices relative to each other is critical, should be kept fairly constant, and must be documented in writing.

Rarely do all market prices move against us by 2SD at the same time, and therefore, the total VAR will be lower than $5 million—in this case, $3 million. This lower number is called the covaried value at risk because it allows for changes in market prices which reduce the total VAR.

It is safe to say that the covaried VAR is always lower than the noncovaried VAR. The real question is, How much lower? The key to the answer lies in the diversity of the price risk positions. The more diverse the positions, the lower the resulting covaried VAR, and conversely, the less diverse the positions, the higher the covaried VAR. The following may serve as an example. Imagine that we have net long foreign exchange positions in dollars against marks, guilders, Belgian francs, Austrian shillings, and French francs. These five European currencies usually move close together in anticipation of a European monetary union. Therefore, $5 million of noncovaried VAR may translate into $4.8 million of covaried VAR. By contrast, if the five price risk positions are in dollar interest rates, German equities, the dollar/yen foreign exchange rate, oil, and Brazilian interest rates, the $5 million noncovaried VAR may translate into a significantly lower amount of covaried VAR.

Finally, the extent to which covarying is applied is important. For example, we may covary *within* individual families of price risk, such as foreign exchange rates, interest rates, and equities. However, a more aggressive strategy is to covary VARs *across* different families of price risk, which produces an even smaller covaried result. This covarying across different families of price risk is statistically more involved and requires special attention from an institution's quantitative staff.

It is undesirable for the risk management function to give covaried limits to transactors because these businesspeople would have to do their own uncovarying on the basis of the types of price risk in which they plan to position. Situations could occur in which $1 million of covaried VAR through the application of esoteric but not necessarily incorrect mathematical and statistical acrobatics was uncovaried and/or translated into an excessively large amount of noncovaried VAR. To avoid such situations, limits should be provided to the trading function either in sensitivity language or in noncovaried VAR language. The conversion of noncovaried VAR limits into position sensitivity limits will take place with volatilities supplied by the risk management function, and the covarying of VARs reported by the businesses also should be done in the risk management area at a central point.

One must take care when one is attempting to reduce the amount of covaried VAR. If there are 10 noncovaried amounts producing, say, $1 million of covaried risk, it is possible that a reduction to zero of one of the 10 noncovaried VARs will produce an increase in the covaried VAR amount of $1 million. The reason for this counterintuitive phenomenon is the possibility that for covarying purposes the eliminated price risk partially offset another type of price risk so that the elimination of the first type of price risk actually increases the covaried risk of $1 million.

Setting Overnight Limits

If one limits the size of the risk instead of the size of the position, the question is how to set that limit. Exhibit 6-6 shows that traditionally a position limit was stated in terms of volume, for example, $10 million. If

---

Controlling FX Rate Risk

- Limits for overnight Risk
— Volume limit for position $10,000,000
— Limit for value at risk $ 100,000

- Daily volatility assumptions
— 1% → Derived position limit $10,000,000
— 2% → Derived position limit $ 5,000,000
— 1/2% → Derived position limit $20,000,000

- Constant amount of $100,000 at risk

Exhibit 6-6. Deriving the position limit from the VAR limit.

we apply the technique demonstrated in the Grandmother Story, we can set the master VAR limit and then *derive the position limit from the VAR limit through volatility.*

In the example, when the daily volatility is 1 percent, we can calculate a volume position limit of $10 million, because if we lose 1 percent of the $10 million, the loss will be $100,000. If volatility rises to 2 percent, we continue to look to the master limit for VAR of $100,000 but now have to reduce the position limit for the traders to $5 million; if we lose 2 percent of the $5 million, it will be within the $100,000 VAR limit. Similarly, if volatility goes down to 0.5 percent, the $100,000 VAR limit will produce a position limit for the traders of $20 million. We can see that the VAR amount is the master limit and that the position limits for traders are derived from volatility: Higher volatility means a smaller volume position limit for the traders, and lower volatility means a higher volume position limit.

The important point here is that we have a constant amount of dollars at risk—the VAR is the limit and remains unchanged—and that is what the system is all about. It highlights again that it is not important how big the position is; it is the size of the risk that counts. It also highlights the importance of an accurate volatility discovery process and indicates that volatility has to be updated as soon as political or economic events in the market change.

It is important to understand the difference between having VAR as the master limit and having sensitivity or volume amounts as the master limit. We have just seen that when VAR is the master limit, the VAR amount remains unchanged, and the position limits expressed either in sensitivity limits or as volume limits may change because they are derived from the constant VAR limit based on volatility. This is very different from a situation where sensitivity limits are used as the master limit. In this case, volatility is applied to the sensitivities under the sensitivity limits, which is the same as applying volatility to the positions under the position limits. The important point is that traders who use sensitivity limits as master limits multiply them by volatility and then note with interest what the VARs are: The VARs sometimes may be high and sometimes may be low, depending on the volatility.

In this scenario, the sensitivity limit remains unchanged, which does not optimize this entire system. Remember, sensitivity limits are camouflaged volume limits. Sensitivity limits are somewhat easier to understand than are volume limits, particularly because they facilitate the multiplication by volatility to derive the VAR. This represents progress; it is much better than simply using the volume limits. However, the best approach is to go the final step and not only calculate the VARs from time to time based on fixed sensitivity limits but also actually make VAR the limit. When this methodology is used, the VAR limit is constant and the sensitivity limits or volume limits are flexible and are derived from the prevailing volatility.

> *The value at risk limit is constant, and the sensitivity limits or volume limits are flexible and are derived from the prevailing expectation for volatility.*

Obviously, the VAR limits that have been assigned to the respective risk-taking units must be converted into position limits. If the trader calls another bank to buy French francs, the bank will ask how many French francs he wants. He cannot say, "I would like to buy an amount of French francs that will guarantee that I won't lose more than $300,000." Obviously, he needs a position limit for French francs.

Volatility is used to convert VAR limits into position limits. In the case of commodities, the position limit may be expressed in volume amounts. For interest-sensitive products and certainly for volatility, the position limits have to be converted to sensitivity limits. If volatility changes every day or almost every hour and the position limit is changed whenever there is a change in volatility, there will be great uncertainty and discontinuity in the size of the position limits. Therefore, we track volatility changes at a central point in the risk management function and change the derived position limit only when there is a cumulative change in volatility that is large enough to justify a change in the derived position limits. A good number for this buffer may be 15 percent, which means that if we observe a cumulative change of 15 percent in volatility since the last time the derived position limit was changed, the risk management function announces a change in the position limits. The position limits will become either 15 percent larger or 15 percent smaller, depending on whether the volatility moves down or up, but the VAR master limit remains unchanged.

Limits for Options

Often exchange traders or equity traders use options to speculate (anticipate the trend) on expected changes in exchange rates and stock prices. In those cases the focus of the speculation is the exchange rate or the stock price. The option is used only as an instrument to speculate on those market prices. These traders are therefore not option traders; they are foreign exchange traders or stock traders who use the option for directional trading in these commodities.

For these traders, we have to ask what kind of limits should be established and whether there should be any limit for volatility. For example, if a trader buys a 10-million-pound 3-month pound call option at the money (without any delta hedge), the trader views this as risking all or part of the option premium on a speculation in favor of the pound. Another way of looking at it is to say that the trader bought implied volatility and, in the absence of a delta hedge, has a net long position of 5 million pounds. (The delta hedge of a purchased at-the-money call option requires the sale of 50 percent of the option amount. The trader did not do that and therefore is net long 50 percent.)

The risk management functions of some banks insist that these types of traders have limits for implied volatility and net exchange positions. The traders say that they are not speculating on implied volatility, do not have any net exchange position at all, and are risking only an amount equal to the option premium that was paid when they bought the option.

In light of this discrepancy between the positions of the traders and the risk management function, let me summarize my personal perspective on limits for options. If a bank runs a real option book with a focus on trading implied volatility, I recommend the establishment of one limit for VAR covering both implied volatility risk positions and, because of the inability to be perfectly delta hedged, net positions in exchange options or interest rate level positions in interest rate options. However, to ensure that the focus of the option business is on implied volatility trading, I recommend establishing a 15 percent sublimit for exchange rate risk or interest rate risk. In other words, the sublimit ensures that at least 85 percent of the option book VAR limit is used for implied volatility trading and speculating.

As was discussed in Chap. 5, it is vital that the sensitivities and VARs for implied volatility and exchange/interest rates be tracked separately. Having a combined VAR limit does not change that recommendation.

If traders wish to use the option instrument for directional speculation, I recommend the following limit structure (see Exhibit 6-7):

- In buying options, there should be a limit on the total amount of premiums paid per month.

- That premium amount should be subtracted from the VAR limit otherwise available to the trader.

- In selling naked options, an amount equal to the extent the trader is not delta neutral should be converted into VAR and then subtracted from the VAR limit otherwise available to the trader.

- Finally, there is the gamma limit focused on trading liquidity. Each institution should determine its total trading capacity for each major

Value at Risk Limit	Month-to-date losses (Realized and MTM)	Adjusted / Remaining Value at Risk Limit
$1,000,000	$100,000	$900,000
$1,000,000	$300,000	$700,000
$1,000,000	$800,000	$200,000

Exhibit 6-7. Hierarchy of option limits.

market factor. Thereafter, allocations should be made to all users of this trading capacity, including the option unit.

Loss Limits

If we were allowed to have only one limit, it should definitely be a loss limit: the maximum amount of money that can be lost in a specific period of time, such as a day, a week, a month, or a year. This limit may be set anywhere between 20 and 50 percent of budgeted earnings for the specified period of time and can be changed only by the risk management function, which of course is completely separate from the dealing function. This point is important because it does not matter how senior the managers in the dealing function are; they may be too much in love with a money-losing position to reduce or eliminate it.

The following story may illustrate the point. In the last game of a United States National Basketball Association final a player who had been very successful with 3-point field goals in past games made at least 20 attempts to score 3-pointers without any success.[2] If we assume that in at least half those ball possessions his team would have scored a normal two-point basket, this would have amounted to 20 more points than were actually scored. His team lost the final by 7 points. If we raise the question of who is responsible for this loss, we must conclude that it is *not* the player but his coach. The player was perspiring and breathing heavily with effort in the heat of the match, whereas the coach on the sideline was a cool observer of the action. The coach should have taken the player aside and told him to play regular basketball (no 3-point attempts) or sit down for the rest of the game. Never mind how big a star the player might be; this simply was not his night. The analogy to loss limits in the hands of the risk management function not connected with the dealing function is obvious.

Loss Limit "Cannibalistic" Variation. Some financial institutions implement loss limits by subtracting month-to-date losses (both realized and marked-to-market) from the VAR limit, which automatically leads to smaller position limits for the traders. The larger the losses, the smaller the

---

Gamma Limit

Determine total trading capacity of institution

Distribute allocations to various RTUs, including options

VAR Limit

One combined limit for delta and volatility

Sublimit for delta may be 15%

VAR Calculation

Separate sensitivities for delta and volatility

Separate volatilities for delta and volatility

Resulting VARs are additive and may not exceed combined VAR limit for the option book

---

Exhibit 6-8. "Cannibalistic" variation.

remaining VAR limit and the smaller the possibility of incurring additional losses (Exhibit 6-8).

Management Action Triggers

Most managers want to be alerted to modest trading losses before the actual loss limit is reached. For this purpose, many institutions employ management action triggers (MATs), which do exactly what the name suggests. When a certain amount of money has been lost, it triggers management to initiate some type of action. The manager may decide to force a reduction in the risk position, possibly to zero, or decide to do nothing because she basically likes the type of price risk position currently causing a loss and/or because other units under her supervision are doing well so that the loss limit for the entire trading center is not endangered.

MATs are not intended to be limits; they are meant to protect the loss limit by alerting management to actual losses. Trigger points are established for the total trading activity in a country and individually for each risk-taking unit to alert senior management when there are modest losses irrespective of the size of the positions or when there are small losses combined with large positions.

Actual Loss MAT and Value at Risk MAT. If the actual losses in a business unit exceed a designated trigger loss (usually represented as a *percentage* of the unit's VAR sublimit), a senior manager must be notified even if the unit has no position. The actual loss MAT is a warning signal.

In the past, if the position limit was $50 million, senior management would be satisfied if the unit stayed within that volume limit. If the unit had a $45 million position, it was okay; at $55 million it was not. Now the senior manager has to be involved and actively manage. In our example, if the trigger is set at 40 percent ($200,000) of the unit's $500,000 VAR sublimit and the US$ unit has actual losses of $300,000, the senior manager is informed, can intervene, and may cut back all the VAR limits, even to zero.

How does management establish the size of an actual loss MAT? That is part of the *art*. In Exhibit 6-8 the $1 million country VAR limit is the *science*; it is completely nonjudgmental because it simply represents 1 month of budgeted earnings. Management action triggers are subjective. For instance, if the aggregate VAR sublimits are equal to the country VAR limit of $1 million, management can be more generous with the MATs, but the more the units are leveraged, the more management needs early-warning signals.

There are actual MATs for risk-taking units and desks within the risk-taking units, and there is also a MAT for the country or trading center as a whole. It tracks net marked-to-market losses for the whole trading activity in a country or trading center. This allows profits in one unit to be taken into consideration to cover losses in other units.

If potential losses from existing positions plus actual losses that have been identified as a result of the mark-to-market process exceed a trigger figure (usually represented as an amount equal to a unit's VAR sublimit), the unit head must inform the senior manager. This is the value at risk MAT.

For example, suppose one business unit makes full use of its position sensitivity limit, which was derived from its VAR sublimit of $500,000. This means it has a VAR of $500,000. Further assume that the unit actually loses $50,000. The $500,000 VAR added to the $50,000 actual loss puts the unit over the $500,000 value at risk MAT, and the unit head must inform the senior manager. Alternatively, the unit may decrease its position sensitivities, which will reduce the unit's VAR. As a result, the VAR plus actual losses no longer will exceed the value at risk MAT.

Significance of Loss Limits and MATs.   Loss limits must be respected in all circumstances. Actual and VAR MATs provide early warnings so that if necessary, risk positions can be reduced before loss limits are exceeded. Actual loss MATs are activated when there are modest losses irrespective of the size of position sensitivities. The VAR MAT is activated when there are small losses combined with large position sensitivities and resultant VARs.

It is the purpose of both MATs to assist management in protecting the loss limit. A MAT is not a limit. The T stands for *trigger* and thus a MAT is a warning signal that alerts management when the traders have reached a certain point. While breaking a limit represents a serious breach, it is acceptable to hit a MAT. A MAT causes management to review the situation, and then, if everyone is comfortable, business continues as usual. Traders should not worry about hitting the MAT or engage in acrobatics to avoid hitting it, but they must avoid breaking a loss limit.

This risk management technique highlights the importance of a well-functioning mark-to-market process. It is now clear why the senior manager requires up-to-date knowledge of mark-to-market results and VAR amounts on existing position sensitivities to effectively manage the VAR limit for the trading center as a whole.

Loss limits and MATs should be monitored only against professional revenues resulting from proprietary trading; customer revenues should not be part of these calculations. The idea is to avoid excessive speculation that puts customer revenues at risk. For example, if the US$ unit has a $200,000 loss limit, it is possible that on the twentieth of the month $300,000 in losses from proprietary trading are being offset by $250,000 in profits from customer-related trading. As a result, the $50,000 net loss for the unit is within the loss limit of $200,000. However, the senior manager should be informed anyway, because the $300,000 loss from proprietary trading exceeds the $200,000 loss limit. This is an important distinction because without it, customer-related trading profits could be put at risk and used to cover losses from proprietary trading.

Profits and losses are derived from realized and unrealized results. Realized profits and losses result from reversed/liquidated positions. Unrealized profits and losses are derived from the mark-to-market value of unliquidated risk positions. For example, if a unit buys at 10 and sells at 9, it loses 1; and the loss of 1 is a *realized* loss. If the unit buys at 25 and maintains the position and the market price moves to 23, the mark-to-market result is a loss of 2; this loss of 2 is an *unrealized* result. The realized loss of 1 and the unrealized mark-to-market loss of 2, for a total of 3, go into the loss limit and MAT calculations. For further illustration, see the sample price risk report later in this chapter.

Summary: Controlling Price Risk in Trading Positions

Trading positions are controlled by setting a single VAR limit for a country or trading center on the basis of expected earnings and distributing VAR sublimits for each risk-taking unit. This is done by analyzing the diversity of the price risk, the degree of similarity of the market factors involved (correlation), the mix between customer and professional revenues, people skills, audit results, systems, and the development, sophistication, complexity, and depth of the market. This analysis may allow the aggregate VAR sublimits to exceed the country VAR limit. Each risk-taking unit may then distribute portions of the VAR sublimit to the various desks within it by following the same approach. At the end of this distribution chain the traders are finally responsible for respecting position sensitivity limits.

The size of trading positions may be affected by loss limits which must be respected at all times. Trading positions also may be affected by MATs, which alert senior management to mark-to-market losses and/or positions involving VAR. The actual loss MAT is activated when there are modest losses irrespective of the size of positions. The VAR MAT is activated when there are small losses combined with large positions.

Controlling Price Risk in Accrual Accounts

In the process of controlling price risk in accrual positions, banks focus on the amount of dollars actually at risk and set limits on earnings at risk (EAR) for each country or major trading center. These limits usually are based on associated next-year budgeted profits.

Setting EAR Limits

The process of setting EAR limits for accrual positions based on the associated return on risk is not as straightforward as setting VAR limits for trading positions, where the relationship between risk and return is easily identifiable. Accrual positions represent the majority of the balance sheet, and the risk embedded in these positions affects many time periods. With this understanding, what are the correct revenues to consider in setting EAR limits? One-year revenues? Forecast 5- or 10-year revenues? Treasury revenues? Total revenues? In reality, EAR limits are often set judgmentally on the basis of different factors, and all of them combined affect the decision regarding the size of the limit. Factors that are analyzed in the limit-setting process include the volumes and types of assets and liabilities, the average duration of the portfolio, the size of total revenues, and the size of Treasury revenues, among others. Also considered are some of the criteria mentioned in Exhibit 6-2.

Because EAR is a forward-looking approach, two EAR limits are set: *undiscounted rolling 12-month EAR* to control the potential earnings impact of the portfolio during the next four quarters and *discounted full-life EAR* to control the total potential earnings impact of the portfolio.

Management is interested in limiting both types of price risk. The rolling 12-month EAR affects the next income statement (management does not want any surprises), while the full-life EAR affects all future income statements during the life of the portfolio. These limits complement each other. It is necessary to make sure the risk for a 1-year period (especially the first year) is reasonable, and the same thing must be done for the total risk distributed over time.

An example will show why both limits are necessary. Assume that a business decides to fund 10-year loans with 1-year deposits at a very generous spread. In the first year this business will have high revenues with no risk (the spread is fixed during the first year), resulting in a very good risk/return performance. However, this is done at the cost of exposing the bank for the remaining 9 years, when the funding cost may be substantially higher. In fact, this may be the cause of the higher spread during the first year (steep yield curve).

Note that in the definition of the EAR limits, the rolling 12-month EAR is *undiscounted* and the full-life EAR is *discounted*. This is done to take into consideration the value of time. Having $100 at risk tomorrow is different from having $100 at risk for a 5-year period. Near-term risks have a higher value than long-term risks. For the first year, the value of time is considered nonmaterial and therefore the EAR is not discounted. However, for more distant interest rate risks, EAR is discounted to present value. An exception is a high-interest rate environment. In that case, the first year EAR should be discounted as well.

In addition to the time frame segregation of the EAR limits, they are segregated for portfolios in different currencies, since the market factors involved (the interest rates and their respective volatilities in different currencies) clearly are different.

Loss Limits for Held-for-Sale Accounts

As was explained earlier, held-for-sale accounts have a special feature: They are accounted for as accrual accounts but are marked-to-market every month. The difference between the market value marked-to-market (MTM) and the book value (accrual value) of these portfolios does not affect the income statement but does affect the capital account. A loss limit for this type of account therefore is intended to protect the capital account from sudden MTM variations during a month. This loss limit is monitored in the same way that one monitors the loss limit in trading positions.

There are two loss limits for held-for-sale accounts. One focuses on month-to-date losses, and the other focuses on losses incurred since the asset was acquired. The purpose of the latter lifetime loss limit is to alert management when a particular held-for-sale asset suffers modest monthly losses which recur month after month and eventually will amount to a noteworthy and possibly painfully large loss. It may be advisable to establish a MAT to serve as an early warning before the loss limit is reached.

Daily Price Risk Report

We have discussed methods for controlling price risk in both trading and accrual accounts. The sample price risk report later in this chapter is a simplified version of a report that a bank can use to document these price risk positions on a daily basis. It conveys how this report can be structured and allows one to visualize how limits and triggers are applied to the price risk positions taken by the various risk-taking units. We have provided a list of the headings and defined them to help you understand the report. Note that the headings are different for trading accounts and accrual accounts. After the report there is an analysis of how the risk-taking units in the example are performing.

Trading Accounts

Risk-taking unit (RTU). The name of the unit or department closest to the business level that has budget responsibility. In the trading account section there are four RTUs: FX, securities, money market, and equities.

Market factor. The market variable or market price that causes the value of a position to change. Market factors include exchange rates and interest rates.

Unit shift. The standard increase in the market factor used to determine sensitivities. They are 1 percent for exchange rates and equities, 1 basis point for interest rates, and 10 basis points for implied volatility.

Month to date (MTD). The total of all realized and unrealized results of a position during a month, including the carry of a position.

Loss MAT (LM). The management action trigger for each unit. Since this is not a limit, it is acceptable to reach or hit this trigger. When that happens, the respective trader must consult the next level of management, which must take action.

Factor sensitivity limit (FSL). The maximum amount of impact that is allowed to occur if the market price shifts by 1 unit.

Factor sensitivity (FS). The actual impact that will occur if the market price to which a position is sensitive shifts by 1 unit. Obviously, FS may not exceed FSL, just as previously positions could not exceed position limits. Active dealing rooms have several different factor sensitivities in each RTU. To keep it simple, we assume a single sensitivity in the RTUs for securities, money market, and equities.

O/N 2SD. Overnight two-standard deviation volatility.

VAR. Value at risk: the amount that would be lost if the market price moved by 2SD volatility against us.

VAR limit. Limit for value at risk.

Accrual Accounts

The horizontal headings for accrual accounts also include risk-taking units and market factors/unit shifts. The remaining headings include the following:

Gap. The volume amount of positive or negative mismatches. Gaps are shown by maturity.

Position/factor sensitivities. A combination of amounts, time, and an increase by 1 basis point in the level of interest rates.

Defeasance factor. Daily 2SD volatility multiplied by the square root of time for the period likely to be required to liquidate the position.

Earnings at risk (EAR). Potential decrease of earnings because of an adverse change in interest rates. Result of multiplying position sensitivity by the defeasance factor.

EAR limit. EAR is tracked, and EAR limits are established for two periods:

- *Rolling 12 months.* Not discounted to present value.
- *Full life.* Includes first 12 months, goes up to 5 years, and is discounted to present value.

Sample Price Risk Report

The following is an analysis of the performance of each risk-taking unit:

FX. No excesses in the covaried amount.

Securities. The VAR limit is exceeded—usage of $900 versus a limit of $750.

Money market. Actual loss MAT is triggered—MTM loss of $450 versus an actual loss MAT of $100.

Sample Price Risk Report

DAILY PRICE RISK REPORT
As of:
Figures in $000

TRADING ACCOUNTS

Risk-Taking Unit (RTU)	Market Factor/ Unit Shift	Month to Date (MTD)	Loss MAT (LM)	Factor Sensitivity Limit (FSL)	Factor Sensitivity	O/N 2SD	VAR	VAR Limit
FX	FX Rate 1%	(50)	(200)				(1,300)	(1,400)
	FX Rate 1	20		600	(500)	1.0%	(500)	
	FX Rate 2	(40)		600	(400)	0.5%	(200)	
	FX Rate 3	(30)		700	(600)	1.5%	(900)	
				Noncovaried			(1,600)	
				Covaried			(1.300)	
Securities	$TSIR 1bp	100	(250)	25	(30)	30 bps	(900)	(750)
Money Mkt	$TSIR 1bp	(450)	(100)	50	0	30 bps	0	(600)
Equities	Index Price 1%	(100)	(150)	50	30	4.0%	(120)	(200)
TOTAL		(500)	(700)					(2,950)
Loss Limit		(1,000)						

ACCRUAL ACCOUNTS

Risk-Taking Unit (RTU)	Market Factor/ Unit shift	Gap ($MM)	Position Sensit. (1bp)	Defeas. Factor*	EAR	EAR LIMIT
Funding & Gapping	$TSIR 1bp					
0/3 Mths		-200	-5	30	(150)	
4/6 Mths		-400	-10	30	(300)	
7/12 Mths		-100	-5	30	(150)	
Rolling 12 months			-20	30	(600)	(700)
Year 2		-150	-15	30	(450)	
Year 3		-50	-5	30	(150)	
Year 4		-50	-5	30	(150)	
Year 5		-50	-5	30	(150)	
FULL LIFE			-50	30	(1,500)	
DISC. FULL LIFE EAR					(1,400)	(1,200)

Cost-to-Close (end of previous month)	4000
Cost-to-Close today	3500
MTD	150
Change in Cost-to-Close	-350
Accrual Limit	-700

(*) Total volatility during the defeasance period

Equities. No excesses.

Total trading. No excesses—trading losses of $500 versus a country MAT of $700.

Loss limit. Actual loss of $500 within a loss limit of $1000.

Rolling 12-month EAR. Usage of $600 within a limit of $700.

Full-life EAR. Discounted full-life EAR limit is exceeded—usage of $1400 versus a limit of $1200.

In FX, there are factor sensitivities in three different currencies. We see three factor sensitivities and three noncovaried VARs of 500, 200, and 900 for a total of 1600. We assume that the 1600 noncovaried VAR equals a 1300 covaried VAR. Covaried VAR limits are established for each family of price risk, as seen in the four RTUs. There is no covarying across families of price risk in this case.

There is a loss MAT of 700 and a loss limit of 1000 each month for the entire dealing room. There are no loss limits for individual RTUs.

Accrual Accounts

Cost to close (end of previous month). At the end of the previous month, there was a profit of 4000. That means the bank would have locked in a profit of 4000 if all accrual gaps had been closed.

Cost to close today. See month to date.

Month to date. So far this month there is a realized profit of 150. If the market had not changed and given that at the beginning of the month we had a positive 4000, the current MTD of 150 would suggest that we now have a cost to close of 3850. However, that is not so. We have a cost to close of 3500, which is 350 less than we would have had if the market had not moved against us to the extent of 350. For these types of losses (negative change in the cost to close) there is a limit of 700, which one can call the accrual limit. It may be wise to have an accrual MAT so that management receives an early warning and can take action to avoid breaking the accrual limit.

Stress Testing

The expression of value at risk has been defined as a 2SD movement in the corresponding market factors, which provides a 97.7 percent confidence level, and it has been explained how banks limit the size of price risk in trading accounts and accrual accounts. However, these risks represent exposures to *probable* market conditions. Even though these measurements are appropriate for day-to-day monitoring and evaluation against limits, the full scope of risk evaluation is complete only if it is extended to account for significant event risk or stress scenarios that may further affect portfolios. This additional evaluation is known as *stress testing*.

Stress testing in price risk is equivalent to the contingency funding plans in liquidity risk (see Chap. 12). Both analyze the corresponding risk, assuming stress or exceptional scenarios. Stress testing in price risk includes both the VAR for trading accounts and the EAR and market value sensitivity for accrual accounts.

Who Is Responsible?

This question must be answered with great clarity in each bank. Management must decide whether stress testing should be done at the business level or at the portfolio level, depending on the particular structure of the business. It also must be decided which stress scenarios may affect the portfolio strongly and which market variables may trigger these scenarios. The main idea behind stress testing is to make senior management inside the business aware of all potential price risks if exceptional conditions occur. Therefore, this exercise should be "custom-made": It should fit the specific characteristics of the business under observation.

Process

There are three basic steps to follow for stress testing a portfolio. The *first step* in analyzing a portfolio under stress conditions is to identify all the stress scenarios that may affect the portfolio adversely. This is the foundation of the exercise and should be carefully defined. Stress scenarios usually include political or economic events that may cause serious disruptions or distortions in the market that will adversely affect the particular business under analysis.

A typical example of the effect of political or economic disruption is the withdrawal of money by foreign investors and the export of capital by locals, usually generated by the deterioration of the country's economy or by political turmoil. Conventional wisdom states that these potential events are limited to emerging markets, but consider the following. Suppose there is substantial political turmoil in Russia with a possible spillover into Germany. This will encourage foreign investors in Germany to withdraw their investments, and the Germans themselves will put their money outside of Germany. Such a development is not likely, but after all, we are talking about stress testing.

In countries other than the United States the FX rate is the first thing to react when investors try to buy back dollars. In an attempt to keep dollars in the country, the government increases the local interest rate to a level where investors will reevaluate the withdrawal. Depending on the credibility of the government, the interest rate may be set so high that it causes the country's economy to collapse, further escalating the crisis. Even banks in the United States could experience a crisis scenario if the Japanese massively liquidated their holdings of U.S. dollar government bonds. This could drive up U.S. dollar interest rates and possibly cause a crisis in terms of liquidity and price risk.

The *second step* is to quantify the consequences of the stress scenarios on the portfolios, in other words, to calculate VAR and EAR/MVS under stress conditions.

For trading portfolios, the expected movement in market factors, the potential disruption in some correlations, and the lack of liquidity during the defeasance period should be part of the calculation. As a general gauge, to quantify the impact of a stress situation, many banks assume an adverse 5SD move on all noncovaried risk positions. Special attention is required for option portfolios in which a market disruption may preclude the ability to hedge some risks (for example, volatility risk that is hedged only through opposite options).

For accrual portfolios, banks usually do not assume parallel movements in interest rates. Instead, they assume different 2SD movements across all points in the yield curve, usually by using the market value sensitivity (MVS) approach. Special attention should be given to the impact on earnings during the next 12 months; the crisis may be temporary, affecting earnings only in the short term.

The *third step* is to analyze the results. It is possible that relatively low VAR/EAR numbers (under business-as-usual assumptions) may become large numbers under stress conditions. Increasingly, regulators demand an uninterrupted information flow from the trader on the phone to the most senior management, including the board of directors, in terms of price risk based on business as usual as well as price risk based on adverse 5SD moves in a stress situation.

Risk/Return Analysis

Mr. Jones was in the orange juice business at a time when mechanical juicers did not exist. Business was booming, and he required additional workers. He advertised in the local paper for prospective orange juice squeezers to come to his bottling plant for an interview. Two men with big muscles showed up to apply for the job. Each man was given six oranges to squeeze. The first man extracted one cup of juice from the six oranges, while the second one squeezed two cups of juice from six oranges. Which one would you hire? Obviously, you would hire the one who extracted the most juice from the oranges. The same is true for the allocation of value at risk limits. We give the largest risk-taking capacity to the departments or units that earn the highest trading profits on their VAR limits. In other words, if two departments have identical VAR limits and one department has higher earnings on that limit, the department with the higher earnings is more likely to be allowed to take more risk so that it can make even more money.

At the Dealing Room and Unit Level

In the discussion about analyzing risk it was said that the new system provides the ability to convert a meaningless volume limit into a meaningful VAR limit. This limit serves as a basis for

- Determining the extent of price risk leveraging. (To what extent may aggregate VAR limits exceed the VAR country limit?)

- Deriving position sensitivity limits and volume limits for specific trading desks using the appropriate volatility

As a result of these interdependencies, we can relate the VAR limit to the expected earnings, which allows a risk/return analysis and helps us understand why just making money is not good enough. Let us examine two dealing desks. One desk makes $10 million, and the other makes $15 million. Obviously, $15 million is more than $10 million, but the desk that makes $10 million risks $1 million, or 10 percent of budgeted earnings, every night and the desk that makes $15 million risks $3 million, or 20 percent, every night. This kind of risk/return analysis was not possible when we talked in terms of volume limits.

Exhibit 6-9 shows a chart of VAR limits and budgeted trading profits for four units in a trading area. It shows how one can relate the VAR limits to the budgeted trading profits and then make a judgment about the relative attractiveness of each risk-taking unit.

This process allows us to judge the relative attractiveness of these revenues. We can relate the budgeted profits (the money a business says it will make) to the VAR limit (the amount of dollars a business may put at risk every night) and express the result in terms of how many days of revenues are at risk every night.

It can be seen, for example, that the FX people say they are going to make $5 million. To make that amount of profit, they are going to put

Unit Name	Annual Budget	Volume Limit	Sensitivity Limit	Volatility	VAR Limit	Days of Revenue at Risk
FX	5,000,000 Daily: 20,000	60MM	1% = 600,000	0.9%	540,000	27 days
12-Month Money Market	4,000,000 Daily: 16,000	600MM	1 B.P. = 60,000	8 B.P.	480,000	30 days
Stocks	3,750,000 Daily: 15,000	50MM	1% = 500,000	1.8% = 900,000	900,000	60 days
6-Month T-Bill	7,500,000 Daily: 30,000	1 Billion	1 B.P. = 50,000	9 B.P.	450,000	15 days
Total	20,250,000 Daily: 81,000				2,370,000	29 days

Exhibit 6-9. Risk versus return analysis based on 250 business days a year.

$540,000 at risk every night, which is 27 days of revenues at $20,000 per day. The money market desk has a similar risk/return performance with 30 days of revenues at risk ($480,000/$16,000 = 30).

The stock and Treasury bill units are distinctively different. The Treasury bills unit shows not only the highest earnings of $7.5 million but also the lowest consumption of VAR limits with $450,000, which translates into a risk/return ratio of 15 days of revenue at risk. This is fantastic.

The problem is the stock unit with 60 days of revenues at risk, which is not acceptable and requires analysis and/or action. First, we check to see whether the budgeted revenues can be doubled with the same VAR limit of $900,000. If this is not possible, we find out whether the budgeted revenues can be achieved by cutting the VAR limit in half from $900,000 to $450,000. Both approaches would reduce the days of revenue at risk from 60 to 30. If cutting the limit without changing the annual budget is not possible, we have to look at the quality of the people in the stock unit. If they are good people, we know that the stock business is structurally unattractive. We should scale down our risk taking in this area and allocate our risk-taking capacity to an area that delivers revenues that are commensurate with our risk/return ratio targets. For example, we might reallocate $800,000 of the $900,000 VAR limit, leaving the stock unit with $100,000. The stock people can now focus on research and customer service, trading in the market during the day but maintaining only modest overnight risk positions.

In addition to the individual unit analysis, we can look at the entire trading area with the four risk-taking units combined. With 29 days at risk, they meet our risk/return objective in spite of the substandard performance of the stock unit. This example also shows that the risk/return analysis must be applied to the lowest (most junior) level of the organization. Any trader with a revenue budget and a VAR limit should be analyzed in terms of risk/return. If we apply the risk/return analysis at a higher, more senior level, it is possible that attractive units such as Treasury bills will offset unattractive units such as stocks and we will never recognize the bad apple in the basket.

The technique demonstrated in Exhibit 6-9 also can be used by institutions which are currently using a volume limit system to manage price risk but would like to convert from volume limits to VAR limits. For example, the third column shows volume limits of $60 million for foreign exchange. As a first step, these volume limits must be converted into sensitivity limit equivalents, such as 1 percent sensitivity limit of $600,000. The sensitivity limit is then multiplied by a volatility of 0.9 percent, which leads to a VAR limit of $540,000. In other words, a trader who has a $60 million volume limit for a commodity that has an overnight volatility of 0.9 percent may risk $540,000 overnight. If this VAR limit is reconverted into position limits, we again get a $60 million volume limit, or a 1 percent sensitivity limit of $600,000, as long as the volatility is unchanged at 0.9 percent. In other words, the sensitivity limit should be set at a level where traders can take the same size positions under the newly defined sensitivity limits that they were able to take under the previous volume limits. It usually is easier to implement the VAR limit system when, at the outset, VAR limits are established which lead through volatility to the sensitivity limits and volume limits that prevailed before. Against the background of a risk/return analysis, one can then reduce VAR limits if the combination of VAR limits and budgeted earnings from trading and positioning produces unacceptable risk/return results.

At the Corporate Level

In the risk-return analysis at the dealing room or country level we quantified the size of price risk by relating it to trading profits and stated the risk/return in terms of how many days of revenues we have at risk. The ultimate risk/return analysis involves analyzing the size of price risk not against income but against the capital of the bank. This analysis—relating price risk to capital—is not useful at the country or regional level because the amount of capital banks maintain in various countries is not based on the size of the price risk they are taking in those countries. Instead, the volume of capital banks have in their branches and subsidiaries depends on the local regulatory requirements, which often relate to the bank's loan volume in a country but not to its trading activities. Therefore, we have to go to the corporate level and do an institutional analysis of the size of price risk relative to capital.

Before describing how to aggregate price risk at the corporate level, let us share a down-to-earth analogy. Assume that I ask you how much salt there is in your kitchen and that you take me seriously. You point out all the salt shakers and then the container of salt from which you refill them. At this point you may think there is no more salt in the kitchen. However, I go to the pantry, grab a can of beans, and point out from the label that there are 3 grams of salt in the beans; then I do the same thing with the corn, peas, bread, and cookies. Thereafter, we perform the same exercise with regard to how much sugar is in the kitchen. In other words, we aggregate each ingredient separately whether it is available in pure form or as part of another product.

We do exactly the same thing with financial market factors when we aggregate price risk. We identify the individual market factor sensitivity across all product lines and across the entire geography. Wherever in the world a bank has a price risk position, the individual market factors are identified and reported to a central point. It is important to identify whether respective positions are long or short, and this is best accomplished by assuming for the entire organization an upward movement in the respective market factor. Thus, anybody who has a short position will assume that there is an upward movement by 1 unit, such as 1 percent or 1 basis point, and report a negative sensitivity to move 1 unit upward in this particular market factor. People who are long will of course report a positive sensitivity to an upward move in this market factor.[3]

Once the market-factor-specific sensitivity has been reported at the central point as both positive and negative, we can net the positive and negative sensitivities for each specific market factor. Once we have the netted individual market factor sensitivities, we can apply volatility to them to calculate market-factor-specific VARs. These VARs then can be covaried to a varying extent and ultimately, if it is desired, produce a single number for covaried VAR.

This process of aggregating VARs at a central point is illustrated by the following example. Assume that three risk-taking units—foreign exchange, securities, and FRA derivatives—have the risk positions stated in the old volume language in Exhibit 6-10 and that these risk positions are broken down into their individual market factors as shown in Exhibit 6-11. Our focus is on the factor sensitivity summary. We see for dollar interest rates (red)[4] a negative sensitivity of 4 resulting from positive 1 in the FX department and negative 5 in the securities department, for yen interest rates (green) negative 5 resulting from neg-

FX	Swap Position: Long US$ 10 million spot vs. Yen Short US$ 10 million one year vs. Yen
SECURITIES	Long Yen bonds one year equivalent US$ 40 million Long US bonds 6 months US$ 100 million Long LCY bonds 4 months equivalent US$ 100 million
FRA	Short LCY 12 months in 1 equivalent US$ 100 million

Exhibit 6-10. Price risk positions in the old language.

US $000

Trading Unit	Market Factor	FS↑	2 SD volatility	VAR		
FX	US$ Interest rate	1 red	10 bp	10		
	Yen Interest rate	(1) green	8	8		
SECURITIES	Yen interest rate	(4) green	8	32		
	US$ interest rate	(5) red	10	50		
	LCY interest rate	(2) blue	20	40		
FRA	LCY interest rate	(10) blue	20	200		
FS SUMMARY	US$ Interest rate	(4) red	10	40		Approx
	Yen Interest rate	(5) green	8	40		200
	LCY Interest rate	(12) blue	20	240		covaried
				320 noncovaried		

Exhibit 6-11. Price risk report in the new language.

ative 1 in the FX department and negative 4 in the securities department, and for local currency interest rates (blue) negative 12 resulting from negative 2 in the securities department and negative 10 in the derivatives department. The three net sensitivities shown in the summary multiplied by their respective volatilities produce a total VAR of noncovaried 320,000. This number has to be covaried and might result, for example, in an amount of 200,000.

Equity Capital Allocation for Price Risk

Regulators have decided that banks must allocate equity capital against the price risk positions—both trading accounts and accrual accounts—assumed in the dealing room. The structural price risk in the balance sheet, mostly consisting of accrual risk, will be subject to equity capital allocation at a later point. While the final decisions have not yet been made, it appears that the calculation of the equity required against dealing room–related price risk will be as it is shown in Exhibit 6-12a. We see that the confidence level is 99 percent, or 2.3SD. The defeasance period is determined to be 10 days irrespective of the type and size of position. As the square root of 10 is 3.16, we get a defeasance period–adjusted volatility equivalent of 7.27SD (2.3 × 3.16 = 7.27). Regulators feel that there are additional risks of an operational and processing nature, and to be sure that all these risks are properly covered, the 7.27SD will be multiplied by 3, resulting in 21.80SD volatility. This volatility percentage will be used to calculate VAR for equity capital allocation purposes.

The examples in Exhibit 6-12b show the impact of such calculations on

Confidence level	99% or 2.3 SD
Defeasance Period 10 days	$\sqrt{10}$ = 3.16
Volatility equivalent of	7.27 SD (2.3 x 3.16)
Multiplier	3
Final result	21.80 SD (3 x 7.27)
(Approximately 11 x the common 2 SD)	

Exhibit 6-12a. Volatility for value at risk versus equity capital.

Volatility Assumptions	
1 SD volatility	8% p.a.
2 SD	16% p.a.
2 SD overnight	1% flat
22 SD overnight	11% flat

Conversion Of Price Risk Into RAAP Assets	
Derived value at risk multiplied by 12.5 to get RAAP assets added to balance sheet	
Implied 8% RAAP capital asset ratio	
FX $100 million at 11% = 11,000,000 VAR x 12.5 = 137,500,000 RAAP	
GAP $500 million for 1 year - 10% interest rate level at 11% volatility = 1.10% = 5,500,000 x 12.5 = 68,750,000 RAAP	
Incremental RAAP assets = $206,250,000	

Exhibit 6-12b. Equity capital for price risk—Basle proposal.

a foreign exchange position of $100 million and a money market gap of $500 million for 1 year, using a volatility that often prevails in the market. For the FX position, an assumed annual 2SD volatility of 16 percent equals 1 percent volatility overnight or 11 percent volatility to reflect the mandated 22SD volatility. Applying the 11 percent daily volatility to the $100 million net foreign exchange position creates $11 million of VAR. For the $500 million 1-year money market gap, if we assume a 10 percent interest rate level, 11 percent volatility equals 110 basis points of overnight volatility, which translates into a 5.5 million VAR (for volatility calculations, see pages 102–103.) This is a total of $16.5 million of VAR for which we need equity capital on a one-for-one basis. These very stiff capital requirements indicate that regulators may want to punish institutions which engage in possibly excessive proprietary trading activities without any noteworthy customer business. Regulators also demand an internal control process that corresponds to the level of trading activity. In fact, regulators reserve the right to increase the multiplier from 3 to 4, producing approximately a 29SD (7.27 × 4) equivalent, if they find that an institution's internal control process does not meet the minimum standards.

One could simply subtract the $16.5 million VAR from a bank's capital. This will produce less equity capital, and if the risk assets remain unchanged, it also will produce a lower capital/asset ratio. However, that is not how regulators want it done.

The entire risk adjustment and equity capital allocation process[5] is driven by the reduction or increase in the amount of risk assets. As it applies to price risk, banks are asked to multiply the VAR number calculated for equity capital allocation purposes by 12.5, simulating an assumed 8 percent capital ratio. The amount derived by multiplying VAR by 12.5 must be added to the risk-adjusted assets, and this leads of course to an increase in risk-adjusted assets and a decrease in the capital/asset ratio. In Exhibit 6-12b we calculated a total of $16.5 million of VAR, which when multiplied by 12.5 produced an incremental $206,250,000 of risk-adjusted assets. We could calculate this backward and say that in order to support $206,250,000 with 8 percent capital, we need $16.5 million, which is the total amount of VAR that was determined earlier for these two positions.

This example and the calculation of $16.5 million VAR assume no covarying. According to the latest word from regulators, *covarying is permitted*, which reduces the need for equity to some extent. However, covarying for this purpose is allowed only within families of price risk, such as foreign exchange, interest rates, and equities.

Exhibit 6-13 illustrates the process of converting VAR into risk-adjusted assets for capital allocation purposes.

		Scenario A VAR 800	Scenario B VAR 800
Risk Assets	90,000	90,000	90,000 10,000 (800 x 12.5) 100,000
Capital	7,200	6,400	7,200
Capital Ratio	8.00%	7.11%	7.20%

Exhibit 6-13. Equity capital allocation for price risk.

In the left column we see risk assets of 90,000 supported by 8 percent capital of 7200. Assume that we have 800 of VAR for which capital must be allocated. One could subtract the 800 VAR from the 7200 capital, which yields 6400 of capital, or 7.11 percent of the 90,000 in risk assets (scenario A). However, that is not what regulators ask us to do. In scenario B, we are multiplying the 800 in VAR by 12.5 to create an incremental 10,000 of risk assets. This increases total risk assets from 90,000 to 100,000. The equity capital is unchanged at 7200. However, the capital ratio is reduced from 8.00 percent to 7.20 percent because of the increase in risk-adjusted assets.

If this disturbs a bank's targeted capital ratio (sweet spot), the bank has to generate more equity capital or reduce the amount of risk assets, possibly through the sale of assets. Another alternative, of course, is to reduce the price risk position, possibly to zero.

Business Plan

A business plan is developed by senior management to provide a direction for the activation of all the resources that are needed to achieve the bank's identified objectives. A business plan must be in writing and should include the following:

- A description of the current and future economic, political, and regulatory environment

    It is very easy for managers to describe the current environment. The real challenge is to envision what the environment will be for the next 15 to 18 months. This is one of the most important tasks for managers, because if they have a correct view of the future, the business is likely to be successful. It is like planning what type of clothing to take on vacation. If we go skiing but have packed for the beach, we will be in trouble.

- A description of the planned activity given the expected environment

  Given the environment, what products should we offer? We want to sell water in the desert and heaters at the north pole, not the other way around.

  To what types of customers do we want to offer these products (target market)?

  What kind of speculation do we want to do (proprietary trading)?

  The description of the expected environment (scenario analysis) and the identification of products, customers, and speculative activity must be integrated and connected with each other. This cannot be overemphasized. If a senior manager gets this part of the business plan right, she has performed a large part of her entire duties. All she needs is good staff people to execute her plan. Such a manager does not have to spend many hours working in the office. She can periodically review the progress under her plan and, if necessary, take corrective action. By contrast, if these points are not properly planned and integrated, the manager can work 18 hours a day and accomplish nothing.

- Status reports

  Product program (see Chap. 15), operations/systems, controls, audit results

- A description of the competition

- A staffing plan

- A budget summary

  Given the volume of business we plan to do in this environment, what revenues do we expect and what is the risk/return ratio for these revenues against the VAR limit?

  The limits requested

  VAR limits and sublimits and management action triggers

- The volatility discovery methodology

  Options, the historical database, and reasoned management judgment

- The volumes and types of assets and liabilities planned

If you are failing to plan, you are planning to fail.

Business plans are produced not only for an institution as a whole but for all the managed entities within the organization. For example, a foreign exchange department in an institution should have its own business plan. Obviously, the departmental business plans must be integrated into the broader general objectives for the institution as a whole.

Integrated Business Approach

Exhibit 6-14 shows how the management of financial trading/positioning comes together in an integrated business approach. We take risks through our customer-related business and speculative trading and then make sure we benefit from the riskier environment. The new language described in the Grandmother Story allows us to measure return on risk, and loss limits help prevent big losses.

Product programs closely examine products for any kind of risk—not only price risk but also other risks, including processing, legal, and regulatory risks. They also protect us against operating errors and fraud. (See pages 273–276.)

We tie that all together with a business plan that sets forth our objectives and the action plans for accomplishing them.

We have to understand the business in order to recognize the risk and assess the magnitude of that risk. After that we can control the risk with VAR limits and position sensitivity limits derived from volatility. We evaluate earnings in terms of the risk/return ratio because just making money is not enough: we have to maintain capital adequacy commensurate with the targeted bank's specific sweet spot and increase earnings per share.

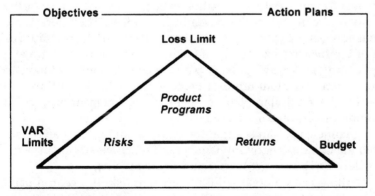

Exhibit 6-14. The management of financial trading/positioning—an integrated business approach.

Managing Foreign Exchange Reserves

The concept of management implies a process aimed at achieving a clearly defined set of objectives. In managing a country's foreign exchange (FX) reserves, I strongly advocate that safety and liquidity be the main objectives; they must be considered more important than the profitability of the portfolio. The rationale for this view is that FX reserves represent the nation's savings account, and funds in the savings account should be invested very carefully.

A country's foreign exchange reserves must be viewed as a nation's savings account. Safety and liquidity must be the prime investment objectives.

Many people believe that U.S. dollars invested in short-term Treasury Bills, such as 91 days, meet all the above criteria to a very large extent. The currency is stable, the credit standing of the issuer is absolutely first class, and the trading liquidity is unsurpassed. The only problem is that with that kind of quality, the return is not high; it is the risk-free rate of return.

The following paragraphs explain how a central bank can simultaneously retain the safety and liquidity characteristics of an investment in U.S. Treasury Bills and use derivatives to assume more price risk and/or credit risk in order to enhance returns on some of the investments.

For exchange rate reasons, a central bank may wish to have, for example, part of its FX reserves in yen. The central bank will simply buy forward yen, resulting in a net long position in yen. When the yen rises, the central bank will gain; when the yen falls, it will lose. The interest rate differential between yen and dollars will be reflected in the premium or discount of the forward exchange rate. For example, if dollars are at 6 percent p.a. and yen are at 2 percent p.a., the central bank will have to buy forward yen at a premium of 4 percent p.a. while it continues to earn 6 percent p.a. on dollars. This is a net yield of 2 percent p.a., which is the amount the central bank would earn if it invested in yen in a more traditional manner. You can see that the bank maintains the safety and liquidity of the U.S. dollar government bond while diversifying into yen through a derivative contract for exchange rate reasons.

The same thing can be done with interest rate risk. If a central bank wants to benefit from a positive yield curve or expects interest rates to decrease over the next few weeks and months, it cannot stay in short-term instruments and do nothing else. However, instead of committing the cash for a longer period, which might impair liquidity, the central bank could stay in short-term instruments and enter into a fixed versus floating interest rate swap. Specifically, the central bank would agree to receive a fixed interest rate for a period of time, say, 5 years, and pay a floating interest rate which will be reset every 3 months. Now the central bank is positioned to benefit from a positive yield curve and/or a decline in interest rates while maintaining its cash in safe and liquid instruments.

In addition to the derivatives described above, the market for credit derivatives soon will be sufficiently developed to provide higher yields for investors through the assumption of responsibility for one type of debtor in exchange for the swap partner's assumption of responsibility for another type of debtor (see Chap. 9).

Obviously, the assumption of risk beyond the risk-free rate of return through the use of incremental exchange rate risk, interest rate risk, and credit risk must be rigidly limited to protect the management objectives—safety and liquidity—for FX reserves. In the past the central banks of some countries participated in the market as vast speculators, which in one case led to a loss of as much as 5 billion U.S. dollars.

To avoid such disasters, benchmarks should be established for the diversification of FX rate risk and interest rate risk. For example, a benchmark portfolio could be apportioned to have 30 percent each in U.S. dollars, yen, and German marks. The remaining 10 percent could be divided among miscellaneous other currencies and assets, including precious metals and equities, with sublimits per asset class or specific commodity, currency, or equity ranging from 1 percent to 0.1 percent. Once the benchmark portfolio has been established, limits for departing from each benchmark within the portfolio would be set. For example, since the benchmark for yen is 30 percent, the limit might be set at $\pm$ 10 percent. This means that the portfolio can never consist of less than 20 percent or more than 40 percent yen.

The same could be done with interest rate risk for each approved benchmark currency. For example, the benchmark may be 25 percent each in 1-month, 1-year, 3-year, and 5-year instruments. Thereafter, limits for departing from the benchmark would be established. The 1-year benchmark may vary between 6 months and 18 months, the 3-year benchmark between 2 years and 4 years, and the 5-year benchmark between 4 years and 7 years. These benchmarks for foreign exchange and interest rate risk should not be viewed as actual recommendations. We are using these numbers to make it easier to understand the concept.

Once benchmarks and limits for departing from the benchmarks are in place, it is very important to measure the portfolio management performance against the benchmark. This involves the following steps:

1. Identify the currency in which the value of the portfolio will be measured. In many private sector organizations this would be the equivalent of the local currency. For many central banks this currency may be either the U.S. dollar or the local currency. In fact, it can be any currency as long as it is only one currency.

2. Determine the initial value of the portfolio in the chosen currency at a specific point in time, for example, as of the end of the year.

3. One month after the initial valuation of the portfolio determine the value of the portfolio as if it had been invested strictly following the benchmarks. In other words, assume that no judgment has been applied to manage any aspect of the portfolio and that the benchmarks in all risk areas have been maintained rigidly. The simulation on a benchmark basis in steps 1 through 3 produces a hypothetical portfolio value of x.

4. Mark-to-market the actual portfolio to reflect the results of portfolio management decisions during the last month.

This last step should produce a value larger than x, which means the portfolio has a profit. If the result is less than x, the activities last month produced less than the nonjudgmental maintenance of the portfolio at benchmark would have yielded. This clearly is not a desirable performance.

Let us be optimistic and assume that the portfolio manager produced a portfolio value larger than x. The increment over x is really the "trading profit." It is the result of having intentionally departed from the benchmark because the portfolio manager thought she could make more money by investing differently from what the benchmark suggested. To the extent that she departed from the benchmark, she took risk, and this risk must be converted into VAR by using the technique described in the Grandmother Story (see Chap. 4).

Once the portfolio manager has the increment of the portfolio value over x and the size of the VAR, she can relate these two numbers and determine how many days of earnings were at risk (see Exhibit 6-9). In other words, was it worth it? Remember that just making money is not good enough anymore.

In the context of safety, credit risk is also very important in managing a portfolio of FX reserves. One must be careful in selecting issues to buy and in deciding where the securities will be maintained for safekeeping. It does not make sense to buy bonds issued by an AAA entity and then lodge these securities with a facility with lower credit quality.

In selecting issuers and the location of the institution providing the custodial services, one should take into account the question of country risk, which is the political and economic stability of a country (see Chap. 10). For this reason, many countries use the custodial services of the Federal Reserve Bank of New York in the United States for investment in U.S. government debt and the safekeeping of those instruments. Otherwise, depending on the type of countries involved, diversification of custodial countries may be a good way to reduce country risk.

Risk versus Return Analysis for Mutual Funds

The same fundamental technique of risk versus return analysis described for the management of FX reserves can be applied to the management of any pool of cash, including the thousands of funds in which people invest their savings for retirement and other purposes. When it comes to equity investments, one must apply the principles for calculating VAR that were described in Chap. 4.

For many of the stocks in equity funds there are options traded at organized exchanges. In those cases we can use option-implied volatility to calculate VAR, provided that the trading liquidity is deep enough. Alternatively, we can use the interpretation of historical data described in Chap. 5. The VARs for all stocks in a fund can be aggregated, which leads to an overnight VAR for that fund. In other words, it is possible to determine an overnight VAR with a 2SD volatility for each equity fund. Of course, defeasance periods and their increasing impact on VAR also must be considered.

For these VARs to be meaningful, the mutual fund industry would have to establish a standard for volatility discovery, confidence levels, and covariance criteria together with a common standard for aggregating price risk. The next step would be for the industry to agree to a risk scale of, for example, 1 to 10, with 1 being low (risk-free rate of return) and 10 being the highest risk imaginable. Each fund would make it very clear to the public where it ranked on this scale and would be audited for its adherence to these risk classification criteria.

Following the implementation of such a system, I can see a few widows playing bridge in a country club. Between hands, one player tells the others that she has decided to move 20 percent of her portfolio from risk level 5 to risk level 6. Most important, I can see that this statement would mean something to the lady making it and to her friends who are listening.

Obviously the funds with the higher risk levels are expected to generate higher returns, and if they do not do that, their customers (the ladies in the country club) will make the same critical comments that the senior manager of a dealing room makes when a risk-taking unit takes risks equal to 5 months' earnings; i.e., an amount of risk that is totally unacceptable.

Today the mutual fund industry uses language that is not very meaningful to describe individual funds. This language includes nonspecific terms such as *balanced growth*. Mutual fund investors must learn to identify the risk-taking level of a particular fund and decide if it fits their investment goals. They also must distinguish between equity risk and interest risk on one side and credit risk on the other side. For example, some fixed-income funds describe themselves as AAA, creating the impression that it is very difficult for customers to lose money on these investments. The AAA refers to the credit quality of the issuer, who is extremely safe and probably will not go out of business. However, if this fund invests in long-term fixed-rate bonds and interest rates rise, the price of those bonds will go down and the investors in the fund will lose money. One can see that funds must clearly communicate to investors the size of the credit risk, which may be nominal, and the size of the price risk (interest rate risk), which can be very substantial.

Notes

1. *Speculation* is a negative-sounding word. You might prefer to refer to the activity as *anticipating the trend*, which means the same thing.

2. For those who are not familiar with the rules of basketball, a field goal (basket) is rewarded with 3 points when the player is a certain minimum distance away from the basket. All other field goals count as 2 points.

3. Obviously, the whole thing can be done in reverse so that everybody reports a downward move as long as it is a common direction, either up or down.

4. In the chart, the color matches the market factor. For example, if this book were printed in color, I would have printed the US$ interest rate data in red, the yen interest rate data in green, and LCY interest rate data in blue.

5. Refer to the section on the risk adjustment process in Chap. 13.

7
The Use of Derivative Products

Hedging an Already Existing Price Risk

Paul Volker became chairman of the Federal Reserve Bank in 1979, during a period of high inflation. Over one weekend in October he increased the discount rate by 3 percent—a very big move. To illustrate how big it was, Allan Greenspan created a huge shock in February 1994 by increasing interest rates by 0.25 percent—and 3 percent is 12 times that size. The 3 percent increase in the discount rate caused huge swings in dollar interest rates during the following 3 years, from single digits to above 20 percent, down to single digits, and again up to 20 percent. In this volatile economic environment businesspeople looked for ways to protect their core businesses against interest rate fluctuations, and banks responded by developing hedge instruments for that purpose. Derivative products—products that are derived from something and whose value depends on the cash value of that underlying something—were developed initially by banks to protect their customers against already existing interest rate risk.

Creative Borrowing and Investing

Although these hedge instruments were developed to protect customers against adverse changes in interest rates, traders soon discovered that they also could be used for creative borrowing and investing. It became apparent that they could provide a lower cost in the case of borrowing and a higher yield in the case of investing.

The common thread among the uses of derivatives in these creative packages is that people intentionally do something different from what they actually want. As a result, they do someone else a favor and benefit from the lower cost or higher yield. There are many ways traders can benefit from doing something different from what they really want to do. Here are three examples:

- Borrow a *currency different* from the one you really want.

- Borrow at a *different* type of *interest rate.*

- Include in the structured deal an option that the trader does not want and then sell off the option.

The first example—borrowing a currency different from the one that is needed—is a long-term foreign exchange swap. To illustrate how it works, assume the following market rates:

Dollar interest rate	13 percent p.a.
Swiss franc interest rate	6 percent p.a.
Swap rate	7 percent p.a.

Boeing has a contract to sell two jumbo jets to Swissair. The payment terms state that Swissair will pay Boeing Swiss francs in 5 years. From Boeing's viewpoint, it has a receivable in Swiss francs and therefore wants to sell Swiss francs 5 years forward.

Let us introduce a second market participant called the "swapper," which for the purposes of this example is a utility company that is in the market to borrow U.S. dollars at a fixed rate for 5 years. An investment bank persuades the swapper to borrow Swiss francs and then swap the Swiss francs with forward cover for the principal and interest amounts into dollars. Thus the company that wants dollars begins by borrowing Swiss francs—almost as if it were borrowing the wrong currency—and then sells spot the Swiss francs it borrowed and buys forward Swiss francs. That is what Boeing is looking for: someone who is a buyer of 5-year forward Swiss francs.

In this case, we have created a customer. Somebody once said that "the purpose of any business is to create a customer." This utility, which is about as local as any company can be, is a participant in the long-term forward exchange market—a buyer of 5-year Swiss francs—because it originally borrowed the "wrong" currency. Of course, this deal is structured so that the utility has an advantage. Instead of paying 13 percent for the dollars, it probably pays only 12.70 percent, for a savings of 30 basis points, which is accomplished by intentionally borrowing a currency other than the one it really wants.

The second example involves a company that intentionally borrows at a different type of interest rate.

A private company with excellent credit standing is looking for 5-year fixed-rate money. Since it is privately held, the company is unknown to market participants and therefore has limited access to the fixed-rate market. A Coca-Cola-type company, a global corporation with almost unlimited market access, is in the market for floating-rate borrowing. If the private company goes directly to the fixed-rate market, it may be able to borrow at 13 percent fixed, while the global corporation can perhaps borrow at a floating rate of $\frac{5}{8}$ percent over LIBOR.

Let us see how the interest rate swap can be applied creatively in this case. The global corporation uses its borrowing capacity and market access to borrow in the fixed-rate market at 12 percent, which is lower than the 13 percent rate at which the private company might have been able to borrow. When the company has the money in its pockets, it does an interest rate swap, giving the fixed-rate pricing at 12.60 percent to the private company (note that it retains 60 basis points). Simultaneously, the private company borrows at $\frac{3}{4}$ percent over LIBOR from a bank that knows it and then fulfills its part of the interest rate swap by giving the floating rate over to the global corporation.

Now everybody is happy. Both companies started with the "wrong" interest rate, but after the interest rate conversions each company has the rate it originally wanted. The private company started with a floating rate of $\frac{3}{4}$ percent over LIBOR and exchanged it for a fixed rate of 12.60. Since it was facing a possible cost of 13 percent fixed, it not only now has the right type of interest rate, it also is economically happy because it has saved 40 basis points. The large corporation started with a fixed rate of 12 percent. When it gave that fixed rate away, it retained 60 basis points and also got the floating interest rate it wanted at 75 basis points over LIBOR. If the large corporation subtracts the 60-basis-points pass-through profit from 75 basis points over LIBOR, it ends up with a floating rate of 15 over LIBOR. This is a good example of how a company benefits from intentionally borrowing at an interest rate other than the one it really wants.

The third example involves an interest rate option embedded in a debt instrument.

Assume that a company borrows $200 million for 5 years through a floating-rate Eurodollar public issue called an FRN (floating rate note). Since the company is well established in the market, it pays $\frac{5}{8}$ percent over LIBOR. Also assume that today LIBOR is 7 percent. Now it comes up with something new. It says, "We want to add a cap—an interest rate ceiling—to this instrument. We never want to pay more than 9 percent." The investor will say, "Under those conditions, I can't give you the money at $\frac{5}{8}$ percent over LIBOR. I'll do it at $\frac{5}{8}$ percent without this ceiling, but if you say that over the next 5 years you never want to pay more than 9 percent, I want more than $\frac{5}{8}$ percent now." The word *option* is not used, but in effect the issuer of the FRN—the company that borrows the $200 million—is buying an interest rate option from the investor with a strike price of 9 percent. In exchange, it pays more than the usual $\frac{5}{8}$ percent over LIBOR. It says, "Okay, you are right. I will pay you $\frac{3}{8}$ percent more for a total of 1 percent over LIBOR." The borrower has purchased an option with a strike price of 9 percent and a premium of $\frac{3}{8}$ percent.

An important feature of this transaction is that the smallest denomination of the issue is, for example, $10,000. This is a clear indication that the issue is aimed at retail investors. Sometimes the smallest denomination of a bond issue is $1 million, in which case the target market consists of wholesale institutional investors. However, in this case we assume that the target market consists of retail investors, which is the most important point, as we will see in a moment.

After the company successfully places the paper and gets the $200 million at a rate of 1 percent over LIBOR, it says, "We never wanted this interest rate option. We are selling the option, which we bought for $\frac{3}{8}$ retail, at the market rate of 1 percent." (It is assumed here that the fair market rate for wholesale options is 1 percent.) To summarize, it borrowed the money with the option attached for 1 percent p.a. over LIBOR, which is $\frac{3}{8}$ percent more than it usually pays, and now it calls an investment bank and sells the option for the entire $200 million wholesale at 1 percent p.a. What is the cost? The cost is LIBOR, because when the company borrows at 1 percent over LIBOR with the option attached and then sells off the option at 1 percent, it actually is borrowing at LIBOR without a ceiling. Since it never really wanted a ceiling, it has effectively reduced its borrowing cost by $\frac{5}{8}$ percent, because it had an option-trading profit: It bought the option retail at $\frac{3}{8}$ percent and sold it wholesale at 1 percent.

These examples demonstrate how instruments that originally were designed for hedging are used creatively for borrowing and investing, providing lower costs to borrowers and higher yields to investors. The key is intentionally doing something different from what is ultimately wanted: a different *currency* in the case of the utility that wanted dollars but borrowed Swiss francs and used a long-term foreign exchange swap to convert the Swiss francs with forward cover into dollars, a different type of *interest rate* in the case of the large corporation and the private company that borrowed at interest rates other than what they wanted and then used the interest rate swap to adjust those interest rates, and an unwanted embedded *option* in the case of the borrower with a floating-rate note who arbitraged between the retail and wholesale prices of options.

There is no end to the complexity and number of variations of derivatives. However, derivatives all have one thing in common: People do something *other* than what they really want—different commodity, different interest rate, or buying an unwanted option embedded in the debt instrument that is issued. Then, after they do something different from what they really want, they correct the situation with a derivative product, that is, swap the "wrong" currency for the currency they really want, swap the "wrong" type of interest rate for the interest rate they really want, or sell the option which they never wanted to own. These derivative transactions may sound simple, but how these transactions are orchestrated can be very complex. It is necessary to understand what the customer wants and then take the raw material of derivative instruments and mold and cut and polish the instruments in such a way that they fit the customer's need exactly. This creative combination of financial engineering and imagination with derivatives is a process I call *financial imagineering*. We can identify here with the German philosopher Kant, who said, "The important thing is to hear and see things that everybody can hear and see, and to think something that nobody has thought before."

The following is a thought process and approach I have used to solve customer problems through the development of a new product or idea:

- Identify the most salient point in a problem situation, simplify it, and understand exactly why what we wish to do cannot be done in the usual way.

- Acquire all (100 percent, not 99 percent) pertinent information, including applicable regulations, policies, exact customer needs, and the bank's objective, and thoroughly understand how these factors relate to the problem.

- Rotate the problem and look at it from several different angles; then think about it in a questioning, revolutionary way.

- Find a solution and put it into action (the creative act).

- Promote the solution with stick-to-itiveness in the bank with the personnel in all the affected departments, overcoming resistance to change ("We have never done it that way before") and developing the new idea into a salable product.

If you have not changed a major opinion or adopted a new one in the last few years, check your pulse; you may be dead.

Highly Leveraged Speculation

In addition to hedging and financial engineering, traders have discovered a third use for derivative instruments: speculation. Since derivatives were designed originally to hedge risk, they can be used with equal ease to assume risk. For example, if a trader has a long position in commodities, interest rates, or volatility and does not want to be long, he sells, and that is called *hedging*. However, when a trader is not long, the same action of selling is called *speculation*. The action is exactly the same, but if someone who is not long does it, she is building up a speculative short position.

As all these products become more convoluted and exotic, it is important that customers become more sophisticated and really understand what they are doing. In other words, it is the bank's responsibility to assure that the customer is suitable for the use of a particular product (when a dealer sells a Ferrari to a 16-year-old and that person has an accident, it may be the fault of the Ferrari salesperson) (see "Customer Appropriateness" in Chap. 15).

Counterparty Credit Risk

The examples presented here are straightforward, relatively plain derivatives designed to demonstrate the basic concepts, which are the building blocks for more complex instruments. In fact, there is no limit to what can be done to make derivatives fancier in order to squeeze more basis points out of them or to satisfy specific customer needs. For example, if you layer derivatives—i.e., if you have a derivative with a value that is based on the value of another derivative—you are creating a much more complex product. But if you disaggregate any creative use of a complex derivative instrument, you will find that it cannot be anything other than a commodity, interest rate, or option that is different from what is ultimately wanted.

Derivatives were invented as instruments for hedging against fluctuating market rates. Then their use was expanded to include creative borrowing and investing. Finally, traders discovered that any instrument which is appropriate for hedging can with great ease be used for speculation. All these uses for derivatives ballooned the counterparty credit risk.

A bank stood as the principal counterparty between Boeing and Swissair in the foreign exchange swap and again as the principal counterparty between the world corporation and the private company in the interest rate swap. Therefore, it can be seen that in most cases banks are principal counterparties in derivative transactions and as such face the counterparty credit risk that will be described in the next two chapters. In fact, the major purpose of this brief summary of derivatives is to impress readers with the fact that the bank absorbs a credit risk in all these mostly desirable uses of derivatives. The examples also show that the typical derivative transaction has a maturity of several years, which further increases the size of the counterparty credit risk.

Banks usually are principal counterparties in derivatives transactions and face counterparty credit risk.

It is critical for participants in derivative markets to understand the difference between the role of principal counterparty, which means that they are subject to counterparty credit risk, and the role of an arranger of derivative transactions. Arrangers act like true brokers, introducing two counterparties who pay a brokerage fee to the arranger and then do a trade directly with each other. In this situation, the arranger obviously is not a principal counterparty and therefore does not have counterparty credit risk. Frequently, traders describe a transaction as being brokered when they actually mean that they have the two counterparties on the phone at the same time and buy from one counterparty and sell to the other one. Even though traders refer to this as brokering a deal, it is clear from this description they are not brokering; instead, they are buying and selling as a principal counterparty and therefore face potential counterparty credit risk with both clients.

Use of Derivatives by Central Banks

Central banks participate in the foreign exchange market primarily to even out imbalances in the demand and supply of the local currency. Typically, this participation occurs in the spot exchange market for settlement 2 business days after the transaction takes place.

Central bank foreign exchange transactions, usually in U.S. dollars against the local currency, affect the country's foreign exchange reserves (FX reserves) and local money supply. When a central bank other than the central bank of the United States buys dollars against the local currency, the FX reserves increase and the local currency money supply increases as well. When the central bank sells dollars against the local currency, the FX reserves decrease and the local money supply decreases.

Periodically, the demand for or the supply of a currency becomes extremely strong, and substantial central bank intervention is required to keep the local currency at a particular value (if it is pegged to or fixed against a foreign currency such as the U.S. dollar) or at a price level at which the local regulators (often acting through the central bank) would like to maintain it. Often this disequilibrium between supply and demand creates market pressure for the local currency to devalue, which requires the central bank to purchase its own currency and sell dollars. This type of intervention is aimed at keeping the FX rate at the level the central bank would like to maintain. However, even though the target of the intervention is the FX rate, two undesirable side effects usually result from the traditional intervention of purchasing local currency and selling dollars in the spot FX market: The local money supply will be reduced, and FX reserves will be reduced (see Exhibit 7-1).

The reduction in the local money supply occurs because the central bank is purchasing its own currency in the process of selling dollars. This action has the same effect that would occur if the central bank sold government bonds as part of its open market operations in an effort to take liquidity out of the market. Even though a central bank may want to tighten the money market and drive up interest rates as part of the total effort to defend the local currency, an excessive reduction of the money available to the system may not be desirable. After all, the economy must continue to grow to restore confidence in the country's currency. In summary, selling spot dollars to defend the local currency may lead to an excessive shrinkage of the local money supply which could be difficult to correct. However, this correction can be made through open market operations in which the central bank buys government bonds and injects back into the market the liquidity that was removed through the spot sales of dollars.

The reduction in FX reserves is a much more serious problem, because each country has only so many billions of dollars. Usually these reserves are not large, which may be one reason why the market anticipates a devaluation of the currency. If the spot dollar sales continue, a point will be reached where there are no reserves left and the country is forced to devalue.

It can be seen from this discussion that even though the central bank's objective is to stabilize and defend the exchange rate, intervention in the spot exchange market has major negative side effects on the local currency money supply and the FX reserves.

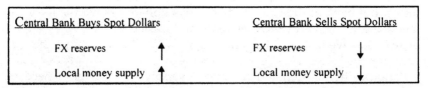

Exhibit 7-1. Impact of central bank intervention on FX reserves and the local money supply.

Historically, in most cases the duel between a central bank and market forces was won by the market, which raises the question why that is so. We can explain this phenomenon with an analogy. At the beginning of time, when people had differences to settle, they fought each other with their bare hands and punched each other in the face until one party to the dispute came up a winner. Then somebody invented the sword, at which point the person fighting with his hands no longer had a chance. Soon after that the shield was developed, and the opponent also began to use the sword. The escalation of weapons continued up to the sophisticated defense systems we have today. Sophisticated attackers invented new weapons and were superior for a brief period, until the attacked entity came up with something just as good or even better, restoring the equilibrium.

This analogy relates directly to the traditional intervention techniques of central banks. The market has learned to use cashless derivatives for its attacks, while the central banks defend themselves with cash-based instruments. In the absence of cash-related limitations, the market's only limitation is price risk, i.e., how much money it can lose if the speculation does not work. For central banks the main question is: How many dollars do we have, and for how long can we intervene at a particular volume per day until we run out of dollars? In many cases the market is aware of the size of the FX reserves and also knows the daily volume of intervention. On that basis, it is easy to anticipate the point at which the central bank will have to throw in the towel. Using the analogy, the market attacks with the sword and the central banks defend themselves with their bare hands. In this scenario they do not have a chance.[1]

The solution, of course, is for the central banks to counterattack by defending their currencies with cashless derivatives. Earlier in this chapter we explained the fundamentals of interest rate swaps and forward interest rate agreements. These cashless instruments are focused strictly on the interest rates applied to notional amounts. There is no commitment to provide cash or take cash. I recommend that central banks use what I would call a *forward exchange rate agreement* (FERA). The private over-the-counter market already uses these instruments and calls them *nondeliverable forwards*, which basically conveys the same meaning. Here is how it could work for a central bank whose currency is under pressure to be devalued. Like all other serious interventions, the central bank must know whether it wants only to smooth the decline in the local currency or actually wants to defend a particular fixed/pegged FX rate. Defending a fixed rate should be done only if there is something to defend. If the currency really is overvalued, as is often the case, the most sophisticated strategy will not be successful.

However, assume there is an unwarranted attack. Assume a spot rate of 100 local currency units equal to a U.S. dollar and an interest rate differential of 12 percent p.a., with the dollar interest rate being lower. This differential creates a premium of roughly 1 percent per month or a forward exchange rate of 112 units of the local currency to a U.S. dollar for 1 year. If the local currency becomes a candidate for devaluation and the market wishes to buy dollars, the central bank can offer 1 year dollars as a nondeliverable forward at 112. This will keep the spot exchange rate at 100 as long as the interest rate differential remains at 12 percent p.a. If the interest rate for the local currency rises, producing an interest rate differential of, say, 15 percent p.a., the central bank will offer dollars value 1 year forward at 115, and so forth. As long as the central bank offers forward dollars at a premium equal to the interest rate differential, the spot exchange rate will stay at 100.

Upon maturity of the FERA, the transaction will be settled for cash in the local currency against a preagreed, clearly defined settlement indicator. This indicator is very important in preventing a disagreement about the rate against which the FERA is settled.

Conducting a foreign exchange intervention with this product does not affect a country's local money supply and FX reserves. However, it does have the same impact on the demand/supply balance as does the spot exchange intervention. The FERA allows the central bank to focus exactly on what it wishes to focus on: defending the spot FX rate *without* affecting the FX reserves and the local money supply.

If a central bank uses this new instrument wisely (to fight off unjustified attacks), it is unlikely that the market will be able to force a devaluation of the local currency. Without the impact on the local money supply and FX reserves, the central bank's constraints are the same as those of the market: "How much money will I lose if it goes wrong?" Now the central bank is in a better position than is the market. First, the profitability of a central bank should not be a major objective (even though it often is). Second, weak currencies which are candidates for devaluation usually have high interest rates and are therefore at a discount in the forward exchange market. Strong currencies which are candidates for revaluation usually have low interest rates and are therefore at a premium in the forward exchange market. Intervening central banks usually buy weak currencies at a discount (sell strong currencies at a premium) and sell strong currencies at a premium (buy weak currencies at a discount). It follows that central banks will always make money at maturity when FERAs are settled for cash, provided that they pick their moments wisely, i.e., use this instrument only when they are sure that they are right rather than to defend an indefensible fixed point.

Even if the central bank loses under a FERA, the loss will occur in the local currency, and it is this amount that will affect the local money supply. The FX reserves will never be affected because the dollar or the other major currency is the "dealt amount," which will always be a wash. The settlement will be in the local currency.

As a practical matter, central banks should introduce this instrument to their local markets in quiet times when the local currency is not under attack. A few deals should be done so that the operating departments of the central bank and the market participants will become familiar with the instrument, do their product programs (see Chap. 15) for the instrument, and understand how it is booked and processed.

Notes

1. The combined FX reserves of all central banks are about $2 trillion, and the daily turnover in the global foreign exchange market exceeds $1 trillion. This is another clear example showing why cash-based intervention in the spot market usually does not work.

8

Lending and Settlement Credit Risk

Chapter 2 described how banks have made the transition from lending as their primary business to placing more emphasis on trading and explained why it has become necessary to devise a more sophisticated system for managing price risk. As a result of this increased emphasis on trading, it also has become necessary to understand contract amounts and counterparty limits and recognize the counterparty credit risk arising from distant-date contracts.

Recognizing, Assessing, and Controlling Lending Risk

In the case of loans and placements, it is very easy to understand the business and recognize the credit risk. A bank gives money to another entity, and the risk is that at the maturity of the loan the bank will not receive repayment of the principal and interest. In terms of assessing the amount of risk, if a bank lends $100,000 at 10 percent for 1 year, it is commonly assumed that the amount at risk is $100,000. However, this is not the case. Since the bank actually expects $110,000 in principal and interest a year from now, it should track and have approvals for a risk amount of $110,000.

Assessing the riskiness of a counterparty is a traditional credit judgment, which is not the focus of this book. Obviously, one has to take into account a company's balance sheet, its management and reputation, and the type of business or industry it is in. In many countries there are official credit ratings for corporations which offer a quick way to judge the credit quality of a counterparty. Modern banks have established internal credit ratings for all counterparties to which credit is extended. As a result, each counterparty may be rated anywhere from 1, which equals AAA, to 10, which equals an almost certain write-off. These internal credit ratings are then used to price loans to customers. The higher the credit quality is, the less likely it is that the counterparty will go bankrupt, and therefore less equity capital has to be allocated to loans extended to the customer. Since the better customers require less equity allocation, loan spreads to those customers may be smaller than spreads to less creditworthy customers. Banks also establish portfolio limits for maximum credit extensions to specific industries, which helps to avoid excessive outstandings in a specific industry, for example, real estate.

The maintenance of a well-diversified portfolio as described above has been facilitated considerably by the emergence of credit derivatives, in particular, credit swaps (see Chap. 9 for a more detailed discussion).

Issuer Risk

Earlier in the book we described the reluctance of banks to engage in the traditional lending business, given the requirement for a minimum interest rate spread to justify putting these assets on the books. The alternative for borrowers is to issue debt instruments which banks purchase from the borrowers and then sell to investors who previously were depositors. The bank's profit margin on these transactions is very thin because the loans are priced to be sold off quickly, not to stay on the balance sheet. The bank's role in this process, often referred to as *underwriting*, has special risks associated with it.

Assume that a bank purchases an IOU from a customer at a fixed interest rate with a maturity of 5 years and intends to sell this paper in a matter of days or weeks at the most. This relatively short period of credit risk may create the impression that the process of assessing the creditworthiness of the borrower can be less rigorous and detailed because, after all, "we only need to analyze whether the client will be alive in a few weeks when we sell the loan." This is appealing, but it is completely wrong. The reason for selling a loan is not that we doubt the credit standing of the borrower at the time of the sale. The reason is that the loan is priced to be sold, and this thin pricing makes it unattractive to keep the loan on the balance sheet. While it holds the IOU, the bank faces exactly the same credit risk it would face if it had made a traditional loan; only after the bank sells the paper without recourse does the credit risk end. However, in spite of this, the bank must analyze the credit quality of the issuer as if the bank would hold the loan to maturity. Otherwise, the paper should not be offered to investing customers.

The reason for selling a loan is not that we doubt the credit standing of the borrower at the time of the sale. The reason is that the loan is priced to be sold, and this thin pricing makes it unattractive to keep the loan on the balance sheet.

In this context, we also must look at the maximum holding period. The people responsible for selling the loan typically fund it for a few days or weeks with short-term money. In a normal yield curve, this creates "positive carry" because short-term funding costs less than the return on 5-year fixed-rate money. As a result, these people often intentionally defer the sale in order to benefit from the positive carry for a longer-than-necessary time period—a very dangerous practice. Interest rates could rise during the holding period, and because these types of loans are very thinly priced, any rise in interest rates is likely to produce a loss. A loan can be sold or cannot be sold, and if it can be sold, the paper should be sold quickly, usually within 1 or 2 weeks. One way of coping with this problem is to take the results of a positive carry away from the salespeople so that this tempting but undesirable incentive is eliminated.

In addition to the risk of rising interest rates, the same borrower may issue additional IOUs through another bank which will flood the market before we offer our paper for sale. Another possibility is that interest rates in general will remain unchanged but because there is negative publicity about the borrower, interest rates for this borrower move higher, causing a loss for the bank. For all these reasons the paper should be sold as quickly as possible.

The bank's approval process for underwriting also should be clearly established with a separate set of rules. In addition to an assessment of the creditworthiness of the borrower (credit skill), an analysis of the prevailing market conditions for the type of paper in question is needed (market skill). The obvious questions include the following: At what price (yield to investor) can the paper be sold? In what amounts can it be sold? Within which time frame? Legal or regulatory questions

LOAN RISK	ISSUER RISK
Intent is to hold the loan. Length of the holding period is for the life of the loan. Credit is primary risk.	Initially it is the same as a loan. Intent is to sell the security. Length of holding period is shorter. Price risk is the dominant risk. ▪ Interest rates change in the market ▪ Company's market share ▪ Negative news about the company
Continuous balance sheet impact. Minimum profit margin required. Commercial banking rules apply.	Limited balance sheet impact. Profit margin may be smaller. Securities rules apply.

Exhibit 8-1. Comparison of loan risk and issuer risk.

often must be addressed in terms of the type of investor that is eligible to buy the paper. In other words, we should not offer to a client an instrument that we are not allowed to distribute or that the client is not allowed to buy.

Finally, care must be taken in exerting sales pressure on investors. For example, when talking about nonrecourse paper, a salesperson may tell an undecided investor, "You can always sell it back to us." The customer will have heard, "I can always sell it back *at the same price,*" while the salesperson will have meant that the bank will be making a secondary market in that paper and will be prepared to buy it back *at the market price.* In this case, there is a big difference between the salesperson's intention and the customer's perception. Salespeople must balance their desire to sell what is called "story paper"[1] against the need to make it extremely clear to customers exactly what they are buying (refer to "Customer Appropriateness" in Chap. 15).

Exhibit 8-1 shows the characteristics that differentiate loan risk from issuer risk.

Credit Risk in Trading

In trading, the credit risk that a counterparty will default on a contract can be divided into two categories of risk. The first category is settlement risk, which is defined as the risk of default *on* the settlement date, when the entire contract amount is at risk. The second is presettlement risk, which is the risk of default *before* settlement, when only the cost of replacing the defaulted contract is incurred. The remainder of this chapter will address the issue of recognizing, assessing, and controlling settlement risk; presettlement risk is discussed in Chap. 9.

Recognizing Settlement Risk

On the maturity date of a contract there is a risk that after we have settled our side of the transaction, the trading partner will fail and 100 percent of the transaction amount will be lost. For example, suppose you buy a pair of shoes in a department store and the salesperson directs you to the cashier to pay for the purchase and then to another area to pick up the shoes. You pay $100 to the cashier, get the receipt, and proceed to the pickup area. At this point the public announcement system comes on and says that the store is bankrupt and no more business can be transacted. You run to the cashier to get your money back, but nothing can be done. Then you run back to the pickup area to try to claim your shoes. You see the shoes and point them out to the salesman, but he says, "Sorry, I have instructions not to do any more business, and therefore I can't give you the shoes." This is settlement risk: You paid, but you cannot get what you bought.

In addition, if the contract rate is more attractive than the prevailing market rate, the risk at settlement is actually more than 100 percent. For example, assume that we sell pounds at $2.00 to ABC Bank and that this bank fails on the maturity date of the contract. Also assume that we pay the pounds to the bank on the maturity date, but because it is bankrupt, the bank does not pay dollars to us. If the market rate has moved so that it is less attractive by 20 percent, the total counterparty risk at settlement actually will be 120 percent. The increased risk represents the cost of replacing the contract at the now-prevailing market rate of 1.60, which is 20 percent less than the original rate of $2.00 per pound.

Assessing the Size of
Settlement Risk

In a foreign exchange trade, we buy something that is being delivered to us and sell something that we have to deliver. We will use the example of a contract on Monday for a spot exchange of German marks and British pounds to illustrate how to assess the size of settlement risk. The timeline in Exhibit 8-2 will explain the sequence of events in this transaction and the period during which the settlement risk exists.

On Tuesday we send a payment order (P) to our correspondent bank in Germany requesting that it debit our mark account and pay the counterparty value Wednesday. Usually, we have to send the payment order at least a day before the settlement date, particularly when there is a large time difference. For example, if we are in the United States, this time difference is 6 hours. Tomorrow morning, when Americans start at 9 a.m., it is already 3 p.m. in Germany.

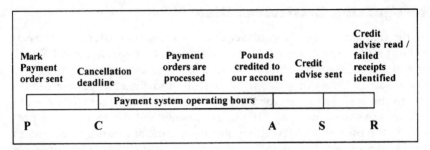

Exhibit 8-2. Payment timeline.

The cancellation deadline (C) is the point at which the payment order no longer can be rescinded or changed. If we send this payment order on Tuesday at 10:00 a.m. for value Wednesday and 5 minutes later realize we made a mistake, we can call the correspondent bank and say, "Change the message we just sent. Where we said $10 million, that's really supposed to be $8 million" or "Where we said Barclays Bank in London, it really should be Paris." Obviously, five minutes later there is no problem, but there is a point where the bank will say, "Sorry, it's too late to cancel or change." That is the cancellation deadline, and that is the time when the risk period begins.

It must be emphasized that these are two different points: Point P is when we send the payment order, and point C is the time when we can no longer cancel the payment order *with confidence.* "With confidence" means the point where we can be absolutely certain we can still stop the payment. There is a gray zone where we can call and say, "Please stop this payment." The correspondent banker then says, "Well, I'm not sure if it's too late; let me check." He may come back and say it is too late, or he may say, "Oh, yes, I still can catch the order before it is executed." One has to identify in advance the time when we know with confidence that we can still stop the payment.

The payment will be executed after point C (the cancellation deadline) during the operating hours for the payment system in Germany. In each country it is a little different, but for each country, and therefore for each currency, we know the earliest and the latest times when our correspondent can actually make the payment. After point C, the outgoing payment for marks no longer concerns us because it is definitely gone. The credit risk for the entire amount of the transaction has begun. When will it end?

Now we switch the focus to the currency we are receiving. In this context we are concerned with the time at which the pounds will be credited to our account with finality.[2] This involves three separate actions. First, the British correspondent bank credits our account; second, the British correspondent sends a credit advise to us; and third, we read this credit advise—i.e., reconcile our account—and in that process identify amounts which we expected but did not receive. The analogy would be to a situation in which a mother has critical surgery. The first step is that surgery is successfully concluded, the second is that the doctor telephones us, leaving the good news about successful surgery on the answering machine, and the third is that we listen to the message on the tape (see Exhibit 8-3).

We have identified the critical points in settlement risk. In this case, settlement risk does not begin when we send out our German mark payment order but when the cancellation deadline for stopping the payment order passes. The credit risk does not end when our account is credited or when the credit advise is sent; it ends when we read the credit advise and reconcile our account.

A 1994 survey conducted by the New York Federal Reserve Bank's Foreign Exchange Committee showed that over half of market participants lose the right on Tuesday to call back a payment for value Wednesday settlement, and they do not reconcile until Thursday amounts that are credited or not credited to their account value Wednesday. This means they are at risk for 2 days, from Tuesday to Thursday, for the settlement of a foreign exchange transaction value Wednesday. That is an astounding piece of news. We can almost stop here because it means that the settlement risk is at least 2 days. Some banks do not reconcile until Friday, and some even reconcile receipts before they are final, which of course is totally wrong.

As can be seen in Exhibit 8-4, settlement risk begins after time has passed to the point where, per the agreement with the correspondent,

1. Account credited with finality	1. Surgery successfully completed
2. Credit advise sent	2. Doctor phones and leaves message
3. Credit advise read, account reconciled	3. We listen to message and are relieved

Exhibit 8-3. Steps in receiving and reconciling incoming payment: an analogy.

Mark Payment order sent	Cancellation deadline	Credit advise read / failed receipts identified
	Settlement Risk	
P	C	R

Exhibit 8-4. Period of settlement risk.

we no longer can call back the payment (point C). Our settlement risk ends when we *realize* we have received the dollars (point R), not at the moment when we *receive* the dollars. As long as there is the possibility that we could be informed of a failed receipt, we are at risk. This simple example points to a market-based definition of settlement risk: *"The full amount of the currency purchased must be considered 'at risk' from the time a payment instruction for the currency sold becomes irrevocable until the time the final receipt of the currency purchased is confirmed."*[3]

Many people think that settlement risk applies only during business hours on the value date of a contract. Consequently, they may say that when traders buy yen and sell dollars, they do not have settlement risk because of the 12-hour time difference. On the surface this sounds fine, but now you know that it is not true. The dollar payment has to be released irrevocably before receipt of the yen can be confirmed, and the time frame of the risk is longer than the 12-hour advantage traders have when they buy yen. In other words, the period from when the traders irrevocably release the dollar payment—when the risk begins—until they realize they have received the yen is typically longer than 12 hours so that even in the most favorable case of a time difference, the traders are still at risk.

We have identified the length of the settlement risk. It begins when the cancellation deadline passes and ends when we reconcile the account. In the sample trade on Monday for value Wednesday, the cancellation deadline is typically Tuesday and the account reconciliation typically occurs on Thursday. This risk period is too long, and steps must be taken to shorten it. Exhibit 8-5 lists improved services we should request from our correspondent banks and actions we can take in our own banks. The correspondent bank must give us later cancellation deadlines, for example, 1 hour before the payment system opens in our case on Wednesday. We also need the names of individuals and their home and office phone numbers so that cancellation requests can be issued before the deadline passes. All this should be part of a written agreement that specifies cancellation deadlines.

Also, the correspondent bank should advise us as early as possible on Wednesday of credits to our account and do so again several times during the day. It is not acceptable for the bank to accumulate credit advises during the day and then send them all to us at the end of the day. Ideally, there should be an electronic credit advise delivery system that interfaces with our electronic ability to receive credit advises and reconcile them with our records.

Our bank must be ready to receive and reconcile credit advises as soon as they come in (we want to be home when the doctor calls and reports on Mother's surgery). Continuing with the example of the trade on Monday for value Wednesday, the above-described process would

---

FX Settlement Risk Reduction

Demand from Correspondent Bank:

Cancellation deadline:

- One hour before payment system opens
- Names of three individuals
- Home and office phone numbers
- Written agreement

Intraday notification of receipts

- Frequently
- As early as possible
- Proper system interface (electronic delivery) facilitates reconciliation

Do yourself:

Early reconciliation of receipts

- Automated reconciliation of electronic bank statements
- Complete reconciliation before cancellation deadline for next day
- Reduce risk to one day

Netting

Exhibit 8-5. FX settlement risk reduction.

assure receipt of credit advises and reconciliation of accounts late on Wednesday and during the night from Wednesday to Thursday so that amounts that are due to us and that we did not receive are identified before the passing of the cancellation deadline at 7 a.m. on Thursday for outgoing payments for value Thursday. This process would reduce the settlement risk from 2 or more days to 1 day.

This leads to an additional complication in the management of settlement risk: the fact that active counterparties trade not only on Monday for value Wednesday but also on Tuesday for value Thursday, and so on. We go through this settlement process for all these trades, sending the payment order, passing the cancellation deadline, receiving an advise of payment, and reconciling that payment. Let us say the cancellation deadline for Monday's trade is 4 p.m. on Tuesday for value Wednesday. Our account is credited on Wednesday, and we are advised of this credit on Wednesday afternoon. It is critical that the reconciliation of Wednesday's incoming payment be completed before the cancellation deadline for Thursday's outgoing payment has passed on Wednesday at 4:00 p.m. If the cancellation deadline for outgoing payment value Thursday passes before we reconciled Wednesday's receipt, 100 percent of this second trade is at risk.

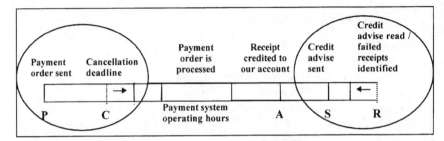

Exhibit 8-6. Payment timeline for identifying risk points and solutions.

We can conclude from this discussion that *the period of settlement risk is longer than assumed and, because of the duration, is higher for people who trade with each other every day.* In fact, the survey referred to earlier showed that settlement risk can rise as high as 265 percent. In other words, if a bank does $10 million a day, the constant peak of settlement risk is $26.5 million, because the bank is consistently paying before it realizes it has been paid. This is bad news for banks.

Fortunately, settlement risk may be reduced significantly if we realistically move the cancellation deadline to a later point and reconcile credits to our account earlier. The timeline is the key to managing settlement risk. It can be used to identify the problem and also to indicate where solutions may be found (Exhibit 8-6).

For instance, if we are the paying bank and think a later cancellation deadline will reduce our risk, we may say to the correspondent bank, "Look, I will agree to send you the payment order as early as I can." This is good for the correspondent bank because the earlier it receives the order, the more time it has to enter it into the computer and do all the processing except for making the payment. Now that the bank is happy, you can add, "In exchange for my sending you the payment order as early as possible, you must give me a later cancellation deadline, such as 7 a.m. on the settlement date."

Payment Risk Faced by Clearing Banks

Before leaving the subject of settlement risk, we will describe payment risk, which is a related risk that results from a different business activity. Payment risk does not arise from settling our own transactions but from making payments on behalf of customers.

There are thousands of organizations in the world that trade U.S. dollars and use big banks (clearing banks) in the United States as their correspondent banks. Every morning in New York these clearing banks pay each other dollars to settle all the payment orders they have received for their customers' foreign exchange, money market, and securities transactions. For example, MegaBank is a clearing bank in New York that maintains dollar accounts for many major banks all over the world. ForeignBank advises MegaBank that it will receive $6 billion value Tuesday from several specified sources and gives MegaBank payment instructions for approximately the same amount of dollars on the same value date. Even though MegaBank is the correspondent bank for ForeignBank and is not a counterparty to the transactions, there is a certain amount of risk involved. The risk is similar to the settlement risk in an FX transaction where there is risk from expecting a payment and making a payment in two different currencies. Settling an FX transaction has the added complication of time zone differences, but this does not affect payment risk because the payments are received and paid out in the same country. Another difference is that payment risk amounts are much larger than settlement risk amounts. Payment risk involves many billions of dollars, reflecting the total of all customer transactions; settlement risk is limited to the size of a bank's own transactions.

The same philosophies discussed for settlement risk relative to the extension of the deadline for cancellations and the acceleration of payment reconciliation can be applied to payment risk. In other words, clearing banks receive money for their customers' accounts which they have to pay out according to the customers' payment orders. To reduce payment risk, they have to accelerate reconciliation at the point where they receive the money and extend the cancellation deadlines for as long as possible for the payments they have to make.

In terms of operating efficiency, it would make sense for clearing banks to execute all their customers' payments first thing in the morning, since they usually receive the payment orders the day before. However, in terms of credit risk, it would not make sense for these banks to pay early because they then would have risk until all the receipts came in from their customers. Also, these banks face requests from their customers for delayed cancellation deadlines. If they pay everything first thing in the morning, it may be a little more difficult to give delayed cancellation deadlines to their customers.

The size of the limit for settlement risk and payment risk is critical. The Federal Reserve Bank has established daylight overdraft limits for the accounts banks have with it. As an example of how these limits work, assume that the Federal Reserve Bank established a $5 billion daytime overdraft limit for our bank. Since we know what payments we have to make, from an operations efficiency viewpoint it would make sense to pay out the entire amount early in the morning. If credit risk and liquidity risk were not an issue, we would prepare the payments on the previous day and press a button the next morning to complete and execute the transactions. By 10 a.m. we would be ready to prepare for the next day and also to handle additional customers' payments for value today.

However, we cannot pay the entire amount first thing in the morning because of the $5 billion Fed overdraft limit and our need for protection against excessive credit and liquidity risk. We wait until money trickles in from the payments we are due to receive; as it comes in, we pay it out, making sure that we always remain within the $5 billion limit.

Because of the need to expedite payments and reduce payment risk, I believe the time is coming when the value date will be broken up so that we no longer will designate payment for value Wednesday. Instead, we will specify value Wednesday early or value Wednesday late, and the break between early and late will be, say, 11 a.m. It would effectively mean that the number of value dates in a year would double, because for every traditional value date there would be two value dates: one early and the other one late.

This division of the value date will replace the current value date designation as an integral part of any money market or financial contract and also will affect the pricing of these contracts. In the foreign exchange market, when a currency is discounted, the longer the forward period, the greater the discount. An 80-day forward has a larger discount than does a 79-day forward because the interest differential has a larger impact when the time period is longer. Following that logic, we can say that for the same value date, value Wednesday late would have a larger discount than would value Wednesday early. As all this business is done more and more by computer, it does not make much difference operationally how many periods we have. In fact, there is no limit on the number of subvalue dates we can have within a calendar day.

I predict that initially there will be only early and late payments, but if we break this down into smaller time units, it also will be applied to loans and deposits and interest rates will be charged accordingly. Currently, the shortest known period is from one value date to another—more or less 24 hours—but there is no reason why banks should not make loans for 2 hours and charge interest for them.

In this business environment, the better one understands settlement risk, the more one can see that all these issues are interrelated. There is a time value of money not only from one value date to the next value date but also at any moment. The trading of intraday money and the putting of a price on the value of that money are coming. In fact, the Federal Reserve does it already. It not only has a daylight overdraft limit, it charges banks a small amount of interest for the actual amount borrowed during the day. In other words, the nature of this business is that somebody has to pay out first before receiving the funds, and the Federal Reserve Bank checks the amount of overdraft every 15 minutes and charges banks interest for overdrafts in each 15-minute period.

The Fed has broken the day down into 15-minute units and charges interest on that basis. The actual interest rate charged by the Fed is very low but could be increased. At that point banks would have to pass on some of that cost to customers who send orders to debit their accounts and make payments on their behalf.

For every value date more than $1 trillion is traded for foreign exchange alone, of which only about 5 percent has a commercial base; for example, a U.S. importer from Japan sells dollars and buys yen so that she can pay for the imported goods. The remaining 95 percent of FX transactions are purely financial transactions that involve receiving and disbursing payments. Securities trading and money trading also require an exchange of payments. The idea here is that the volume of our payments requires that we institute the breaking up of value dates into multiple periods and that new technologies provide the means to do it. Twenty years from now people will laugh about this. They will look back at the days when the smallest measuring unit for the time value of money was 1 day and say, "Can you imagine there were days like that?"

Since traders do not want to be overdrawn or have idle balances, they more or less maintain square positions by buying as much as they sell for any given value date. That means that as a value date begins in the Far East and moves on to the Middle East, Europe, and eventually the United States, trillions of dollars of payments in different currencies have to go through the payment cycle. There is resistance to being the first one to pay, but somebody has to start paying so that other people will follow. Finally, as the sun sets over California, the global value date is over and everybody breathes a little easier because another payment cycle has been completed. Of course, when the last payments are made in California, the first ones are already being made in Australia for the next value date. This cycle occurs every business day of the week.

The timeline in settlement risk is a good indication of how the system works. However, this system requires a lot of trust, and unfortunately, people today trust the system because they have no idea how big the risk is; they do not know how big the risk is because they do not know the beginning and ending points of the risk period. As they develop a greater understanding of the time duration and size of the risk, they will become more careful about approving limits for those risks and will charge properly for them. More management time will be spent trying to reduce risk by shortening its duration and implementing payment netting (see the section on netting in Chap. 9).

Capital Allocation for
Settlement Risk

Let me share my philosophy regarding the appropriateness of equity capital allocation. Initially, the only way banks could lose money was to have an asset that could not be collected. Since they could lose money on those uncollected assets, banks needed equity capital and retained earnings so that they would have something to charge the losses against. The result was the mandated capital/asset ratio. Then, for the reasons explained in Chap. 1, banks realized that there is another source of revenue: proprietary trading. When money is made through proprietary trading, there are no assets on the balance sheet and therefore no need for capital reserves. Traders went along for a few years making money with off-balance-sheet transactions until the regulators realized that there is credit risk in trading and that capital has to be allocated against it, as defined in the Basle Accord. The Basle Accord addresses only presettlement credit risk, but if banks do not reduce settlement risk dramatically, regulators may ask for capital against that as well.

Regulators have already decided that price risk is subject to capital allocation (see Chap. 6, Exhibit 6-11b). As we move into the future and develop new forms of business that involve other types of risk, both regulators and management will recognize that where there is risk, there is a chance of losing money, and where there is a chance of losing money, there should be a capital allocation to cover all potential losses. Banks do not need regulators to mandate capital allocation; they should recognize the value of having adequate capital so that the aggregate risks in all areas do not exceed the amount of capital a bank has or even constitute a notable percentage of it.

As a matter of fact, private industry should be the forerunner here. From an internal pricing viewpoint, we should constantly be on the lookout to understand the business and recognize the risk. The moment we recognize the risk, we should quantify it, and once we know how big the risk is, we should allocate capital to it. We may find that a business involving risk and requiring capital allocation is profitable but not profitable enough relative to the size of the risk and the amount of capital allocated to it. First we try to charge bigger spreads, and if that is not possible, we may have to stop doing the business. In other words, if there is risk, we have to put capital against it, and the business has to be profitable enough to create the appropriate return against the amount of capital that is required for this kind of risk. Once again, the point is that just making money is not good enough.

> *We may find that a business involving risk and requiring capital allocation is profitable but not profitable enough relative to the size of the risk and the amount of capital allocated to it.*

Controlling Settlement Risk

Setting limits for settlement risk is an easy process if one accepts the proposition that settlement risk is equivalent to an overnight loan. However, the problem with settlement risk is that very often senior credit officers in banks do not fully appreciate the fact that even when the process is well managed, as was suggested earlier, the length of the risk period is at least 1 day. As a result, the settlement risk limit for a counterparty should be set at a level that would be comfortable for the approving credit officers if the same line also was used for overnight loans to the same counterparty. In other words, maturing exchange contracts involve a level of settlement risk that equals the risk involved in an overnight loan. The best way of making sure that credit officers have this attitude toward settlement risk is to have one omnibus line for settlement risk and overnight loans, which means that any amount under such a line that is not used for settlement risk could in fact be used for overnight loans to the counterparty. In such a situation, credit officers are more likely to take the proper steps toward setting limits for settlement risk: First, judge the creditworthiness of the counterparty, and second, approve an amount with which one is comfortable given the type of counterparty in question.

Unfortunately, many banks do not follow this thought process. Very often the amount approved for settlement risk is based on the size of the limits needed by the traders to continue to do a transaction volume on a business-as-usual basis. In other words, instead of the size of the settlement risk line being based on the quality of the counterparty, it often is based on the needs of the users. If lines are based on the creditworthiness of the counterparty and particularly if they also can be used for overnight loans and placements, these lines usually will be substantially smaller than they are today. This will lead to a shortage of lines later in each trading day and force a bank's management to look into the entire spectrum of good practices to reduce settlement risk. For a complete analysis of settlement risk and the best practices for reducing it, refer to the New York Foreign Exchange Committee booklet "Reducing Foreign Exchange Settlement Risk."

> *The size of lines for settlement risk must be based on the quality of the counterparty, not on the needs of the users.*

Notes

1. It is good paper, but it is not so obvious. A story must be told to explain the attractions of the paper to investors.

2. Some countries have special complicated "finality rules." This means that even though an amount has been credited by the correspondent bank to a bank's account, under certain conditions this credit to the account may be reversed. In those countries one must make a distinction between the time when the account has been credited and the time at which this credit is final.

3. *Reducing Foreign Exchange Settlement Risk,* New York Foreign Exchange Committee, October 1994.

9

Presettlement Credit Risk

Traders have presettlement credit risk from the time when they negotiate a distant-date contract until the settlement date of that contract. Specifically, a trader worries about two events that can occur before the settlement of a contract. First, the trader worries that the market rate may change adversely. Then, when the trader is happy pricewise, he or she worries that the trading partner may fail before the maturity date. If both events occur, the contract must be replaced at a prevailing market rate that is less attractive than the contract rate. The following story illustrates this point.

A high-powered businessman who needs a rest travels to a mountain resort for a relaxing week of fishing. On the first morning, just as the sun is rising over the still, clear lake, he pushes his boat off and heads for one of his favorite fishing spots. He sits in the boat with rod in hand, waiting for the first bite. Nothing happens, but he is relaxed and happy, and for a change his blood pressure is low. Suddenly the fishing rod jiggles. At first he is elated, but then he gets very nervous. The good news is that a fish is on the hook; the bad news is that it is still in the water, and he worries that he will not be able to get it into the boat. The bigger the fish is, the more he worries, and if he does not get this big fish and still wants a fish, he will have to replace the fish he lost off the hook with one purchased at the market.

There are definitely similarities between this fisherman and a trader with presettlement credit risk. The fisherman is calm until he hooks a big fish and the fishing expedition moves in his favor; only then does he worry about losing the fish and the possibility of having to replace it. The trader of distant-date contracts is calm until the market moves in her favor; only then does she worry about the survival of the counterparty.

Presettlement risk makes it possible to sustain a loss resulting from the bankruptcy of a counterparty before maturity without ever having paid out any money. If the counterparty fails, the size of the loss equals the cost of replacing the contract. For example, suppose a trader takes the following action today:

- Buy from a customer 1 million pounds value 6 months forward at $1.99.

- Sell to a bank 1 million pounds value 6 months forward at $2.00.

Two months later the following things occur:

- The rate of exchange for the pound drops from $2.00 to $1.60.

- The trader's position is square; therefore, she is not affected by this price change.

Four months later (2 months *before* the contract matures) the following things occur:

- The bank to which she has sold 1 million pounds at $2.00 fails and will not perform under the contract; i.e., it will not buy the pounds at $2.00.

- The trader still has to honor the contract to buy 1 million pounds from her customer at $1.99.

- To square her position, the trader has to sell the pounds one more time, but at the now-prevailing rate of $1.60.

- The trader loses $400,000 without ever having paid out any money to the bankrupt counterparty because the exchange rate at which she sold the pounds the second time is much less attractive than the exchange rate at which she originally sold.

In these types of cases, even though the contract looks good in terms of price risk, traders have to worry about losses resulting from presettlement counterparty risk.

The situation described in this example of forward exchange contracts also applies to interest rate contracts such as forward interest rate agreements (FRAs) and interest rate swaps. For example, a counterparty agrees to pay 10 percent fixed for 5 years and goes broke after 2 years;

the 3-year market interest rate at the time of bankruptcy is 8 percent. We have to replace the 10 percent contract with the bankrupt counterparty at the now-prevailing 8 percent market rate for 3-year money, and consequently, we suffer a loss of 2 percent p.a. for the remaining 3 years.

Presettlement risk also is incurred when one *buys* options. For example, suppose we have the right to purchase something at 100. Assume that the market rate rises to 120, the option is in the money, and the counterparty from which we bought the option fails. Again, we have a loss because the replacement cost of this option will be at least $20. There is no *presettlement* risk when we *sell* options, but we face *settlement* risk in the purchase and sale of commodity options such as foreign exchange, securities, and metals. In this case, if the option ends up in the money and is exercised by the option buyer, it will create the same settlement process with the same associated settlement risk as will any other maturing contract of this kind. There is no risk at all in selling interest rate options except during the period of time between the closing of the transaction and the receipt of the option premium in cash, which usually is not more than 24 hours.

In the context of presettlement credit risk, when we are happy pricewise, we worry about the credit quality of the counterparty.

Assessing the Size of Presettlement Risk

In the discussion of the traditional bank environment we described a conversation with a bank president who wanted to know what it would mean for us if our counterparty failed. In the past, when the president called to say that ABC Bank seemed to be in trouble and wanted to know the status of our outstandings with that bank, the response was given in volume terms. We told him, for example, that we had outstandings of $2 billion in forward contracts, which did not say anything about the size of the *risk*. (Again, this is 100 percent correct but totally useless. Recall the airplane analogy in Chap. 4. Now we are trying to understand what the $2 billion outstanding with a counterparty means to us in terms of a *loan equivalent amount*.

The size of presettlement risk in forward contracts is determined by two elements: the creditworthiness of the counterparty with which the forward contract is done and the conversion of meaningless notional/volume transaction amounts into meaningful estimates of loan equivalent amounts. We have briefly discussed the creditworthiness of counterparties and will not pursue it further at this point. This section focuses on the conversion of transaction amounts in forward and derivative contracts into loan equivalent amounts.

Loan Equivalent Amounts

Given the emphasis on risk/return analysis in this book, the process of converting transaction amounts into loan equivalents is obviously critical because the size of the loan equivalent amount affects the pricing of forward and derivative contracts. We will see that the same fundamental technique applied to estimating value at risk can be used to estimate potential loan equivalent amounts.

Suppose a trader wants to close a transaction for $100 million value 12 months forward with a counterparty for which he has no trading line. We know that this transaction could potentially involve credit risk, but the question is, how much? Analyzing the situation, we find that it is the change in the market rate that can create loan equivalent amounts. As a result, if we can estimate how much the market rate will change, we will know the size of the loan equivalent amount that may develop in the future.

Do we know how much the market rate may change in the future? The answer is yes. That is what most of our discussion in the chapter on price risk was about, and the key components of estimating value at risk also can be used to estimate potential loan equivalent amounts resulting from distant-date products. In both cases we have to estimate how much the market rate will move, and in both cases we use volatility to make that estimate. Just as in price risk management, all aspects of volatility must be applied in the same way to calculate potential loan equivalent amounts. We use the same volatility discovery methodology and certainly the same confidence level: 2SD volatility. The only thing that is different is the period of time involved. In price risk the focus is overnight (unless there is a longer defeasance period), and therefore we use overnight volatility. In calculating potential loan equivalent amounts resulting from distant-date transactions we apply volatility for a time period equivalent to the maturity of the respective forward contract, i.e., 3 months' volatility for a 3-month forward, 10 months' volatility for a 10-month forward, and 10 years' volatility for a 10-year forward.

Look at the following transaction:

> *$100 million 1-year forward transaction at 100*
>
> *One-year volatility of 5 percent*
>
> *Potential loan equivalent amount of $5 million*

You can see that we calculate the potential loan equivalent amount ($5 million) at the time when the transaction is done by applying a volatility-based conversion factor (5 percent) to the transaction amount ($100 million).

> *There is intellectual integrity in estimating the value at risk of a price risk position and estimating the potential loan equivalent amount resulting from a distant-date contract because both are based on expected volatility.*

At any time between the contract date and the maturity date of a contract, the aggregate loan equivalent amount can be divided into a current loan equivalent amount based on marking-to-market all outstanding contracts and a potential loan equivalent amount based on the expected price volatility, as was discussed above. The current loan equivalent amount is exact. We compare the contract rate with the market rate at which the existing contract could be replaced, and if the contract rate is more attractive than the market rate, we convert the differential into dollars and treat the dollar amount (the replacement cost) as a loan equivalent. We have current loan equivalent amounts when we buy and the market price rises before maturity and when we sell and the market price falls before maturity. This amount is derived from the mark-to-market process. For example,

Purchase 100 pounds for next June at	$160
Market rate	$170
Current loan equivalent amount (replacement cost)	$ 10
Sell 100 pounds for next June at	$160
Market rate	$150
Current loan equivalent amount (replacement cost)	$ 10

The potential loan equivalent amount is estimated by using the same type of volatility that is used to estimate value at risk in price risk positions. The appropriate volatility is multiplied by the amount of a new contract or the mark-to-market price of outstanding contracts. The aggregate loan equivalent amount equals the current loan equivalent amount plus the potential loan equivalent amount. The following example shows in simplified numbers how we can respond in a more meaningful way if a senior person in the bank worries about the potential bankruptcy of a client and wishes to know what our outstandings are with that counterparty.

Purchase forward, value 6 months at	85
Four months later the market rate is	<u>100</u>
Current loan equivalent amount resulting from marking-to-market	15
Potential loan equivalent amount resulting from application of 10 percent volatility to market rate of 100	10
Aggregate loan equivalent amount	<u>25</u>

Our response is that we have a current loan equivalent amount of 15 (we bought 4 months ago at 85 6 months forward, and the current market rate is 100). This means that if the counterparty fails today, we actually will lose 15 because the purchase at 85 can be replaced only at the now-prevailing market rate of 100. However, the counterparty is *not* bankrupt; we are just worried. Therefore, we have to see what additional potential damage can be done by likely changes in the market rate. In the above example, we assume a volatility of 10 percent for the remaining 2 months of the contract. This 10 percent volatility must be applied to the market rate—not the contract rate—and it results in a potential loan equivalent amount of 10. Consequently, we have an aggregate loan equivalent amount of 25, of which 15 is current and 10 is potential.

The relationship between the current loan equivalent amount and the potential loan equivalent amount changes over the life of the contract. For example, the graph in Exhibit 9-1 represents a 12-month contract.

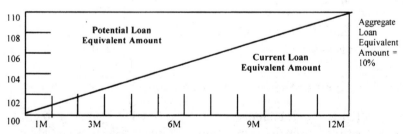

Exhibit 9-1. Distribution of current versus potential loan equivalent amounts.

The spot rate is 100, the forward rate is 100, and we assume that the conversion factor based on 2SD volatility is 10 percent. On the day we make the contract, the only amount we worry about is a potential loan equivalent amount, because the contract is closed at the market rate. In other words, if we were to mark-to-market the position, the difference between the contract rate and the market rate would be zero, and consequently, there is no current loan equivalent amount.

As time passes, the market rate changes and the contract rate becomes more attractive than the market rate. Throughout the year the total exposed amount is always 10 percent. Initially, the 10 percent is entirely potential loan equivalent amount; as time progresses, it gradually becomes more current loan equivalent amount and less potential loan equivalent amount until it is entirely current loan equivalent amount at maturity. If there is no time left, there is also no time for volatility to have an effect.

In the real world the market rate obviously does not move the way it does in the exhibit. For example, after 3 months the market may have moved 4 percent instead of the prorated 2.5 percent we projected for the first quarter. Also, the volatility for the remaining 9 months may be 8 percent flat. If we recalculate the aggregate loan equivalent amount, we find a $4 million current loan equivalent amount (because the market has moved 4 percent) and an $8 million potential loan equivalent amount (because the volatility for the remaining life is expected to be 8 percent). All this translates into an aggregate loan equivalent amount of $12 million. This kind of exercise must be done periodically (at least monthly) to maintain reasonably updated aggregate loan equivalent amounts and track them against available credit lines.

Summary: Loan Equivalent Amounts

Even though we are applying volatility to the market price to determine the size of the loan equivalent amount (much as we did with price risk), presettlement counterparty risk is clearly credit risk. The primary risk depends on whether the counterparty will go bankrupt. However, the *size* of the loan equivalent amount depends on how much the market rate will move, and therefore, the size of the loan equivalent amount can be estimated with the use of price risk management techniques.

The current loan equivalent amount resulting from marking-to-market is correct at any one time. We can look at the market at 4:10 p.m. and observe that if the counterparty goes bankrupt right now, this is what the replacement cost will be. The potential loan equivalent amounts in forward contracts cannot be anticipated exactly. A meaningful estimate is the best we can provide, because expected future volatility is the best basis for estimating potential loan equivalent amounts.

To summarize, the generation of loan equivalent amounts in presettlement counterparty credit risk resulting from distant-date forward transactions proceeds as follows:

Before we enter into a distant-date contract, the entire loan equivalent amount is of a potential nature and is calculated by applying the appropriate volatility to the transaction amount.

After a distant-date contract is on the books, the calculation of the total loan equivalent amount involves two steps. First, we mark-to-market the already outstanding contract and determine the replacement cost or current loan equivalent amount. Second, we apply the appropriate volatility to the market rate and the transaction amount and calculate the potential loan equivalent amount. The aggregation of the current loan equivalent and the potential loan equivalent amount will give us the total loan equivalent amount.

Current loan equivalent amount (replacement cost) (correct at any time):

+ Potential loan equivalent amount based on volatility

Aggregate loan equivalent amount

Presettlement Risk for Different Types of Contracts and Customers

You now understand the concept of converting meaningless volume and notional amounts of distant-date contracts into more meaningful (potential) loan equivalent amounts. This stage of understanding can be compared with the point in the discussion of price risk when we acquired a complete understanding of the Grandmother Story. This sensitivity approach to measuring price risk positions combined with volatility allows us to convert meaningless volume amounts of price risk positions into meaningful estimates of value at risk. In the price risk section, we noted that many additional concepts were added which have made the VAR approach much more meaningful, including different volatility discovery methodologies, confidence levels, defeasance periods, and covariance calculations. The point here is that we often must make similar, sometimes complex additions to the basic loan equivalent approach to calculate more meaningful potential loan equivalent amounts.

There are two reasons why it is necessary to estimate potential loan equivalents to the best of one's ability. The first reason is related to making sure that a particular transaction does not exceed the line established by credit officers for generating loan equivalent amounts with a given counterparty. The other, equally important reason is related to the pricing of distant-date transactions. In addition to considering the creditworthiness of the counterparty, only when we have the best possible idea of the size of the potential loan equivalent amount that is likely to evolve from a distant-date transaction can we include a profit margin in a particular deal that justifies putting it on the balance sheet. Remember that *just making money is not good enough anymore.*

One must always bear in mind that the aggregate loan equivalent amount is not as exact as one would like because the conversion factors depend on volatility and the specific features of a given instrument. For example, the volatility percentage applied to single-cash-flow instruments such as forward foreign exchange and forward contracts for other commodities depends on the length of time between the contract date and the maturity. The longer the time period, the higher the impact of volatility and the higher the conversion factor. However, in the case of forward contracts for multiple-cash-flow instruments such as bonds and interest rate conversion agreements, the amount of volatility and the resulting conversion factor depend on two different time periods: the time between contract date and the settlement date and the tenor of the instrument.

For example, we could have two transactions both of which are 3 months forward; one is a 6-month T-bill, and the other one is a 30-year bond. If there is a 1-basis-point change in interest rates, the impact on the value of the 6-month T-bill will be much smaller than the impact on the value of the 30-year bond. Remember, in counterparty risk we do not worry about the change in interest rates; instead, we worry about the size of a change in the value of a contract caused by a change in a market price, such as an interest rate.

Let us look at another example. We trade a 1-year instrument and a 2-year instrument, each for $1 million and for value 3 months forward. A change of 1 percent p.a. occurs in interest rates. The 1 percent change in the 1-year instrument equals a $10,000 change in value, while the 1 percent change on the 2-year instrument produces a $20,000 change in value. (These are approximate numbers because we did not discount to present value.) The percentage change in the market price is the same in each case, but the value change is larger for the longer-tenored instrument than it is for the shorter-tenored instrument. The loan equivalent amount is larger on a longer-tenored instrument than it is on a shorter-tenored instrument even though both are traded 3 months forward.

Fixed/floating interest rate swaps and options have another significant feature: The volatility-based conversion factor is high at the beginning but declines approximately 60 to 70 percent into the life of the contract. This occurs because there are fewer settlements left on the swaps
and less time until an option's expiration date.

Suppose we have a swap with a 6-month floating rate (reset every 6
months) against a 10-year fixed rate. Over this 10-year period the market rate can depart substantially from the 10-year fixed rate in the contract; if we do it for 3 years, there are only 3 years in which the market
rate can change. The longer the deal, the higher the impact of volatility.

Now consider a 5-year fixed rate against a floating rate that is reset
every 6 months. The 5-year rate gives us a certain volatility and therefore a certain potential loan equivalent amount. However, suppose we
are 49 months into the deal and there has been a substantial change in
the market rate; this means that when we reset the 6-month floating
rate, for the last time after 54 months, a substantial interest differential
occurs. However, even though the interest differential is large, the
actual dollar amount to be received (the loan equivalent amount) will be
relatively small. In 5 months the last settlement will be made for the last
6 months of interest. At this point, it does not matter if the market rate
has moved substantially away from what it was when we did the deal
$4\frac{1}{2}$ years ago because the payment that has to be made is interest for
only 6 months. Therefore, as can be seen in Exhibit 9-2, the loan equivalent profile decreases as the contract gets closer to maturity.

As the curve indicates, the loan equivalent amount is quite high initially, then levels off, and finally decreases as there are fewer remaining

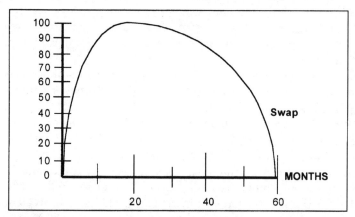

Exhibit 9-2. Potential loan equivalent amount over time for a
fixed/floating interest rate swap.

cash flows. If we apply 5-year volatility to the entire 5 years and the notional amount of the transaction, we will overstate the potential loan equivalent amount toward the latter part of the contract. The basis idea is that *the loan equivalent amount is not constant over the length of the contract.*

The size of the potential loan equivalent amount for different types of contracts is based on the volatility of the applicable market prices and the specific features of different instruments. Complex calculations for the determination of conversion factors are required, depending on the type of instrument involved in a transaction. Occasionally, banks publish user-friendly conversion factor guidelines that contain the appropriate conversion factors for specific currencies, instruments, and time periods. These tables are updated periodically as volatilities change, new instruments are developed, and risk assessment technology evolves.

The size of the conversion factor also can be affected by customers' trading patterns. For example, assume that every month a Mercedes importer buys approximately the same amount of marks 6 months forward to pay for the imported cars. This counterparty can go broke the day after she has done the most recent deal for value 6 months forward, in which case the market rate is almost the same as the contract rate, or she can go broke the day before the longest outstanding (5 months and 29 days) contract matures, in which case volatility may have affected the market price to the fullest expected extent. For a customer, like the importer, who maintains a regular trading pattern, we can use a lower volatility-based conversion factor to calculate the potential loan equivalent amount, because for some of that customer's contracts the market will have changed a lot and for others it will not have changed at all. In other words, we know what the conversion factor should be for this dollar/mark 6-month forward deal, but because this customer's trading pattern is so regular, we can make an exception and take less.

Approvals for these exceptions to calculating the loan equivalent amount must be provided on a customer-by-customer basis and can be given only for counterparties that show an appropriate trading pattern.

Active counterparties that deal with each other in both directions as buyers and sellers (multinational banks) also must treat each other differently. Since they buy from and sell to each other at approximately the same rate levels, the prices of the contracts are irrelevant. For the purpose of loan equivalent determination, it is important only that the contracts be done at approximately the same price. For example, assume that there are two contracts with a counterparty: a contract to purchase at 100 and a contract to sell at 101. Now the market moves to 120. We do not have to worry about the sale at 101, only about the contract that is better than the market rate. In this case our purchase at 100 is at risk because the market rate is 120. If the market goes down to 80, we can forget about the purchase at 100 because it is not at risk. Only the sale at 101 is at risk; if the counterparty fails, we will have to resell at 80. When we buy and sell at approximately the same price, we have a loan equivalent amount on only one of the contracts; the price will go up or down, and we cannot have a loan equivalent amount on both contracts at the same time. If we apply the volatility-based conversion factor to each contract, we will overstate the loan equivalent amount. As a result, a quick solution to estimating loan equivalent amounts in these cases is to consider only half the loan equivalent amounts calculated on a regular basis.

There is a more accurate and professional approach to estimating loan equivalent amounts for a portfolio consisting of two-directional trading. First we mark-to-market all the outstanding contracts with a counterparty, which gives us the current loan equivalent amount, and then we take the appropriate volatility and make two assumptions. First, we assume that the market rate will move *up* by the estimated volatility percentage and note the resulting potential loan equivalent amount. Second, we assume that the market rate will move *down* by the same volatility-based percentage and track this potential loan equivalent amount. We add the larger of the two potential loan equivalent amounts to the current loan equivalent amount resulting from marking-to-market to get the aggregate loan equivalent amount.

In contrast to a regular loan, where only the lender has credit risk, a forward contract involves potential credit risk for both the buyer and the seller. For example, if a buyer purchases 1 year forward at 100 and the market rises to 115, the buyer is faced with a loan equivalent amount. However, if the market drops to 85 a few months later, it is the seller who faces a loan equivalent amount. Therefore, we can say that either the buyer or the seller can have credit risk, depending on the relationship between the never-changing contract rate and the ever-changing market rate.

A forward contract involves potential credit risk for both the buyer and the seller, depending on the relationship between the never-changing contract rate and the ever-changing market rate.

This concept is important when we try to sell and/or assign an existing forward contract. In this case we need the consent of the original counterparty before we can complete the sale because the original counterparty may end up extending credit to the party acquiring the contract. This is different from selling loans, where it usually is not necessary for the investor in the loan asset to be approved by the borrower.

It is clear from this discussion that estimating potential loan equivalent amounts, particularly when more complex instruments are involved, requires the application of sophisticated statistical and mathematical analysis. However, the fundamental idea here is that potential loan equivalent amounts are created by the estimated expected change in market prices and that the volatility discovery sources for these estimates should be the same as those used for calculating VAR. In addition, types of instruments and counterparty trading patterns must be taken into account. Active market participants need to have qualified personnel on staff who can estimate potential loan equivalent amounts. We need the best possible estimates for potential loan equivalent amounts because the size of these amounts, together with the creditworthiness of the counterparty, forms the basis for establishing the pricing and the minimum profit margins for these transactions.

> *The size of potential loan equivalent amounts, together with the creditworthiness of the counterparty, forms the basis for establishing the pricing and the minimum profit margins for these transactions.*

Pricing Forward Contracts

For two reasons, it is essential that the pricing of all distant-date products be appropriate. First, the risk-adjusted asset principles (RAAP) require us to allocate equity capital to loan equivalent amounts. Adequate pricing must provide a large enough profit that the required incremental capital is generated through retained earnings. Second, it is more difficult to sell forward contracts because a sale involves a two-directional credit extension and requires the counterparty's approval. Underpriced contracts are likely to generate loan equivalent amounts in the future for which there are not sufficient retained earnings to support these evolving risk assets from a capital adequacy viewpoint.

Chapter 1 gave some examples to illustrate the point that in terms of real loans, just making money is not good enough anymore. We made some assumptions that were based on management's return on equity objective and the regulator-mandated capital/asset ratio. For instance, if a company wants to achieve a 20 percent return on equity and maintain a 5 percent capital/asset ratio, it needs a 1 percent return on assets after taxes of 50 percent.

Since 1993, regulators have demanded that *additional* capital be kept against the loan equivalent, which they call the asset equivalent. For example, suppose we have a real loan of $1 million with a targeted return on assets of 2 percent before tax and also have a $10 million forward contract with a volatility-based conversion factor of 10 percent and a potential loan equivalent amount of $1 million. The targeted return on the loan equivalent amount is also 2 percent before tax, which means that if we deal with a counterparty with comparable credit quality, the spread needed on the $10 million forward is 0.2 percent p.a. The credit risk is the same whether we make a real loan of $1 million or have a loan equivalent of $1 million that was created when we did the $10 million forward with a 10 percent volatility-based conversion factor. In other words, what we said about just making money not being good enough applies also to the minimum spread we have to make on distant-date products such as forwards, swaps, and purchased options. Assuming counterparties with comparable credit quality, forward contracts create loan equivalents, and these loan equivalents require the same minimum profit margins that actual loans require. This means we ultimately need to fund the incremental equity needs through retained earnings.

Another way of accomplishing this objective is to establish a targeted return on the amount of equity that needs to be allocated to a particular transaction which increases the amount of risk-adjusted assets of the bank. Let us look at an example to illustrate this point.

The Basle risk adjustment criterion (see Chap. 13) requires the inclusion as risk-adjusted assets of 1 percent of foreign exchange transactions maturing within 1 year and 5 percent of FX transactions when they mature beyond 1 year and up to 5 years. As a result, technically speaking, a 2-year forward contract requires a 5 percent conversion factor only for the first year. Thereafter, the remaining life will be less than 1 year and the conversion factor can be only 1 percent. Most banks, however, use 5 percent for the entire 2-year period, as is shown in Exhibit 9-3. The reason is that the Basle volatility substitute of 5 percent for contracts with a remaining life between 1 and 5 years is extremely low if not completely unrealistic. It is very likely that at the end of the first 1-year period the market rate will have moved much more than 1 percent, and the current loan equivalent amounts created through these changes in market prices must be shown as risk-adjusted assets. In anticipation of this likely development, it is unrealistic to assume a 1 percent volatility substitute for the second 1-year period.

Because of what was just said, in the example we apply a 5 percent product risk adjustment as a volatility substitute to the transaction amount of $200 million because the contract is a foreign exchange con-

Wonderful Bank headquartered in France wishes to sell to us pounds 100 million value two years forward outright. Assume that the pound has neither premium nor discount and that in spot and forward the FX rate is 1 pound = 2.0000 US dollars. Further assume that the bank targets a ratio of 10% for capital to risk adjusted assets and wishes to have a pre-tax return on capital of 30% p.a.

	$200 million	Transaction Amount
5% Product risk adjustment	10 million	
20% Counterparty risk adjustment	2 million	Risk adjusted asset
10% Capital / Risk adjusted asset ratio	200,000	Equity capital need
30% p.a. for 2 years return on risk adjusted assets	120,000	Required profit

$200,000,000	Market value of pounds
120,000	Required profit to meet return on equity target
199,880,000	Dollar amount required to purchase 100 million pounds

1.9988 FX rate quoted

Exhibit 9-3. Calculating minimum profit on a forward transaction.

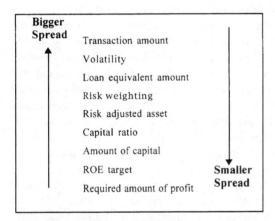

Bigger Spread

Transaction amount

Volatility

Loan equivalent amount

Risk weighting

Risk adjusted asset

Capital ratio

Amount of capital

ROE target

Required amount of profit

Smaller Spread

Exhibit 9-4. Criteria influencing the minimum profit margin.

tract with a maturity date beyond 1 year. This leads to a loan equivalent amount of $10 million. Next comes a 20 percent counterparty-related risk adjustment because we are dealing with a bank in an Organization for Economic Cooperation and Development (OECD) country. This leads to a risk-adjusted asset of $2 million. Thereafter, we apply a capital ratio of 10 percent, which leads to $200,000 of allocatable equity. Finally, we apply the return on equity target of 30 percent p.a. for 2 years, which leads to the required minimum profit margin of $120,000.

Exhibit 9-4 shows a list of all the criteria that influence the minimum profit margin required for a contract. If any one of the criteria is lower, we can be satisfied with a smaller profit margin, and if any one of the criteria is higher, we require a higher profit margin.

The problem with the approach to pricing suggested in the Wonderful Bank example is that it leads to minimum margins which are not accepted by counterparties in the marketplace. The reason for this is that many banks that participate in the long-term forward exchange market are not sufficiently familiar with the potential future impact on the balance sheet and the pricing process suggested above or simply ignore them. It is tempting to engage in this business and focus on the immediate absolute dollar amount of earnings without relating it to the amount of capital that may be required in later months and years, when changes in market rates may force the recognition of very sizable amounts of risk-adjusted assets and the provision of equity to support those assets. The selling of these forward contracts as a solution to the problem is more difficult than selling loans because, as was said before, when one is dealing with a mutual credit extension, the sale of forward contracts requires the agreement of the original counterparty.

In our example we used the Basle volatility substitute of 5 percent for foreign exchange contracts beyond 1 year. Intellectual honesty would require us to apply 2-year option-implied volatility to a 2-year forward exchange transaction. This volatility usually is a multiple of the 5 percent used in the example. As a consequence, we see that the use of market volatility instead of Basle volatility substitutes increases the problem of being competitive in the marketplace. Each institution, and possibly the industry as a whole, must look for creative solutions to this problem. A portfolio approach to estimating loan equivalent amounts "outstanding" with a particular counterparty, as was discussed in this chapter is one alternative for obtaining more realistic aggregate loan equivalent amounts. Another important technique for reducing loan equivalent amounts is netting by novation, which is discussed in the next section.

Controlling Presettlement Risk

There are two types of approval processes for presettlement risk positions. One is the determination of the creditworthiness of the counterparty with which we trade. This is a classic credit decision that is based on a set of prescribed standards for credit evaluation. The other process is the establishment of a volatility-based conversion factor stated as a percentage and its application to a specific forward contract. The conversion factor has nothing to do with the type of counterparty with which we trade because, as was stated before, the size of the loan equiv-

	Market and Product Skills		Credit Skills		Corporate Policy	
Transaction	Conversion Factor	Loan Equivalent	Counterparty	Risk	Capital Allocation	Minimum Profit
100 million	5%	5 million	AAA	Small	Less	Smaller
100 million	5%	5 million	BBB	Large	More	Larger

Exhibit 9-5. Controlling presettlement risk.

alent amount that will develop depends on the movement of the market rate and the special features of the specific instrument that is traded. Thus, if we do exactly the same type of forward transaction with Triple A Company and later with Triple B Company, the size of the loan equivalent amount that will evolve will depend on how the market rate moves, and that will be the same for either transaction (Exhibit 9-5).

Two identical distant-date contracts closed with a triple-A company and a triple-B company will produce identical potential loan equivalent amounts. However, the size of the risk will be different because of the difference in the credit quality of the two counterparties. Consequently, the conversion from a transaction amount to a potential loan equivalent amount requires market and product knowledge. The judgment of the creditworthiness of the counterparties requires credit expertise.

Limits versus Trigger Points

Two limits are needed for counterparty risk: one for presettlement and one for settlement. The presettlement limit was a lump sum. For example, if we had an assumed aggregate contract limit of $10 million, it meant we were willing to accept a presettlement risk of $10 million with a given counterparty. We were not willing to have the entire $10 million mature on the same day, however, because that would have been a 100 percent settlement risk. To avoid that, a company with a presettlement limit of $10 million outstanding might have a settlement risk sublimit of $2 million. In other words, during one business week the company might have $10 million outstanding with $2 million maturing on each of the five business days. If the counterparty fails on Monday, the company loses $2 million. If there is an adverse rate movement of 20 percent on the entire $10 million, the company loses an additional $2 million. Therefore, it could lose a total of $4 million (Exhibit 9-6).

```
┌─────────────────────────────────────────────────────────────────────┐
│ Traditional Limits                                                    │
│                                                                       │
│ Standard foreign exchange line                                        │
│                                                                       │
│       Aggregate contracts outstanding            $10 million          │
│                                                                       │
│       Sublimit for settlement risk               $2 million           │
│                                                                       │
│       Maximum loss                                                    │
│              $2 million Settlement Risk                               │
│              $2 million (20% Presettlement risk on $10 million)       │
│              $4 million                                               │
└─────────────────────────────────────────────────────────────────────┘
```

Exhibit 9-6. Credit risk in foreign exchange.

Note that losses resulting from counterparty failure can actually be more than 100 percent of the transacted amount if we are negatively affected by settlement risk and presettlement risk at the same time. Such a situation occurs in the following circumstances. First, the counterparty fails on the maturity date, and we pay but do not receive payment; in this case the loss equals 100 percent. Second, the contract with the bankrupt counterparty must be replaced at the now-prevailing market rate. If we assume that this market rate is 20 percent less favorable than the original contract with the now-bankrupt counterparty, we suffer an additional loss of 20 percent. This amounts to a total loss of 120 percent with 100 percent resulting from settlement risk and 20 percent resulting from presettlement risk.

In the context of price risk, we demonstrated the methodology for converting meaningless volume positions into VAR and then expressed price risk limits in terms of value at risk. We follow a similar process for presettlement risk. Having determined how to convert meaningless transaction volumes into loan equivalents, we want to limit and control presettlement risk in terms of loan equivalent amounts.

If we track aggregate loan equivalent amounts resulting from distant-date contracts instead of transaction volumes, we can no longer have limits at the trader level because of potential passive excesses. A passive excess occurs when a trader exceeds the limit for loan equivalent amounts for a given counterparty without doing anything—simply because the market rate moves and/or volatility changes. For example, a trader could buy forward at 100 and sell forward at 101 and make 1 point. However, the loan equivalent amount that is going to evolve on one of these two deals depends on how the market rate moves, which is beyond the control of the trader. An unusually large move of the market rate, either higher or lower, may result in a passive excess of the loan equivalent amount limit, for which the trader cannot be held responsible.

We can now understand why *limits* for loan equivalent amounts are no longer practical. As was mentioned earlier, the passive excesses resulting from changes in market rates, including volatility, may lead to larger loan equivalent amounts without actually involving any incremental business. A good way of "limiting" the size of loan equivalent amounts is to establish trigger points which are incorporated in the total credit line for the counterparty. Whenever a trigger point is reached for a counterparty, management is alerted and can assess the total loan equivalent amount plus other credit extensions to determine how further requests from the counterparty will be handled.

There is a huge distinction between limits and triggers. Limits should be spelled with a capital L, and everybody in the organization should know that they must be adhered to at all times. People who intentionally exceed limits must be fired. Against this background, there should be no limits that are taken less seriously than others. This is where the word *trigger* comes in. Triggers cannot be broken; they can only be reached or hit, which leads to a review of the situation at hand. Traders should clearly understand the difference between reaching triggers, which presents no problem for a trader, and exceeding limits, which subjects a trader to the possibility of being fired.

Let us look at an example of structuring loan equivalent triggers. Suppose the total outstandings of $6 billion in distant-date contracts for a counterparty translate into an aggregate (current plus potential) loan equivalent amount of $75 million. The ALERT point (*aggregate loan equivalent risk amount trigger*) is set at $90 million, which is part of an approved total credit line of $200 million. Under this $200 million line, $80 million is allocated and/or reserved for real loans and $120 million is allocated and/or reserved for trading-related loan equivalent amounts. This means that if the currently prevailing trigger point of $90 million is reached and management continues to be comfortable with the credit quality of the counterparty, the trigger can successively be raised up to a maximum of $120 million.

As the aggregate loan equivalent amount outstanding approaches the total amount allocated for trading purposes ($120 million), care must be taken that substantial changes in market prices do not carry the trader over this $120 million allocation. Well before this point is reached, consultations must take place with the credit function to make more room for the future creation of loan equivalent amounts. Possible solutions include the following:

- Increasing the overall $200 million line together with the original $120 million allocation for loan equivalents
- Leaving the overall line of $200 million unchanged but increasing the $120 million for loan equivalents at the expense of the $80 million allocation for real loans

- Leaving all established lines unchanged and curtailing trading or stepping up netting and other loan equivalent–reducing techniques as the trader approaches the existing $120 million allocation for loan equivalent amounts

The beauty of the process described above is that traders can behave almost as if there were no limit as long as the trigger point is not reached. However, as should be obvious to the reader, all the actions taken by the trader occur under a preapproved limit, and therefore, the actions taken by the trader meet internal and external audit standards.

This technique can be used for any kind of distant-date product. The aggregate loan equivalent amount of $75 million for a given counterparty may be the result of all distant-date contracts outstanding with that counterparty, irrespective of products and instruments. Therefore, if we have real loans to the customer of $50 million, the total for real loans and loan equivalents is $125 million.

Providing credit risk information in terms of loans and loan equivalents is much more meaningful than talking about exposures. I recommend that readers eliminate this meaningless word from their vocabulary. It is safe to say that people use the word *exposure* when they do not know exactly which risk they mean or are too lazy to articulate the question in such a way that listeners know what type of risk is meant. Throughout this book we have carefully avoided using this meaningless word and instead have used language that describes the exact risk meant in the area of price, credit, liquidity, or operations.

Ownership of Counterparty Risk

Frequently traders are the first to notice when another financial institution approaches financial difficulties. "It is too easy to make money off of them," a trader once noted, and he then recommended that his bank no longer trade with a particular market participant. A few months later the financial institution failed, and our trader was a hero because his tip to the credit officer prevented a loss. As a result of situations like this, some banks use a system under which the credit function approves trading lines (loan equivalent amounts) on the basis of the perceived creditworthiness of the counterparty. However, any losses resulting from the failure of a counterparty are charged to the bonus pool of the trading function. This encourages traders to adopt "ownership" of the credit risk relationship with counterparties and creates a heightened alertness among traders in regard to detecting and identifying financial institutions which may be in trouble.

Netting

In the early 1990s the International Foreign Exchange Master Agreement (IFEMA) was developed and accepted by many market participants to reduce counterparty risk resulting from foreign exchange transactions. IFEMA has two major parts: close-out netting focusing on the presettlement risk of unliquidated (still outstanding) forward exchange contracts and payment netting focusing on settlement risk resulting from maturing foreign exchange contracts. The reason for the popularity of IFEMA was that regulators allowed the reduction of risk-adjusted assets resulting from outstanding forward contracts after the implementation of the Basle Accord.

Netting is an effective way of reducing loan equivalent risk with a given counterparty. Assume that we buy forward at 100 from a counterparty and sell forward at 101 to the same counterparty. Further assume that the market price moves to 110. If we have a proper netting agreement and there is a bankruptcy, the two contracts are offset; therefore, our net risk is only 1. Without a netting agreement, the counterparty would "cherry pick," or continue to accept the purchase at 101 (given that the market rate is 110) and renege on the sales contract at 100. In this case, our total risk would be 10.

The best legal response to cherry picking is netting by novation, or close-out netting. In the case of a bankruptcy, we automatically combine all positive cash flows irrespective of maturity and currency at prevailing market rates into a single dollar amount discounted to present value. The same technique is applied to all negative cash flows resulting from all outstanding transactions.

The present values of the net positive cash flow and net negative cash flow are again netted into a single legal contract which asserts that we have either a net receivable or a net payable with the bankrupt counterparty. All this is worded in legal language of such a nature that at any point in time only one legal contract is outstanding. The positive value and negative value of this single outstanding contract change continuously as we engage in additional transactions and/or settle maturing contracts with a particular counterparty. This explains the name *netting by novation*, because the one single legally outstanding contract continuously renews itself. However, the most important feature is that the legal existence of only a single contract protects us against cherry picking.

This netting agreement routinely also has a provision for payment netting, which applies when two counterparties pay each other on the settlement date. Active use and implementation of payment netting can substantially reduce settlement risk (see Chap. 8).

Credit Swaps

The final section of this chapter explores the developing market for credit derivatives. This product is available today in very sophisticated markets, but it is not as widely used as it probably will be in the very near future.

Assume the following scenario. AutoBank has $1 billion of loans outstanding to Carmaker, Inc. TechBank has $1 billion of loans outstanding to Compu Company. Both customers wish to borrow more money from their respective banks, with which they have close, long-standing relationships. Even though the banks would like to accommodate these good customers, they are not comfortable lending more money beyond the current outstandings. What can they do?

One possibility is for the banks to sell part of their loans without recourse. However, if this is not practical, the rapidly emerging market for credit derivatives, particularly the credit swap, offers an alternative solution. Here is how it works. AutoBank agrees to guarantee $300 million of TechBank's loans to Compu Company. In exchange, TechBank agrees to guarantee $300 million of AutoBank's loans to Carmaker, Inc.

The result of these transactions is that both banks have

- Reduced the risk of part of their outstanding loans to their top customers
- Acquired new risk assets representing claims on different customers
- Diversified their loan portfolios
- Created room for additional loans to their top customers

This is the basic idea of the credit swap. Now let us look at the details.

Types of Assets

- Each bank has replaced a claim on a corporate customer with a claim on a bank.
- Each bank has added a claim on another customer.

Balance Sheet Impact

- As the $300 million part of each $1 billion loan is now guaranteed by an OECD bank, its risk weighting is reduced from 100 percent to 20 percent (see Chap. 13). Consequently, the amount of risk assets at each bank is reduced from $300 million to $60 million for the original loan.
- Each bank adds $300 million in new risk assets as a result of having provided coverage under a credit swap.

Pricing of a Swap

The pricing of credit swaps is determined by the market's perceived credit quality of the two customers. Beyond that, the pricing is influenced by the eagerness of a specific bank to reduce its outstanding loans with a particular customer. The latter point can be compared with the impact of trading liquidity and defeasance periods as was discussed in the context of price risk in Chap. 5. In a relatively new developing market, this point should not be underestimated.

In the absence of a specific trading-liquidity-related technical condition of the market, the swap will be at par if the two borrowers involved are of comparable credit quality. However, a triple-A-rated borrower against a single-A-rated borrower would require that a premium be paid by the bank receiving the guarantee for the single-A borrower. The reason is obvious. As a result of the transaction, the bank has improved its loan portfolio by replacing a loan to a single-A customer with a claim on a triple-A customer. Academically speaking, it has less risk and has to pay for that.

Miscellaneous Points

This business requires a clear and unquestionable indicator to determine when a borrower has failed and a swap partner is authorized to collect under a guarantee. In other words, it must be very clear what constitutes bankruptcy and what procedures must be followed so that the bank can collect under a guarantee.

At this point, let us establish more appropriate terminology. The industry does not use the word *guarantee*. Instead, a bank obtains *cover* for a loan through a credit swap. Similarly, the industry does not use the word *bankruptcy*. A bank refers to such a situation as a *credit event*.

The current thinking is that only borrowers that have public debt issues outstanding are eligible for credit swaps. Because of the public debt issue, it is obvious when a company is in default. Whenever a borrower fails to make an interest or principal payment on a public issue, the credit event is triggered and the borrower is deemed to have defaulted. As a result, all the banks which have provided cover for loans or other credit extensions through credit swaps must pay up in accordance with their credit swap agreements.

Another questionable point is the treatment of a swap that has a maturity different from that of the loan for which it provides cover, for example, a 3-year credit swap to cover a 5-year loan. What is the balance sheet treatment in this case? Some people say that for 3 years a reduced risk asset may be shown on the balance sheet. Others say that one cannot reduce the risk assets at all.

Perspectives for the Future

A fixed versus floating interest rate swap separates the cash in a money market transaction from the type of interest rate, such as fixed or floating. A borrower does not have to renegotiate a loan with the lender to switch from a fixed rate to a floating rate. Instead, the borrower does a separate cashless transaction, exchanging one type of interest rate for another.

A credit derivative performs a similar function. In developed financial markets, the yields of securities issued by different companies indicate, through the premium over the government yield, their relative strength. Once the credit swap becomes more popular and standardized, it will be this credit swap which announces to the world through the demand/supply-driven yields for specific corporations the relative strength of those corporations. In fact, there is no need for an actual loan outstanding. A bank may agree to a credit swap to cover the hypothetical debt of Company X for $100 million for 5 years. If a credit event occurs, per a specific agreed indicator, the bank must pay the counterparty to the credit swap. This will be a very fine-tuned global market in which everybody knows that at a specific moment that a credit swap for Company X against Company Y costs, for example, 12 basis points p.a.

When one thinks this through and remembers that just making money is not good enough anymore, the pricing of credit extensions becomes very simple. The lender knows his or her capital/risk asset sweet spot, and the market tells us through the credit swap market the specific premium-over-government-yield-based credit standing of a prospective borrower. The combination of these two factors determines the amount of equity we must allocate to the transaction. Add our goal for return on equity, and, voilá, there is the pricing of the credit extension if we keep it on the books. The *it* in this case means the entire loan, or it could mean that we keep the loan on the books but reduce the risk through a credit swap with another bank. This is another revolution in the making, this time not only on the price-risk-related trading side. Instead, the trading is rapidly encroaching the credit function and may soon influence the pricing of credit in a major way.

At the beginning of the credit section it was mentioned that modern banks have established internal risk ratings for all customers using credit. As the credit swaps market evolves and becomes more liquid, it is possible that the premium-over-government-yield-based ratings will provide serious competition not only to the internal credit ratings of banks but also to the official credit ratings of public rating agencies.

Biggest Impact: Portfolio
Diversification

It would not be appropriate to view a credit swap as an instrument with which risk can be reduced directly. In fact, the opposite is true. The example of AutoBank and TechBank shows that before the swap, each bank had $1 billion in risk assets on the books. After the $300 million credit swap, each bank had $1,060,000,000 in risk assets on the books. The numbers work as follows: $700 million remained completely unchanged. The $300 million covered by the credit swap was replaced by the other bank's $300 million in loans that were newly assumed as a risk. The bank's original $300 million is still on the books as a risk-adjusted amount of $60 million. Exhibit 9-7 shows that the total risk assets actually rise as a result of the swap.

Even though there are more risk assets on the books as a result of the credit swap, we would like to suggest that this instrument does reduce risk overall because of its capacity to diversify a portfolio of loans and other extensions of credit. In Chap. 8, the discussion of modern portfolio management for credit extensions to customers explains how limits are set for portfolio subsections in terms of industry and geography and indicates that all customers are risk-rated on a scale of 1 to 10. Given this type of portfolio, the credit swap is very convenient for modeling the ideal portfolio in terms of industry and geography. Beyond that, the credit swap will create an environment in which the relative credit quality of many customers will be more transparent than it is today and the distinctions between the credit standings of companies will be expressed in terms of individual basis points. As a result, it will be possible to express the overall riskiness of a portfolio with greater accuracy and relate the risk assumption to return benchmarks. One can envision the policy committee of a bank discussing whether it wants to add 6 basis points of risk to the portfolio because it believes the incremental 6-basis-point risk equivalent is well within its scope for risk taking and would like to have the incremental 6 basis points in income.

Finally, to the extent that the market is quoting prices for credit swaps

Risk assets before the credit swap	$1,000,000,000
Remainder of loan on the books after credit swap	$ 700,000,000
Risk assets acquired by the swap	$ 300,000,000
Risk-adjusted assets on the books after credit swap	$ 60,000,000
Total risk assets	$1,060,000,000

Exhibit 9-7. Risk assets resulting from a credit swap.

for assets on a balance sheet, it is very easy to mark-to-market these assets. The valuation of a loan on the books of a bank becomes almost as easy as marking-to-market an AAA corporate bond.

When this book is revised in a couple of years, this chapter surely will require the most extensive changes as a result of new developments in the credit derivative market.

Summary

Credit risk is the second most important type of risk in financial trading.

Settlement risk is pure credit risk which begins with the passing of the cancellation deadline and ends when credits are reconciled to our account. This period is longer than is commonly assumed, usually at least 1 day. The industry is working to reduce this risk through the introduction and implementation of clearinghouse and netting mechanisms.

Presettlement credit risk occurs when the counterparty to a distant-date transaction fails before maturity and the market rate has changed so that the contract rate has become more attractive than the market rate. Before entering into a deal, we can apply appropriate volatility to the transaction amount and estimate a potential loan equivalent amount that is likely to evolve from this transaction. After a deal has been booked, the total loan equivalent amount can be estimated in that we will determine the replacement cost of an outstanding contract (current loan equivalent amount). Thereafter, we will apply appropriate volatility to the remaining life of the transaction which indicates the potential loan equivalent amount.

$$
\begin{array}{r}
\text{Current loan equivalent amount} \\
+ \text{ Potential loan equivalent amount} \\
\hline
\text{Total loan equivalent amount}
\end{array}
$$

The conversion of meaningless volume and notional amounts into meaningful loan equivalent amounts allows the risk-related pricing of forward contracts, i.e., minimum spreads large enough to support incremental risk-adjusted assets resulting from distant-date contracts, through retained earnings from a capital adequacy viewpoint.

Limits/triggers and outstandings with individual counterparties are tracked in loan equivalent terms instead of in volume and notional amounts. The potentially painful impact of distant-date transactions on the size of the risk-adjusted balance sheet can be modified through netting and clearing techniques initiated by the financial industry.

There is intellectual integrity in managing price risk and presettlement counterparty risk. In both cases one tries to anticipate the future movements of market rates and relies on volatility to arrive at those judgments. In price risk, a change of the market rate in the wrong direction creates a loss. In presettlement risk, a move of the market rate in the wrong direction creates a loan equivalent amount. Only if the counterparty fails do we lose money.

Presettlement counterparty risk requires the employment of two sets of skills: Conversion from meaningless volume and notional amounts to loan equivalent amounts requires market and product skills, and judging the creditworthiness of counterparties requires credit skills.

Credit derivatives, particularly credit swaps, are rapidly becoming popular. Through this product, two banks exchange credit risk: One guarantees credit risk for the other, and vice versa. This process is ideal for portfolio diversification. In addition, it will soon provide market-driven transparency in regard to the credit standing of market participants and facilitate risk/return-oriented pricing of credit.

10
Country Risk

Understanding the Business, Recognizing Country Risk

Market participants who trade with counterparties outside their own country must be aware of the risk associated with cross-border business and establish lines not only for their counterparties but also for the countries in which those counterparties are located. The following example can serve as a simple illustration of this type of risk. Suppose Big Bank in the United States lends dollars to MegaCorp in Emerging Country and the customer sells those dollars to the local central bank in exchange for the local currency. At the maturity of the loan it turns out that the customer has made good use of the local currency because both the principal and the interest are readily available for reconversion into dollars. The problem is that the central bank does not have the dollars to satisfy MegaCorp's demand, and as a result the customer cannot repay the dollars to the lending bank on the maturity date. In this example, the problem is not the inability of the customer to repay the loan but the failure of Emerging Country to convert the local currency into dollars. This risk is known as *country risk*; sometimes it is referred to as *cross-border risk*. It is easy to see why country-specific credit lines should be established to cover cross-border transactions in which two countries are involved.

However, country risk and the need for country-specific credit lines prevail even if the claim on a particular country is denominated in that country's local currency, such as a claim in pesos on Pesoland, in which pesos are the local currency. Some people assert that country credit lines are not necessary in this situation because the country's central bank can always print its own currency. Nevertheless, there are two reasons why we must consider this a risk just as it would be if the claim were in dollars.

First, it happens occasionally that a country is *able* to pay a local currency obligation but *does not want* to pay. The second reason, which occurs more frequently, is that the local currency may be purchased outside of a country, and this affects the amount of foreign exchange reserves in the country. For example, assume that a U.S. corporation plans to invest $100 million in Pesoland, a country which we assume has severe capital outflow controls and very low foreign exchange reserves. In the normal process the U.S. company must sell the dollars in Pesoland to get the local currency for investment, and this dollar sale will increase the exchange reserves of Pesoland. However, further assume that Pesoland has constraints on foreign currency outflows but freely permits outflows of the *local* currency, pesos. These local currency amounts available outside of Pesoland are purchased at a discount by the U.S. corporation that wants to invest $100 million in Pesoland. Since the outflow of local currency in pesos enables the foreign owners of those pesos to convert them into dollars, the $100 million which the U.S. corporation plans to invest in Pesoland never reaches the central bank and therefore cannot increase the exchange reserves of Pesoland. For this reason, countries that wish to impose strict capital outflow controls also will apply those controls to the local currency. This means that from a bank's viewpoint claims in the local currency and in a foreign currency must both be included in its calculations of country risk for a particular sovereign entity.

Let us look at another situation in which there is country risk for the counterparty and for two countries. Suppose a U.S. bank extends credit to a company in Pesoland which is a subsidiary of a parent company in Emerging Country. In this case the U.S. bank will need a credit line for Emerging Country in addition to credit lines for Pesoland and the customer in Pesoland. The reason for this is that if Emerging Country goes bankrupt, the parent company in Emerging Country may no longer be allowed to support its subsidiary in Pesoland, causing the subsidiary to default on its obligation to the U.S. bank. To summarize, we can say that for country risk purposes, lines are required for the actual borrower, the country where the borrower is located, and the country where the parent of the borrower is located.

Assessing Country Risk

After we have gained an understanding of the business and learned to recognize country risk, the question is how to evaluate countries and detect early-warning signals for the types of problems that were just described. This is a difficult subject, but we will point out a few basics.

We refer to a country's foreign exchange reserves as the *country's savings account*. Similar to an individual's personal savings account, this account reflects the surplus or deficit resulting from the difference between income and expenses. In very simple terms, when you earn more than you spend, the balance in your savings account goes up, and when you spend more than you earn, the balance in your savings account goes down. When the savings account is empty, you are forced to borrow to pay your bills, and when nobody will lend to you, you are bankrupt.

This may sound simple, but something very similar happens to countries. When we want to anticipate the failure of a country, we have to look for indicators that directly or indirectly affect the foreign currency inflows and outflows and ultimately the foreign exchange reserves (the country's savings account).

In this context, the exchange rate—the value of the country's currency in the international foreign exchange market—is an important indicator. In my global travels, whenever I arrived in a country, I used the following simple approach to evaluate the economy:

Question	*Answer*
What is the level of interest rates?	22 percent p.a.
What is annualized inflation?	16 percent p.a.
What is the current exchange rate against US$?	110 local currency for 1 US$
What was the exchange rate 1 year ago?	100 local currency for 1 US$

These are simple questions with answers that usually are readily available, and those answers allow some early conclusions about what is going on in this country. One can conclude that the country in the example has a relatively high real interest rate of 5 percent: The nominal interest rate of 22 percent minus a 1 percent country-specific risk premium minus 16 percent inflation equals 5 percent. This high real interest rate will encourage the local people to keep their money in their own country. Beyond that, foreigners will be encouraged to take advantage of the high real interest rate and move money into the country. Therefore, it can be expected that this country will have significant short-term capital inflows (Exhibit 10-1). Additionally, one can conclude that the local currency may be overvalued in the international foreign exchange market. During the last 12 months inflation at 16 percent has been 6 percent higher than the 10 percent devaluation (the dollar rose from 100 to 110).

In Exhibit 10-2, event A shows what happens to dollar prices if a country has more inflation than its main trading partners have. When the

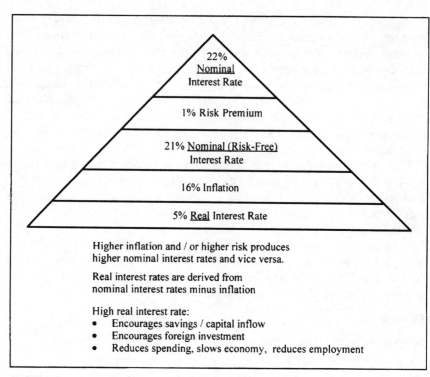

Exhibit 10-1. Economic indicators in a country.

Local Currency Cost of Hamburger	FX Rate	Dollar Cost of Hamburger	Event
0.80	LCY 0.80 = $1.00	1.00	
1.00	0.80 = $1.00	1.25	A. 25% inflation
1.00	1.00 = $1.00	1.00	B. 25% devaluation
1.00	1.25 = $1.00	0.80	C. 25% additional devaluation
		A. Local currency overvalued	
		• Fewer exports, higher imports	
		• Exchange reserves down	
		• Employment reduced	
		B. Purchasing power parity	
		C. Local currency undervalued	
		• More exports, fewer imports	
		• Exchange reserves up	
		• Employment up	

Exhibit 10-2. Inflation and exchange rates.

local currency experiences 25 percent inflation *without* a devaluation, the currency is overvalued and the dollar cost of a hamburger rises from $1.00 to $1.25. Only if the local currency is devalued 25 percent (the same percentage as the assumed inflation) will the dollar price for the hamburger return from $1.25 to the standard price of $1.00 (event B). If the local currency is devalued again (without any incremental inflation), the local currency will be undervalued and the dollar cost of a hamburger will decrease to 80 cents (event C).

Why is this significant? Foreigners do not care about local currency prices. Travelers judge the cost of things in a particular country (hotels, food, items to buy and take home) in terms of their local currencies; for example, Americans in France think in dollar terms. After event A (25 percent inflation without devaluation), a $1.00 hamburger costs $1.25, which is expensive. Only after event B (25 percent devaluation) does the price return to the standard price of $1.00. However, if we return to the original question of how to evaluate countries to detect early-warning signals for the types of problems that contribute to country risk, we can see why this is an important concept.

If a country is in a situation similar to the one after event A (more inflation than devaluation), it can be concluded that the country's exports will suffer because the world will find everything in that country and from that country too expensive. At the same time, imports into the country will boom because residents of this country traveling to other countries will find everything very inexpensive and will purchase a lot of merchandise to bring home. Consequently, because of its overvalued currency, this country will import more than it exports. In other words, it will have a trade deficit—a net outflow of dollars—which will reduce the exchange reserves (savings account).

In summary, in the sample country we have financial capital inflows (high interest rates attract investors) and trade-deficit-related outflows (high prices cause buyers to go elsewhere). All the cash inflows and outflows make up what is called the current account. If the size of the financial inflows and the size of the trade deficit are the same, a country has a balanced current account. This appears to be an ideal situation, but it is necessary to look ahead and question the sustainability of this position. What products are imported? Perfume and television sets to satisfy consumer demand or construction machinery to develop the infrastructure? In this case, perfume is bad and machinery is good. What type of financial inflows are we talking about? Short-term, portfolio-type inflows or long-term investments? In this case, a short-term inflow is bad and a long-term inflow is good.

Long-term inflows and borrowings also improve liquidity, particularly when the maturities of long-term borrowings are staggered and spread over several years. The staggering of maturities is very important because in the event of a crisis specific to the borrower or to a country and/or region, it can be very painful if substantial maturities occur soon after problems have surfaced.

This subject is not the thrust of this book, but to manage the risk associated with cross-border transactions, one has to look at the domestic budget, the policies, and especially the political stability of the country. The International Monetary Fund (IMF), which often acts as a banker and lender of last resort for countries that need help, is working on establishing easier access to information regarding the health of a country's economy. This involves standardizing reports on key data which serve as an early-warning system and allow judgments to be made about the creditworthiness of a country. For example, a good indicator of a country's perceived creditworthiness is the yield of outstanding international debt issues. The lower the country-specific risk premium over the U.S. government yield or Eurodollar yield, the better that particular country's creditworthiness and reputation in the market, and vice versa (see Exhibit 4-4).

In addition to the direct financial risks described at the beginning of this chapter, there are also indirect risks, which can lead to financial loss. These include the quality of the legal status prevailing in a country and the availability of only limited information. It is important to examine the legal foundation, whether the rule of law prevails at all, and if so, what form it takes. For example, what are the rights of security holders when things go wrong?

Concerning information, we know that in western markets investors make informed decisions based on substantial amounts of financial information released by companies because of prevailing laws and infrastructures. Without this information, how do investors know whom to trust?

School for Country Managers and Regulators

The world has become so interconnected and interdependent that a crisis in one country can quickly spill over to another country and even to an entirely different part of the world. Because of this, there is a public world interest that even a relatively small country manages its affairs properly and "keeps its house in order." This responsibility may exceed the capacity of a country's leadership, which often has predominantly political skills and is overwhelmed by the challenges of economic developments and the resulting impact on the financial markets.

I recommend that a body such as the IMF create a school where future leaders (government and central bank) of countries can acquire the skills needed to manage a country's economy. There should be a special focus on what to do when inappropriate economic measures must be taken for political reasons. This would allow anticipation of the undesirable results of those inappropriate measures and hopefully produce less of a negative impact than would otherwise be likely. The training would probably take one year or longer. The faculty could be drawn from a senior central bank staff and politicians around the world, still in offices as well as retired, as well as recognized academicians and practitioners. Real life cases could be used.

The creation of such a school would represent "tree planting." It would take years before the first graduates moved into sufficiently senior positions in their respective countries so as to apply their skills and make an impact. However, I am convinced that no cost for such training can be too high, given the enormous financial and social losses to the specific country, and to the world overall, caused by substandard handling of a political, economic, or event-related crisis.

11
Futures

Futures Exchanges

A futures exchange is an organized forum for the transfer of risk. In some types of business the creation of risk is unavoidable. For example, agricultural businesses that produce vegetables, fruits, or animals are forced to assume risk. Seed must be put into the earth, requiring fertilization and irrigation, and then one must wait until it has grown and has commercial value. The same is true for animals, which must be bred or purchased when they are small and then raised until they can be brought to market.

This is where the futures exchange comes in. Take pork bellies as an example. The original supplier, the pig farmer, sells pork belly futures at, say, 60 cents per pound for delivery in 3 months. This is not an option; it is a formal commitment to deliver pork bellies at a specific date in the future. However, the farmer has no intention of delivering pork bellies to the buyer of the futures contract because the farmer always sells his pork bellies to his good friend the meat packer.

One reason why the farmer and the meat packer are good friends is that they never talk about money. They have an agreement that on the day the farmer delivers the pork bellies to the meat packer, both parties will look at the prevailing spot or cash price for pork bellies and make that the price the meat packer pays to the farmer. Three months later the farmer delivers the pork bellies to the meat packer. They check the cash price and note that it is 70 cents, which is what the meat packer pays the farmer.

When the farmer goes home, he reviews his books and notes that he has an outstanding future sale of pork bellies at 60 cents per pound. This is the pork belly sale he executed to hedge the price of the pork bellies he just sold to the meat packer. The farmer no longer needs the hedge, and so he calls his broker and buys back the sales contract at the now-pre-

Farmer sells three-month pork belly futures at 60 cents per pound	
Spot after three months is	70 cents per pound
Farmer covers future at loss	10 cents per pound
Net spot sale at	60 cents per pound
Spot after three months is	50 cents per pound
Farmer covers future at a profit	10 cents per pound
Net spot sale at	60 cents per pound

Exhibit 11-1. Sale of pork belly futures to hedge a spot sale.

vailing market price of 70 cents. Since the farmer sold at 60 cents and buys back at 70 cents, he suffers a hedge loss of 10 cents. Net net, he receives 60 cents per pound for his pork bellies, which was his objective to begin with.

If the price of pork bellies had gone down to 50 cents, the cash sale of the pork bellies to the meat packer would have occurred at 50 cents. However, the buyback of the futures contract, which had been sold at 60 cents, also would have occurred at 50 cents, generating a hedge profit of 10 cents. This hedge profit, together with the 50 cents from the cash sale in the farmer's pocket, again generates aggregate sales revenues of 60 cents, which was the farmer's objective.

Exhibit 11-1 shows that the net of cash sale minus hedge loss or plus hedge profit will always amount to the targeted net sales price, in this case 60 cents.

Third Participant in the Futures Market

If the farmer's sale and the meat packer's purchase occurred at exactly the same time, the two parties could, through their respective brokers, deal directly with each other. However, such exact timing is very uncommon. This allows us to introduce the third classic participant in the futures market, speculators, such as the doctors and lawyers who have gambling money available and add, as you will see, trading liquidity to the market. Suppose the farmer is ready to sell pork bellies and there is no buyer. As a result, the price for pork bellies drops. The broker sees that, phones his customer, the dentist, and says, "Pork bellies are unusually low. I recommend we buy some." The dentist replies, "Okay, go ahead and buy some." A week later the meat packer is ready to buy pork bellies, but there is no seller. As a result, the price for pork bellies rises. At that point the dentist's broker recommends that the dentist sell the pork bellies, which satisfies the demand of the meat packer.

This story explains why it seldom happens that anybody takes delivery. The farmer does not deliver because he always sells spot to the meat packer, the meat packer does not take delivery because he always buys spot from the farmer, and the dentist is not interested in delivering or receiving pork bellies. You can see how important the role of the speculator is for the functioning of the market. He or she is virtually oiling the wheels of the futures market by providing trading liquidity and willingness to take the risk when nobody else is around to do so.

Creditworthiness of a Futures Exchange

A futures exchange as an organization must be evaluated in terms of credit quality. Just because we deal with a futures exchange, that does not mean we do not have to worry about this particular counterparty's credit standing. Each exchange has its own organizational rules and bylaws, and some of these structures are better than others. Therefore, a detailed analysis and examination of each exchange should be undertaken before one buys a seat and becomes a member of a futures exchange. Exhibit 11-2 lists some of the features to look for as part of an overall review of an exchange. The main focus of the analysis should be on the existence and size of a reserve fund that can be tapped when a member of the exchange fails. In the end, each institution will want to avoid being left as the member with the deep pockets, paying off everybody else who did not manage properly.

FUTURES EXCHANGES
• Owned by members / brokers
• Licensed / supervised by regulators
• Each customer must deal through a broker
• Organizational structure important for
– Quality / liability of members
– Reserve fund
– Trading liquidity
– Settlement process

Exhibit 11-2. Features of a well-organized futures exchange.

Margins in Futures

Banks that deal in forward transactions recognize that forwards are extensions of credit and require credit lines for every counterparty with which they deal. Brokers at organized futures exchanges also under-stand the business and recognize that there is credit risk, but they lack the skill or time to evaluate the financial statements of all the people who trade futures, including pig farmers, meat packers, doctors, and lawyers. Brokers reduce their credit risk by requiring customers to establish margin accounts. As one can see in Exhibit 11-3, there are two types of margin. First, the investor is required to deposit an *initial* mar-gin amount that has been established in the contract. Then, at the end of each day, all the contracts are marked-to-market and the investors with losses have to pay cash into their margin accounts and the investors with gains receive cash. These payments are called the positive and neg-ative *variation* margin, better known as the *maintenance* margin. These daily margin payments "maintain" the initial margin at the level that was established when the deal was done.

Let us look at an example that illustrates these two types of margins. Suppose an investor buys gold futures for $1 million and the initial mar-gin deposit established in the contract is 5 percent, or $50,000. At the end of the day, when the contract is marked-to-market, it turns out that the gold price has dropped 1 percent and the investor loses $10,000. The broker will call him and say, "Sorry, I have bad news. You lost $10,000, and you must send me a check for that amount." The normal reaction would be for the investor to respond, "Yes, I already saw on the news that the gold price fell, and I will send you a check for $10,000." The buyer's broker already may have reached into the initial margin account

Margin in Futures
Initial Margin
▪ Protects against counterparty risk
▪ Size depends on daily volatility of the commodity
▪ Does not have to be cash (government bonds or bank letter of credit)
▪ Usually interest bearing
Variation or Maintenance Margin
▪ Result of daily mark-to-market
▪ Losers pay cash, winners receive cash
▪ "Maintains" initial margin at proper level

Exhibit 11-3. Two types of margins in futures transactions.

to send the $10,000 to the broker representing the seller of the gold, who made the $10,000. When he receives the $10,000 from his customer, he replenishes the initial margin account so that it is maintained at $50,000. That is how it usually works.

The customer may have a different reaction and say, "You know, this is a bad time for me, and I cannot pay the $10,000." The broker then may say, "Look, I don't care about all your problems. I'm only interested in whether you will pay me, because if you cannot pay, I'll find another buyer for this contract. When I do, instead of you sending me $10,000, I'll send you $40,000 and we'll forget about the whole thing." The only reason the broker can use that arrogant approach with the customer is that he has the margin. If the daily price change had been 7 percent, the maintenance margin would have been $70,000, which is more than the initial margin of $50,000, so the broker would have responded differently.

This story highlights the relationship between the initial margin and the maintenance margin. Most people know there are margins in futures, but few understand the purpose of those margins. The initial margin provides protection against counterparty risk. At the end of each day all outstanding contracts are marked-to-market, and this produces positive or negative variation margins that will be received by the winners and paid by the losers of the day. These variation margins maintain the initial margin at the contracted level. The size of the variation margin ideally should be set at a level slightly higher than the "usual" daily fluctuation in market prices. Here again, a good starting point for anticipating the size of daily changes in market prices is volatility. This is the same volatility we have been talking about throughout the book.

Setting the Size of Margins

Against this background, it is clear that the important task of determining the size of margins, including the margins required in forwards transacted with less creditworthy counterparties, requires both market skills and product skills. However, in most banks the size of margins is determined only by the credit function.

The importance of all the details concerning a margining arrangement between a bank and a customer cannot be overemphasized. In particular, the following points must be very clear:

- The size of the initial margin
- The frequency of portfolio marking-to-market
- The frequency of advising the customer of the result of marking-to-market

- How much money the customer may lose until the initial margin has to be reestablished, in other words, how much money the customer can lose until she has to put up additional cash to cover the losses
- At what time has the bank or broker the right to liquidate the contract

My experience has shown that these arrangements often are not clearly articulated and frequently lead to disagreements and even lawsuits between the two parties.

Margin arrangements must be articulated as precisely as possible. Care must be taken to assure that customers understand the margin agreement. This area has a very high potential for lawsuits in case of losses.

Some exchanges are beginning to mark-to-market twice a day instead of daily, perhaps at noon and again at the end of the day. The reason for shortening the time period from one mark-to-market to the next is of course that there is less expected volatility. The shorter the period is, the less volatility there is to be expected during that shorter period; and because volatility is lower, the initial margin can be smaller, which means more leverage for the investor. The table in Exhibit 11-4 shows that when leverage of $100,000 increases (the initial margin drops from 50 percent to 1 percent), possible transaction amounts rise from 200,000 to 10 million. You also can see that the higher the volatility, the larger the value at risk, and the value at risk, expressed as a percentage of $100,000 cash, increases with higher leverage and/or higher volatility.

When investors have more leverage, there is more turnover and therefore more commission income for the broker. From the broker's viewpoint, the question is: Will the incremental commissions earned from higher turnover exceed the incremental expense of double marking-to-market?

% Leverage	Transaction Possible	1% O/N Volatility	% of Cash	2% O/N Volatility	% of Cash	5% O/N Volatility	% of Cash
50%	200,000	2,000	2%	4,000	4%	10,000	10%
10%	1,000,000	10,000	10%	20,000	20%	50,000	50%
5%	2,000,000	20,000	20%	40,000	40%	100,000	100%
1%	10,000,000	100,000	100%	200,000	200%	500,000	500%

Exhibit 11-4. Leveraging $100,000 cash.

It is obvious that the size of the initial margin is a critical question for the broker, who has two conflicting objectives: avoiding credit losses and making more money. The credit voice in the broker says, Let's set the margin as high as possible, because the higher the margin is, the less likely it is that the daily movement will be larger than the margin and therefore the less likely we are to have a credit loss. That is good thinking. The problem is that the higher the margin is, the less leverage there is for customers who trade futures, and the less leverage those customers have, the less they will trade, which of course means less commission income for the broker. The businessperson in the broker says, Let's set the margin very low, because the lower the margin, the greater the leverage for customers and the more volume they will trade and therefore the bigger the commission income for the broker. The problem with the lower margin is of course the probability of a daily movement that is larger than the size of the initial margin, which creates credit risk for the broker.

Putting a Tail on Futures

When futures transactions are marked-to-market, the losers have to pay negative variation (maintenance) margins and the winners collect positive variation margins. This feature plays a role in a mixed transaction in which one side of the deal is futures bought through an organized exchange and the other side of the deal is not futures, such as spot or forward. For example, the market is quoting dollars at 20 percent and a trader who needs dollars is looking for a way to get them cheaper. Instead of borrowing the dollars, the trader borrows 100,000 oz of gold at 1 percent and swaps the gold for dollars. The trader sells the gold spot at $400 and buys 1-year gold futures at a premium of 17 percent. Since the trader paid 1 percent to borrow the gold plus a premium of 17 percent for gold futures, the cost of the created dollars is 18 percent, which means the trader acquires dollars at 2 percent below market cost.

Sometimes there are these kinds of disparities between the forward market and the futures market. In a forward exchange market, premiums and discounts equal the interest differentials. However, with futures, when there is a pronounced move in a given commodity, futures premiums tend to exaggerate the trend of the underlying price. In other words, when commodity prices rise, the futures premium is higher than it should be, and when commodity prices fall, the premium is lower than it should be. In this example the futures premium is lower than it should be because when dollars are 20 percent and gold is 1 percent, the premium for gold should be 19 percent instead of 17 percent.

Remember that the example involves a *future* purchase of gold, not a *forward* purchase, and as we have said, a future purchase is subject to margining. Since the trader has purchased futures as part of the "engineered" swap in which he sold spot gold, if the gold price goes down, the trader has to *pay* variation margin and if the price goes up, the trader *collects* variation margin. In this situation where the trader does not have a net position, these variation margins, positive and negative, do not represent profits and losses because whatever he makes on the futures, he loses on spot, and vice versa. However, the interest on these margins affects earnings and losses. For example, in the case where the trader sold spot and bought futures, when the gold price goes down, he has to pay variation margin. While the margin itself is not a loss, the interest on the margin *is* a loss.

To protect against this loss, one puts a "tail" on futures, which means that the amount of the futures contract is less than that of the nonfutures contract, i.e., the spot contract. In the example, when the trader sells 100,000 ounces of gold spot, he buys a one-year futures contract for only 83,334 ounces. I call this position an *apparent net oversold position.* The transaction looks, feels, tastes, and smells as if the trader were net oversold 16,666 ounces, but it only seems that way, as you will see. The trader seems to be oversold, and when the gold price rises, he has a loss on this apparent net position, but since he bought futures, he collects positive variation margin, which can earn interest. If the gold price falls, he makes a profit on the oversold position but has to pay out negative variation margin, and that costs interest (the cost of carrying the margin). The idea is to set the tail at a level where the profits and losses resulting from the apparent net gold position offset exactly the interest paid or the interest earned on the margin.

Exhibit 11-5 shows that if we seem to be oversold 16,666 ounces and the gold price goes down $10, we make a profit of $166,660. However, if we

Protects against impact of variation margins.	
Spot Sales Futures purchases Net hedge (tail)	100,000 ounces 83,334 ounces 16,666 ounces oversold
Gold price drops $10 Impact on 16,666 ounces oversold position	+ $166,600
Impact on 83,334 ounces futures purchase is $833,340 negative variation margin. Carrying cost at 20%	- $166,668

Exhibit 11-5. Hedge effectiveness: putting tails on futures.

made futures purchases of 83,334 ounces and there is a $10 drop in the gold price, the size of the negative margin will be $833,340. If we assume a dollar interest level of 20 percent, then 20 percent of the $833,340 will create a cost of carrying on the negative margin of $166,668. It can be seen here that the negative margin impact offsets the positive impact of the net position, and that is what it means to put a tail on futures to protect oneself against the negative impact of absorbing interest costs on margins.

The way this is managed is for each futures contract to have a contract-specific tail. Of course, when one runs a futures book, one calculates a master tail for the entire book. The size of the tail changes every day because it is a function of time and the interest level and of course the amount of the book. Even if the size of the book and the interest level remain the same, the tail has to be recalculated each day because the contracts are a day closer to maturity. In the real world the size of the futures book also changes, and very often the interest rate changes as well. It is critical for management to know exactly what the size of the master tail has to be. This is somewhat similar to the delta hedge, where there is the delta-neutral hedge position and one has to know exactly what that position should be. As a practical matter, the trader never is exactly delta neutral, and that is true here as well. The trader never has the exact master tail; he has either more or less tail, and to the extent that he is "undertailed" or "overtailed," he has net positions when there are commodities involved or interest-level-sensitive positions when interest rate futures are involved.

Experienced traders must understand this concept, because failing to hedge the variation margins can be very costly. For example, in the early 1980s the price of gold went down from $800 to below $400, and when there is a pronounced trend in the market, the futures price tends to exaggerate the market price. In this case, the gold price came down and the futures price ran ahead of the market, which means it declined more than it should have. As gold has a premium against dollars, it meant that the premium was not as high as it should have been; i.e., the prevailing interest differential was not respected. As a result, many people took advantage of the profit opportunities by borrowing gold, selling spot, and buying gold futures at a premium lower than it should have been. Some people who did this business were unaware of the need for tails, and you can imagine the negative impact on earnings when gold dropped from $800 to $400. For example, if there was a $100 million book, the margin was $50 million and the interest on the $50 million was very substantial. Even though the traders profited from the disparity between the premium for gold in the futures market and the interest differential between gold and dollars, they lost substantially on the cost of carrying the margin.

Standardization

The common nightmare of organizers of futures exchanges is that there will not be enough trading liquidity in the market. It is for that reason that there is standardization of futures contracts on the basis of

- Quantity
- Quality
- Maturity

Quantity is standardized in that one deals only in predetermined contract sizes, and the dealers know exactly what those quantities are: for gold, it is 100 ounces; for 91-day Treasury bills, it is $1 million; for German marks in foreign exchange, it is 125,000 marks; and so on. One can do nothing, do one contract, or do a multiple of a contract. It is not possible to do part of a contract.

Quality is standardized in that one is very specific about the features of the traded commodity. People do not say 91-day dollars; instead, they specify Treasury bills, Eurodollars, domestic CDs, and the like. Gold is assumed to be 99.5 percent gold (the experts say "two nine five"), and so forth.

Maturity is standardized in that the main contracts are dealt for a particular day in March, June, September, or December. It is not possible to deal for value May 11, for example.

As you can see, there is standardization in the quantity, quality, and maturity of futures contracts. Without this standardization, it could happen that people agree on the price but cannot agree on the maturity or quality. This system assures that when counterparties agree on a price, they have a deal. The intent of standardizing contracts is to provide an optimal environment for the consummation of a deal, i.e., to enhance trading liquidity.

If we add this concept to our understanding of margins, we get the complete picture of how futures work. To summarize this very basic explanation of futures, let us highlight how the various features relate to each other and show the dynamics between the positive and negative aspects of this instrument (Exhibit 11-6).

In conclusion, let us summarize the main features of futures contracts as they compare to forwards. The margins involving daily marking-to-market and the paying and receiving of variation margins are operationally burdensome. However, because of these margins, there is considerably less credit risk in futures compared with forwards, which are much easier to operate but have more credit risk.

Standardization substantially enhances trading liquidity, including

	ADVANTAGE	DISADVANTAGE
Credit Risk	Margins reduce counterparty risk There is no margin requirement for forwards and, therefore, they carry more credit risk	
Hedge Effectiveness		Standardization of contracts forces customers into basis risks. Forwards provide maximum flexibility because they are over-the-counter products that can be tailored exactly to the customers' hedging needs and, therefore, carry no basis risks.
Flexibility For In And Out Trading	Very easy to get in and out for hedging and speculation purposes	
Operational Ease		Must be marked to market daily which creates additional work for the operations area. However, this disadvantage creates the maintenance margin which is the reason why there is less credit risk in futures. There is no margin requirement for forwards and, therefore, they are not marked to market daily, which makes them operationally easier to handle.
Confidentiality	Only the broker knows what a customer is doing in the futures market With a forward, at least one other market participant is aware of transactions	
Trading Liquidity	Standardization of contracts for quality, quantity, and maturity enhances the trader's ability to consummate a deal	

Exhibit 11-6. The advantages and disadvantages of futures compared with forwards.

the flexibility of buying and selling futures contracts. However, it is this standardization which creates basis risks, i.e., the inability to create a hedge that equals in amount, maturity, and type of market rate the features of a risk position.

12
Managing
Liquidity Risk

Price risk and credit risk are issues that constantly must be monitored and managed to assure the success of a business. Liquidity is vital to the life of a corporation because without it, a business can be forced to shut down. This chapter discusses the types of liquidity risk and the process of monitoring future cash flows in normal and contingency environments.

The process of managing liquidity involves two types of risk: funding liquidity risk, which is the risk that funds will not be available when they are needed, and trading liquidity risk, which is the risk that a bank will not be able to liquidate assets quickly enough when cash is needed or liquidate price risk positions when an adverse price change is expected.

Funding Liquidity

Funding liquidity can be defined two ways. It is liquidity for survival—funds are available to meet financial commitments when they are contractually due. It also is liquidity for growth—funds are available to take advantage of attractive business opportunities. The process for achieving funding liquidity to assure the survival and growth of a bank consists of four building blocks:

1. Liability management
2. Liquid assets management
3. Contingency funding plan
4. Liquidity ratios

Liability Management

Until the 1960s banks managed liquidity entirely on the asset side of the balance sheet. Typically, a bank's assets consisted of 60 percent loans and 40 percent government bonds. When money came into the bank (a loan repaid, a new deposit received), the bank would buy bonds, and when money left the bank (a new loan, a deposit withdrawn), the bank would sell bonds.

When financial institutions began to focus on capital adequacy and the size of the balance sheet, the bonds were sold and replaced by loans. That was a time when liquidity management on the liability side of the balance sheet was discovered and specific liquidity-enhancing techniques were developed.

There are three important factors to consider in managing liquidity on the liability side: diversification of sources and instruments, market share, and maturities. We will examine each of these aspects of liability management and then see how they are incorporated into the liability profile, a summary chart of liquidity characteristics, which is discussed later in this section.

Diversification of sources means taking money from as many different types of customers in as many different industries as possible. A source may be the insurance industry, the petroleum industry, or the interbank market. Different customers may be individuals or small, medium-size, and large corporations. We also want to offer a diversity of instruments with which to take money from these different sources. This is mutually desirable: It is more attractive for the investor to have a choice, and it enables the issuer to obtain more money and have more liquidity. By offering instruments such as certificates of deposit, repurchase agreements, bankers' acceptances, commercial paper, and other securitized assets, we have more opportunities to obtain money from the same customer.

> *The ability to get more money is the result of having many different sources and many different instruments to tap those sources.*

Some of the available sources and instruments are listed below.

Sources	Instruments
Individuals	Deposits
Corporations	Borrowings
Banks	Certificates of deposit
Central bank	Repurchase agreements
Nonresidents	Foreign exchange swaps

In countries outside the United States it is particularly important to limit dependence on one instrument. For example, foreign exchange swaps are used to fund local currency loans with dollar deposits by selling the dollars spot and buying forward dollars to create the local currency. There are two reasons why a bank may choose to do a swap instead of borrowing the local currency directly from the local money market to fund the loans: (1) liquidity and (2) cost. We will analyze these two reasons and discuss the limit for this type of business: the cross-currency funding limit.

A bank creates the local currency through swap transactions to enhance its liquidity. Assume that a bank in a particular country is making local currency loans and is having difficulty finding local currency deposits to fund those loans. It borrows dollars, which are usually more readily available, and swaps those dollars with forward cover for the needed local currency. The cost of the local currency is the interest on the borrowed dollars plus or minus the swap cost or swap income. Regulatory changes, a higher cost, or a deterioration in that country's credit standing may make it undesirable or impossible to continue funding local currency loans through swap transactions. That leaves the bank with loans on the books which it may not be able to call plus a tight supply of the local currency, resulting in a liquidity crisis. This is a clear indication of the need for limits on cross-currency funding for liquidity purposes. This limit should be modest because one may be forced to replace the swapped funds locally.

When sufficient local currency is available in the local money market, banks may create the local currency through swap transactions to fund loans at a lower cost. Visualize a country with many exporters who sell their dollar receivables forward to a bank. The bank is buying dollars forward outright from customers and selling spot dollars to another bank. These are "engineered swaps" because they are pieced together: the forward transactions with customers and the spot transactions with another bank. The cash flows are exactly the same as those created by a natural swap with another bank; however, an engineered swap offers the possibility of buying the forward dollars elsewhere at a more attractive price. Through an engineered swap, it is possible to create the local currency at a cost lower than the cost available in the local money market. In this case, the size of the limit may be generous. Cross-currency funding limits are needed to make sure a bank continues to participate in the local money market. It is important to maintain contacts and preserve credit lines for future liquidity needs.

One can see a difference between these two motives for foreign exchange swaps: (1) to create funds that are difficult to find in the local market and (2) to create the local currency at a cost lower than the cost otherwise available in the market.

Thus, the reason for FX swapping is either liquidity or cost. The motivation for a swap transaction should be understood and considered in assessing the cross-currency funding limit.

Cross-currency funding limits:

- *If the reason for cross-currency funding is nonavailability of the local currency, the limit must be modest.*

- *If the reason for cross-currency funding is lower cost, the limit may be generous.*

In terms of risk, if swap transactions have to be discontinued for regulatory or cost reasons, there is liquidity risk. Swaps are done with another market participant, and this means there is counterparty credit risk. In addition, there is country risk, because the swapping entity usually has to borrow the currency, often dollars, from a source outside its own country. Cross-currency funding limits are intended to control the risks inherent in FX swaps.

In the example of foreign exchange swaps, the bank borrows one currency and exchanges it for another currency with forward cover. As the bank accrues interest payables and interest receivables in two different currencies, it is generating a net exchange position. Therefore, in addition to the swapping of the principal amount, an appropriate forward outright contract must be executed to hedge the FX rate risk that results from accruing interest in two different currencies. The premium or discount involved in this hedge must be included in the calculation of the cost of the created local currency liquidity.

Market Share of Sources and Instruments. It is desirable to maintain a large market share of low-interest deposits from nonprofessional market participants. However, when it comes to professional sources and the instruments that access those sources, we are looking for a small market share. In many countries, market shares are well known among professionals. When a bank borrows a large amount from one source or through one instrument, it reduces the liquidity of that source or instrument, and that makes it difficult for the bank to borrow more money. For example, if the money the bank takes constitutes a large percentage of all the money an insurance industry places, that industry may turn down additional requests. However, a smaller market share with an industry source means that that source is more likely to give the bank more money. Also, if the bank borrows 25 percent of the money it needs from the insurance industry and then the money supply from that industry dries up, the bank loses a valuable source and its liquidity is severely affected.

In terms of instruments, a small market share enhances trading liquidity in the secondary market. If 25 percent of all negotiable certificates of deposit (CDs) traded in the market come from our bank, the market participants will be less inclined to buy additional CDs from us because investors also want to diversify their investments.

We want to retain our ability to take fresh money from the market at any time and also want the market to be eager to buy our liability instruments. This is similar to the situation in a fishpond with hungry fish in it. When one throws a piece of bread into the pond, the fish come from all sides to grab it. That is the situation we want to have in the financial market. Fish that are fed all the time may not respond to our bread crumbs.

Having a small market share in sources and instruments enhances the liquidity we gain by being diversified. However, this should not be interpreted to mean that the smaller the market share, the better. It is important to keep the bank's name in circulation and maintain contacts with professional traders so that the bank stays informed about market activity and ensures the availability of credit lines. The bank has to use available lines periodically to make sure they remain open.

One technique is to have a relatively short-tenored borrowing and at maturity pay it back and borrow from the next investor who has a line for the bank. When the lenders want to roll over the loan at maturity, the bank wants to be able to say, "No, at the moment it doesn't suit us; we have to pay you back," rather than saying, "Please roll over the loan because we need money badly for a longer period."

In summary, it is important to have many sources, many instruments with which to tap the sources, and a small market share in each source and instrument without going to the extreme of zero market share. We want to use available lines to keep our name in circulation and ensure that lines are always available.

Maturities. On the liability side, we want to stretch the tenors, making the maturities longer. We also want to consciously stagger deposit maturities, which means there has to be a proactive management to avoid a concentration of those maturities on a given day or even in a particular week.

Depending on the historical rollover behavior of customers and our expectations of the business environment, we may be able to convert the maturities of liabilities from legal contractual maturities to actuarial maturities. For example, savings accounts can be withdrawn at any time, and so the contractual maturity of those accounts is available on demand. However, if we analyze the actual withdrawal patterns and rollover behaviors of the past, we may be able to convert the contractual maturities (which may be "demand") into actuarial maturities (which may be 6 or 12 months). That allows us to treat a percentage of the savings accounts as if it were 1-year money or even longer. The same is true for checking account balances, other demand items, and even time deposits that often are actuarially "evergreen" deposits (1- or 3-month deposits that are rolled over continually).

Liability Profile. A liability profile is a summary chart of liquidity characteristics (Exhibit 12-1). The columns from left to right show the different sources and instruments, fictitious volume numbers, and the percentages of the mix, which show where there is a concentration of a particular source or instrument in the portfolio. In this example there is no concentration of a source or instrument.

Instrument / Source	Volume $ MM	% Mix	Mkt. Share %	Average Tenor Days
Deposits		25		
– Demand	175	7	1	1
– Savings	250	10	2	30
– Time at Market	75	3	3	60
– Time off Market	125	5	4	90
CDs		25		
- Up to 6 Months	250	10	11	100
- Over 6 Months	375	15	18	270
Bankers' Accept.	250	10	40	120
Interbank		20		
- Call	100	4	6	1
- Notice	75	3	90	7
- Time	325	13	10	60
FX Swaps		10		
- Banks	50	2	6	180
- Central Bank	75	3	10	90
- Customer Forwards	125	5	9	60
Other	150	6		
Capital	100	4		
TOTAL	2,500	100%		

Exhibit 12-1. Local currency liability profile.

Next there is the percentage of market share, where you will notice a concentration of the interbank "notice" money. (A predetermined time period is observed after notice has been given before the money may be withdrawn.) We assume that this bank introduced this new product to the market and that this is why there is a large market share. In this situation, a high market share is justified. As other market participants begin to copy our behavior, the market share will decrease.

The tenor is shown last. Here it is important to distinguish between two types of maturities: average maturities in terms of the *original life* of the instrument and average maturities in terms of the *remaining life* of the instrument. For example, when we are establishing a business and funding plan for the next year, average maturities on different instruments refer to the original life of the instruments (7-day deposit, 1-year deposit, etc.). When we analyze our liquidity in a tight money market, we want to know the remaining life of the liabilities: the dates when deposits mature. In this case, the original life of each liability is not relevant and the numbers given represent the remaining life of each instrument or source.

This liability profile is a snapshot taken on a single day. By comparing it to the same summary 1 week ago, 1 month ago, 3 months ago, and 1 year ago, we can gain a historical perspective and recognize trends which we may find acceptable or unacceptable. In the latter case, steps must be taken to reverse an undesirable trend.

Standby Lines. Standby lines—provided to our bank by other banks or provided by our bank to others—are lines of credit that carry different degrees of commitment. In fact, most standby lines are not really commitments at all. Lines that we assume exist on the basis of past experience, that are often offered verbally without a commitment, or that are contingent on the counterparty having money to lend are not reliable sources of funds. An unconditional written commitment with a commitment fee may have some reliability as long as the lending party has the money when we need it.

One should avoid providing standby lines to others. If one does provide them, one should charge very healthy fees, certainly much more than the $\frac{1}{8}$ or $\frac{1}{4}$ percent p.a. fees that are common in the marketplace.

Liquid Assets Management

Liquidity on the asset side is accomplished through the sale of individual assets and the securitization of assets. We begin the discussion of liquid assets management by making a distinction between asset *sales* and asset *securitization.* Suppose a bank lends $100 million for 90 days to IBM in exchange for a promissory note; then the bank decides to sell the promissory note to an investor. This is an example of asset sales. The bank has an asset—the loan to IBM as evidenced by the promissory note—and sells it. Asset securitization is a situation where a bank bundles many loans to create a new security which legally represents all the loans and then sells the newly created security. The best-known example is the mortgage-backed security, which is *one* security backed by *several* mortgages. All asset sales and securitization techniques were developed to improve the capital/asset ratio. Only recently have these techniques been used to improve liquidity.

Obviously, when a single or securitized asset is sold, there is a positive impact on liquidity: A bank sells a piece of paper representing the asset and gets cash. An asset sale also may affect the capital/asset ratio and profitability. When a bank makes a loan, it should prepare documentation that is conducive to the easy sale or securitization of the asset even if that is not the immediate intention. It is important to create complete securitization-friendly documentation at the initiation of the loan; not later, when it is much more difficult to obtain.

Impact on Capital/Asset Ratio and Profitability. In any securitization management should know whether the dominant reason is to improve liquidity or improve the capital ratio. This will determine whether the sale is executed with or without recourse. When a bank sells an asset *without* recourse—which means that if the borrower does not pay, the third-party investor suffers the loss—the asset is removed from the balance sheet and the capital/asset ratio improves. In other words, an unchanged amount of capital appears as a greater percentage of the reduced balance sheet. If a bank sells an asset *with* recourse, there is still a positive impact on liquidity but the capital/asset ratio is not necessarily improved because all or part of the asset is retained on the balance sheet.

The objective of selling single or securitized assets must be very clear. If liquidity is the dominant reason, it may be better to sell the asset *with* recourse because the funding costs may be lower and therefore the retained profits from the loan may be higher. If the driving force is a need to improve the capital/asset ratio, the asset must be sold *without* recourse. The question is: How eager is management to improve the capital/asset ratio at the expense of a reduction in earnings? Strictly from a liquidity management viewpoint, a bank can afford to sell the loan with recourse because of the positive impact on liquidity.

The impact on profitability depends on the price at which the asset is sold. Let us look at an example involving a 5-year revolving loan:

Eurodollar term loan price	LIBOR plus 1 percent
Typical funding cost	LIBOR
Profit	1 percent

Obviously, if this loan could be sold without recourse at LIBOR, the bank could collect the profit up front and eliminate the liquidity risk. In addition, the bank would have fewer risk assets (less credit risk) and an improved capital ratio. However, if this loan can be sold at only $5/8$ percent over LIBOR, the bank's managers have to ask themselves whether they are so eager to improve the capital ratio that they are willing to give up more than half the earnings from this loan. It is important to look at the price and evaluate whether the trade-off for improving liquidity and/or the capital ratio justifies the sacrifice of profitability.

Maturities. An analysis of maturities must be done for assets as well as for liabilities. Can the loan really be collected at maturity, and if it can, what will be the impact on earnings? From a liquidity viewpoint it may be very desirable to collect a loan, but this may not be such a good idea from an earnings viewpoint. Another consideration is the impact on the relationship. For example, if the bank has evergreen loans on the books— short-term (1- or 3-month) loans that are rolled over again and again for years—and tries to collect those loans from the customer, this may affect the relationship negatively.

The contractual maturities of assets also may be converted into realistic *actuarial maturities*, depending on one's view of the business climate. While converting contractual maturities into actuarial maturities has a positive impact on the *liability* side (because longer liabilities make the bank more liquid), this exercise has the opposite effect on the *asset* side. When short-term loans are rolled over and converted from contractual to actuarial maturities, maturities on the asset side also get longer, which makes the bank less liquid.

To summarize the management of assets through sales and securitization, the idea is to have assets in a liquid form. There is always a positive impact on liquidity when a bank sells an asset. Whether there is a positive impact on the capital/asset ratio depends on whether there is recourse to the bank, and the impact on profitability depends on the price at which the bank sells the asset. Shorter asset maturities make the bank more liquid but can have a negative impact on earnings.

Contingency Funding Plan

The third element in liquidity management is the contingency funding plan, which is a written plan for maintaining liquidity under adverse conditions. The contingency funding plan is based on assumptions about possible environmental abnormalities and includes strategies for maintaining liquidity in each scenario a bank may face.

Uses of Contingency Funding Plans.   If a bank operates in a country that places constraints on the flow of funds between significant areas within the same organization, separate contingency funding plans must be produced for those areas. This prevents a situation in which the organization as a whole has sufficient cash but the cash is in the "wrong pocket" and cannot be made available to another part of the bank which is starving for cash. An example of such a funds flow constraint in the United States is Federal Reserve Regulation 23-A, which prevents banks from lending to their parents as a one-bank holding company.

Contingency funding plans also are prepared for systemic and bank-specific problems. For example, one contingency scenario may assume that there is plenty of cash in the market but that the bank's name is not popular in the market and the counterparties do not want to give the bank cash. In this scenario, we might simulate our funding needs if rating agencies would announce a two-notch downgrade of the bank. Another contingency scenario may assume that our name is OK but the market as a whole is very tight. In this case we need two different contingency funding plans that are based on the reasons for the market's tightness. In one scenario we assume that the central bank is tightening in an effort to fight inflation. The other scenario assumes an external event affecting the local market and causing massive capital outflows.[1] The reason for this distinction is that if the money market is tight because of an external event, we can rely on the central bank, whose job it is to help in these types of situations. However, if the central bank is the reason for the tightening in the market—it may be fighting inflation—we obviously cannot expect any help from the central bank and therefore must have other contingency funding sources available (see Exhibit 12-2).

Finally, contingency funding plans also should assume different survival horizons, such as assuming a shortage for 1 week, 3 months, and 6 months.

Contingency Funding Plan Process.   To prepare a contingency funding plan, all assets are evaluated to determine which ones are collectable and at what time. In this conversion process from contractual to actuarial maturities, a bank must avoid upsetting the relationship with its borrowing customers. It also will make realistic scenario-related runoff assump-

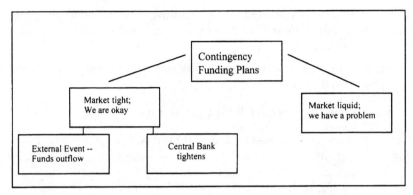

Exhibit 12-2. Different contingency funding plans.

tions about its liabilities. In this context, banks have found, for example, that deposits on which no interest or a below-market interest rate is paid tend to be more stable than are deposits that command the top market rate at all times. Customers who insist on earning top market rates on their deposits are sharper and more proactive and will withdraw money from the bank immediately when there is bad news in the market about the bank. In addition, we identify which of our unused sources of funds we can tap and may even test them to see if our assumptions are correct.

Part of this process on the asset side is that we *perfectionize* the documentation. A good example is mortgages. Assume that mortgages are eligible as collateral for borrowing from the central bank. However, there is no point in having, say, $1 billion in mortgages distributed among the 100 branches and subsidiaries a bank may have in a given country and thinking that the central bank will give the bank $700 million against those mortgages. Perfectionizing is the process of bundling the mortgages together so that they can be used as collateral with the central bank. In fact, it may be wise to borrow against these mortgages occasionally to assure that the process works. In this case, instead of selling the mortgages, the bank is establishing them as collateral and borrowing against them.

Another important aspect of planning for contingency funding is clearly establishing criteria that trigger the beginning of a contingency situation and specifying exactly what needs to be done at that point. The required actions include the following:

- Advise the corporate treasurer and other appropriate senior people.

- Identify the planned contingency situation that comes closest to what actually happened in the market.

■ Review the actions outlined in the contingency funding plan and determine whether modification of the plan is required to cope with the current situation.

■ Establish and obtain approval for a new contingency funding plan to be followed in this case.

To summarize the contingency funding plan process:

1. Develop plans for assumed unusual situations. Create separate plans for different units if there are funds flow constraints, for systemic problems, and for bank-specific problems. Analyze the liquidity implications for different time periods of survival.

2. Analyze existing assets and liabilities in light of each assumed scenario to determine how many assets can be converted into cash and at what time and to establish realistic scenario-related runoff assumptions on the liability side.

3. Mobilize all untapped sources of funds to determine what new money can be brought into the bank from other banks, from customers, or from the central bank.

Banks with operations in other countries must have contingency funding plans for each of those countries. They should not rely on liquidity sources at headquarters and ignore proper funding in their overseas businesses for the following reasons:

■ Earnings reported by and remitted from those countries may be overstated. Liquidity costs money, and if a business in a given country does not follow liquidity-enhancing policies and absorb the associated costs, the earnings generated in those countries will be overstated.

■ If a country-specific problem is causing illiquidity in a particular overseas branch or subsidiary, the parent bank is forced to inject cash into this country when it is least inclined to do so. The reason for the country's problem could be of a political or economic nature and could create a situation where under normal circumstances one would never lend fresh money into that country (see Chap. 10).

■ If it is a bank-specific problem, there will be a global run on this bank's liquidity in all the countries where it operates and at headquarters. In this case the parent bank should have provided for huge contingency liquidity reserves to handle the problem at home and at all the overseas places where it does business.

It is important for one person in each bank to understand the entire cash flow of the bank as well as the different contingency funding plans.

There may be different businesses in a given country, and each business may have its own treasurer. However, there should be only one country treasurer who reports in this capacity to the country head, and these two people are responsible for the liquidity in that country.

It is clearly desirable to pursue prudent liquidity management and contingency funding planning on a country-by-country basis. This is even more desirable because regulators around the world increasingly demand contingency funding plans in addition to imposing a host of other control and fraud-avoidance policies.

> *Contingency funding planning is like a fire drill. It must be taken seriously—then and only then will it work.*

Managing Funding Liquidity Risk

The last section examined the process for achieving funding liquidity to assure a bank's survival and growth. Now we turn to the tools used to manage funding liquidity and control funding liquidity risk. You will see why there is a cost associated with funding liquidity risk in a business-as-usual environment and in a contingency environment and why a bank should require compensation for that cost from the users of liquidity.

Managing Liquidity in a Business-as-Usual Environment

Liquidity can be controlled by limiting the maximum amounts of funding that will be needed during different time periods under business-as-usual conditions. In other words, limits are set for the maximum cumulative outflow (MCO) per time period, assuming a normal environment. A prospective cumulative cash flow can be positive (inflow) or negative (outflow). If it is positive, it represents a bank's expectation that it will have prospective liquidity available for lending. If it is negative, it represents the amount of prospective funding (borrowings) the bank expects to require for certain predetermined future dates. Limits are given for these negative or maximum cumulative outflows.

Maximum Cumulative Outflow Report. The information needed to monitor and enforce liquidity limits on a daily basis is gathered in a cumulative cash flow report—the Maximum Cumulative Outflow report. The

MCO report essentially is a runoff profile of all on- and off-balance-sheet accounts. It does not include new business, which is managed as part of the Funding Plan, which forecasts the future balance sheet structure. However, it does include some rollovers of current balance sheet items (refer to the material on actuarial maturities earlier in this chapter).

The format of the MCO report is a matrix that shows the runoff of all on- and off-balance-sheet assets (sources of funds) and liabilities (uses of funds) for different maturity brackets. Horizontally, assets and liabilities are grouped in sections according to the type of assets and liabilities. Vertically, the outstandings (O/S) in each account and all their runoffs at the different maturity brackets are listed.

A simplified example of this report is illustrated in Exhibit 12-3. The categories of assets and liabilities included in the example are

- *Third-party on-balance sheet assets and liabilities*—all activities with counterparties outside the bank itself, representing the core of the balance sheet

- *Intercompany on-balance-sheet assets and liabilities (if applicable)*—borrowings from and placements with other branches or business units within the bank

	O/S	O/N	2/7 days	8/15 days	16 - EOM	Mth 2	Mth 3	Mths 4/6	Mths 7/12	Year 2	>2 Years
THIRD PARTY (3P)											
Liabilities (uses)											
Assets (sources)											
3P Sources-Uses	0	0	0	0	0	0	0	0	0	0	0
INTERCOMPANY (IC)											
Liabilities (uses)											
Assets (sources)											
IC Sources-Uses	0	0	0	0	0	0	0	0	0	0	0
3P/IC Sources-Uses	0	0	0	0	0	0	0	0	0	0	0
THIRD PARTY (OFFB)											
Liabilities (uses)											
Assets (sources)											
OFFB Sources-Uses	0	0	0	0	0	0	0	0	0	0	0
3P/IC/OFFB Sources-Uses	0	0	0	0	0	0	0	0	0	0	0
INCREMENTAL (INC)											
Liabilities (uses)											
Assets (sources)											
INC Sources-Uses	0	0	0	0	0	0	0	0	0	0	0
NET CASH FLOW	0	0	0	0	0	0	0	0	0	0	0
MCO	0	0	0	0	0	0	0	0	0	0	0

Exhibit 12-3. Simplified MCO report.

- *Off-balance-sheet assets and liabilities*—all cash flows generated mainly by derivatives plus interest payments, margin calls, and cross-currency principal exchanges
- *Incremental sources and uses of funds*—contingent sources and uses of funds

Maturity brackets are detailed for the near term (overnight, 2 to 7 days, 8 to 15 days, 16 to 30 days) and are less detailed for the longer term (month 2, month 3, months 4 through 6, months 7 through 12, year 2, and more than 2 years). When I ask people what they think is the most important day in liquidity management, they usually say year end, quarter end, or month end. All these answers are wrong, because the correct answer is *TODAY.* If we do not make it through today, we no longer have to worry about the end of the month or year. The second most important day is tomorrow, and so on. This is reminiscent of the German soccer team in the final tournament for the World Cup. The Germans said, "In the semifinal we will play Italy, and in the final we will play Brazil," and then they lost in the first round of the elimination tournament to a country relatively unknown in soccer circles. In elimination tournaments, the most important match is the next one, because if a team loses in that round, it does not have to worry about the final anymore. The same is true for liquidity management, where short-term liquidity requires much closer attention than does longer-term liquidity.

> *Day-to-day funding liquidity is more important than earnings.*

The last two lines of the report show the consolidated cash flow for a business unit. The first line represents the net cash flow per time bracket, and the next one represents the cumulative cash flow. The maximum cumulative negative cash flow is the MCO.

Exhibit 12-4 shows how the cash flows resulting from a third-party money market gap transaction—3-month $100 placement funded with an overnight (O/N) 1-day borrowing—are reflected in the MCO report.

Section 1. Place 3-month $100—an inflow (+) in the 3-month bracket. Borrow overnight $100—an outflow (−) in the O/N bracket.

Section 2. There is no intercompany activity.

Section 3. There is no off-balance-sheet activity.

Section 4. Incremental sources and uses of funds apply only to adverse scenarios. In a business-as-usual scenario, new activity is not included.

	O/S	O/N	2/7 days	8/15 days	16 - EOM	Mth 2	Mth 3	Mths 4/6	Mths 7/12	Year 2	>2 Years
THIRD PARTY (3P)											
Liabilities (uses)	100	100									
Assets (sources)	100						100				
3P Sources-Uses	0	-100	0	0	0	0	100	0	0	0	0
INTERCOMPANY (IC)											
Liabilities (uses)											
Assets (sources)											
IC Sources-Uses	0	0	0	0	0	0	0	0	0	0	0
3P/IC Sources-Uses	0	-100	0	0	0	0	100	0	0	0	0
THIRD PARTY (OFFB)											
Liabilities (uses)											
Assets (sources)											
OFFB Sources-Uses	0	0	0	0	0	0	0	0	0	0	0
3P/IC/OFFB Sources-Uses	0	-100	0	0	0	0	100	0	0	0	0
INCREMENTAL (INC)											
Liabilities (uses)											
Assets (sources)											
INC Sources-Uses	0	0	0	0	0	0	0	0	0	0	0
NET CASH FLOW	0	-100	0	0	0	0	100	0	0	0	0
MCO	0	-100	-100	-100	-100	-100	0	0	0	0	0

Exhibit 12-4. MCO report: third-party money market gap.

As you can see, the last line (MCO) indicates that $100 funding (because the cumulative cash flow is negative) will be required from the first day until the third month.

MCO Limits. MCO limits are established for significant individual business units within a country and for the country as a whole. If a bank operates in foreign countries, MCO limits should be established for each subsidiary. In this situation the bank periodically should pull together the cumulative outflows from all the countries at a central point and establish a master cumulative cash flow report which will show the institutional cumulative outflows on a currency-by-currency basis. In organizations and countries with cash flow constraints, separate MCO limits must be established for areas in which there is no funds flow constraint.

MCO limits also are set per tenor and per currency. However, since the MCO report has a focus on liquidity, it is possible to net out positive and negative flows for major liquid currencies. For example, there may be a negative cash flow in pounds and a positive cash flow in dollars for the same maturity bracket as a result of a foreign exchange swap position. If the pound outflow is offset by the dollar inflow, the MCO report will show a net zero cash flow and there will be no funding liquidity risk even though there is still trading liquidity risk.

The control for netting out positive and negative cash flows of different currencies for liquidity purposes is called the universal MCO limit. There is no limit for individual currencies; instead, there is an MCO limit for net cash flows irrespective of currency. The universal MCO system is applied only to highly liquid currencies which can be converted easily into other currencies.

Let us look at an example to clarify this concept. Suppose you are in Japan and have only US$50 in your pocket. You have no liquidity because you cannot spend the dollars, but you can solve the liquidity problem by exchanging the $50 for the yen equivalent. If you did not have the dollars, you would have to solve your liquidity problem by borrowing yen, which would be much more difficult. Purchasing a currency is easier than borrowing, and that is why the universal MCO is allowed.

The MCO report has to be prepared with actuarial maturities. Otherwise, the savings and demand deposits, which are actually very stable, and the continuously rolled over loans will distort the MCO report.

Triggers on Liquidity Ratios. Day-to-day cash management of the local currency over the very near term requires more real-time information than is contained in the MCO report. Practical considerations prohibit the inclusion in the MCO and the limit-setting process of some items, such as customer demand account transactions, because their timing and frequency cannot be forecast with any level of certainty.

The MCO is not designed to replace the unique process of managing the daily funds flows. A better way to manage day-to-day cash flows is through triggers on some liquidity ratios which are designed to manage near-term liquidity risk (up to 30 days). Some ratios that may be considered include

- Maximum overnight borrowing as a percentage of total assets
- Maximum percentage of liabilities from large fund providers
- Maximum percentage of short-term liabilities from interbank sources
- Minimum percentage of realizable liquid assets to total assets

The MCO report, MCO limits, and triggers on liquidity ratios are tools for managing funding liquidity in a normal environment. However, one also must be prepared to manage liquidity in an adverse environment.

Managing Liquidity in
a Contingency Environment

Let us bring the contingency funding plan together with the MCO report. There should be two types of MCO reports: the MCO report that assumes business as usual, which was discussed in the previous section, and the MCO report in a contingency or adverse environment. In the second report it is assumed that some loans are not collectable, that several types of deposits will be withdrawn, and that on the cash supply side, sources that are not used ordinarily may be tapped.

The purpose of preparing the contingency funding plan and the MCO report in a contingency scenario is to show how, even in an adverse environment, a bank can survive for a stipulated period, usually 3 to 6 months. The ultimate purpose of a contingency funding plan is to prevent a net shortage of cash, which would force a bank to borrow at the central bank.

It must be emphasized that liquidity costs money. Let us review our analysis of managing liquidity on the asset and liability sides. Liquid assets usually have lower yields than do nonliquid assets. Consequently, when we keep additional liquid assets for liquidity purposes, we incur a cost. Different sources of funds have different costs, and if we ignore liquidity, we will take all our money from the cheapest source. Not tapping the cheapest source of funds for liquidity purposes means that we have a higher cost. The same is true for instruments. If we ignore liquidity, we will take all our money through the cheapest instruments. Not doing that means that liquidity has a cost.

In terms of maturities on the liability side, if there is a normal upward-sloping yield curve, longer-tenored deposits will be more expensive than those with shorter maturities. If we stretch the maturities of our deposits for liquidity purposes, we are paying up on the yield curve and incur an additional cost. In other words, if we want to ignore liquidity and maximize profits, we must borrow overnight money from professional sources such as other banks. However, if we do this, we may suffer the fate of the bank in the following story.

When a large U.S. bank went bankrupt several years ago, it had 40 percent of its liabilities in short-term Eurodollar deposits from the interbank market. When the first news about problems in this bank hit the market, none of those Eurodollar deposits were rolled over, and the bank had no chance to survive. Other banks had similar problems, but with a much broader retail deposit base, they were able to weather the storm.

All we have said about liquidity costing money is well known to senior bank managers. However, when there is earnings pressure and funding decisions have to be made, it is very tempting in an environment with an upward-sloping yield curve to take money for shorter and shorter periods, assuming that the bank can "get away with it." This is a very dangerous practice and should be avoided.

> *Liquidity costs money. However, not having it costs the life of a bank.*

A bank may lose 10 percent of its capital on bad loans or in financial trading and survive. If the bank cannot meet its contractual obligations, the game is over.

In 1994 Mexico auctioned government bonds with maturities between 3 months and 18 months. The 18-month paper was heavily oversubscribed because the market wanted to give Mexico a lot of money for 18 months. However, Mexico curtailed the 18-month issue and took the money at shorter maturities. A few months later, after the devaluation and massive capital outflows, Mexico was eagerly looking for longer-term money and had difficulty finding it.

> *Liquidity must be taken when the market offers it, not just when we want it.*

It should be clear that liquidity costs money. As a result, senior bank managers should not hesitate to charge a price for liquidity to the parts of the bank that consume liquidity (see "Return on Liquidity Risk," below).

Liquidity Ratios

To maintain liquidity, some banks have introduced structural liquidity guidelines for "mandatory term funding." With this system, a certain percentage of all third-party assets, irrespective of maturity, are funded with money that has a remaining life on an actuarial basis of at least 1 year. Since there is a high probability that the original borrowers will roll the loans over, the original tenors of the loans are ignored. If the loans are paid off, the bank most likely will lend the money to somebody else. In other words, since the balance sheet never shrinks, a bank may simply say that, for example, 25 percent of all loans must be funded with money that has a *remaining* life on an actuarial basis of at least 1 year. This "25 percent rule" may apply to loans that are in perfect shape. As soon as there is a question about the quality of a loan, the percentage will go up. When a bank is not collecting any interest on a loan, the percentage may be as high as 75 percent.

To fund a minimum percentage of all loans with money that has a remaining life of at least 1 year, it may be necessary to take 2-year to 3-year money. The yield curve environment, which usually creates higher costs in the funding portfolio, must be reflected in the interest charged on loans. This is a powerful reminder that liquidity costs money.

By combining all these liquidity management tools—the MCO report, the contingency funding plan, and mandatory term financing—a bank should be able to survive for 6 months without being forced to borrow from the central bank. In addition, a bank can improve its funding ability for 6 months in a contingency environment by having more liquid assets.

Return on Liquidity Risk

Return on price risk is identified through the relationship between value at risk/earnings at risk and budgeted profits (see Chap. 6). Similarly, in the credit area the bank converts meaningless volume and notional amounts into meaningful estimates of loan equivalent amounts for which it establishes minimum profit margins.

Similarly, the bank wants to know the return on liquidity risk. The risk of not having liquidity pushes people into longer-tenored liabilities, more diversified sources and instruments, and more liquid assets. This behavior has a cost. When we price term loans, we take into account the cost of liquidity to determine the required amount of profit. For example, consider a 5-year revolving-term loan that gets repriced every 3 months. In the past, the markup over the interbank rate was just enough to compensate for the credit risk. However, the 5-year loan involves liquidity risk in addition to the credit risk. It is a commitment of liquidity for 5 years, and the assumption of liquidity risk also requires compensation. If loans traditionally were made at 1 percent over LIBOR to compensate for the credit risk, perhaps the charge would be $1\frac{1}{4}$ percent, consisting of 1 percent for credit risk and an additional $\frac{1}{4}$ percent for liquidity risk.

The first cost of liquidity is the elimination of gapping profits on a certain percentage of the loans. If the interest rate on a loan is reset every 3 months, from a price risk viewpoint, the most conservative form of funding is to take a deposit for 3 months. However, it is possible to fund the loan with an even shorter deposit—a 1-month deposit against a 3-month interest rate period—and this provides an additional opportunity for gapping profits. Suppose there is a requirement that a minimum of 25 percent of all performing loans be funded with money that has a remaining life of at least 1 year—in other words, the money is taken for a tenor longer than the interest period. This requirement provides for liquidity but eliminates the opportunity for gapping profits on that 25 percent. The second cost of liquidity is the cost of taking money for a longer period of time than the interest period of a revolving-term loan (3 months in the example). There is a yield curve cost—a higher cost of money strictly from a maturity viewpoint.

Consider a situation where we lend long in one currency and borrow short in another currency, therefore acquiring all three risks: credit risk because we are lending, liquidity risk because we are lending long and borrowing short, and price risk because we are borrowing unhedged in a foreign currency.

In such a case we need compartmentalization of risks and rewards; each risk has to be identified, and the return has to be sufficient to compensate for the assumption of each risk. A decision may be made to not seek compensation for each risk because of customer relations or for another reason, but at the very least, the profit margin required to justify the assumption of all these different types of risk should be identified.

Role of the Asset and Liability Management Committee

The role of a bank's asset and liability management committee (ALCO) is to maintain adequate liquidity for the survival and growth of the business. The members of ALCO should include the president, the corporate treasurer, the financial controller, and the managers of all the major businesses in the bank. The committee members review the liability profile to compare the most recent numbers with the corresponding historical numbers for the past 3-, 6-, and 12-month periods. They also may look at more detailed profiles for specific sources and instruments that are significant for the bank. In addition, ALCO should track on a monthly basis the volumes and types of assets and liabilities projected in business plans and budgets against the actuals. For liquidity purposes, it will look at the volume of liquid assets and scrutinize the development of liabilities, considering all aspects of liquidity management on the liability side as discussed earlier in this book: sources, instruments, market shares, and maturities.

Another important responsibility of ALCO is to set the interest rates used in the transfer pool. This pool absorbs excess funds from parts of the bank with more deposits than loans (suppliers) and provides funds to parts of the bank with more loans than deposits (users). Obviously, the level of these rates often is disputed. The suppliers want higher rates, and the users want lower rates. The correct pool rate should reflect the marginal cost of funds, which is the cost of readily available funds for the respective tenors. If an institution has excess funds, the definition of the marginal cost of funds will be "investment yields readily available for the respective tenors."

The marginal cost of funds may be dramatically different from the average cost of funds, which must never be used to set the pool rate. If Treasury has taken deposits in the past and market interest rates are now 1 percent higher, loan and deposit pricing must be based on the now-prevailing higher level with Treasury recognizing a profit. In the same situation, if interest rates have dropped, the lower level must be used for pool rates, with Treasury recognizing a loss.

Periodically, Treasury should provide fixed pool rates for the popular tenors, such as 7 days, monthly, quarterly, and annually. In addition, there should be a floating pool rate to accommodate assets priced on a floating-rate basis, such as Prime rate or Base rate. The pool rate should be the same for suppliers and users; i.e., there should be no spread for Treasury.

For capital adequacy purposes, ALCO will look at the volume of risk-adjusted assets and the size of the capital, including the most recently retained earnings and dividends paid. This exercise is really focused on managing the "sweet spot"[2] capital ratio each bank should establish as a target. This means that in terms of capital, a bank wants to have enough that it is accepted by the world without question but not too much, because if it exceeds the amount defined as enough, it has unnecessarily low leverage, which makes it more difficult to achieve attractive returns on equity. Sweet spot management is one of the most important exercises in the bank. It begins with business plans and budgets and must be maintained continuously in the monthly reviews of the business. Sweet spot management definitely requires that the volume of risk-adjusted assets be part of business plans and budgets. (Also see page 264.)

Banks with large amounts of assets denominated in foreign currencies must translate those assets into local currency. This translation may lead to increases or decreases in assets, which disturb the management of the sweet spot capital ratio. The solution to this problem is to maintain equity capital proportionately in the same currencies as assets. For example, if an American bank has half its assets in yen, it should also maintain half its capital in yen. A 20 percent appreciation of the yen will produce a 10 percent increase in total assets as well as total capital, but leave the sweet spot capital ratio unchanged. A depreciation of the yen will decrease assets and capital by 10 percent and again leave the capital ratio unchanged. This process is referred to as hedging the capital ratio.

If we project risk assets, earnings, and dividends, we will know the amount of capital and retained earnings available at year end. If the resulting capital ratio exceeds the targeted sweet spot, we must decide what to do with the excess cash and must choose among the following alternatives:

- Grow risk assets in our existing businesses
- Buy another company if that complements our overall strategy
- Increase dividend payouts if that does not disturb the established dividend policy
- Buy back our own stock, a practice that has become popular in a world that increasingly focuses on shareholder value

Before leaving the subject of ALCO, we will propose a new name for this committee to highlight the need to focus on balance sheet management, including risk-adjusted assets as defined by the Basle Accord and the size of capital. Very often a change in name also sharpens the focus, and for that reason our preferred name is BALCO, or the Balance Sheet and Liability Management Committee. Another possibility is to use the acronym ALCCO, standing for Asset, Liability, and Capital Committee.

This management process for the corporate balance sheet is preferable to having decentralized businesses in the same country or even in several countries that do not communicate and may even be competing with each other while contributing to a single aggregate balance sheet. A decentralized organization is acceptable for price risk purposes, business strategies, and earnings, but for liquidity and balance sheet purposes there can be no decentralization. That is why the country treasurer has to make sure that the country liquidity remains as it is outlined in the business plan and that the *appearance of the balance sheet is built into the funding plan and is part of the budget.*

In the past, the balance sheet often was a derivative of completely decentralized activities in the same currency and the same country, and when all these activities were totaled up in one balance sheet for the bank, there was a surprise factor. Now the activities in each country must be thoroughly planned and coordinated. When everyone tries to reach the same goal, the result may vary from the goal, but it will be closer if each country has a plan for the volumes and types of assets and knows how it wants to fund them.

Summary: Managing Funding Liquidity Risk

Banks set limits on the amount of cumulative negative cash flows (outflows) for a given period (MCO limits). These negative cash flows are monitored and enforced through information gathered in the MCO report. Daily compliance with limits may be assured through a close analysis of near-term cash flows and the setting of triggers on liquidity ratios. MCO limits may be set irrespective of the currency when one is dealing with easily convertible currencies. These limits are known as universal MCO limits.

Liquidity limits should be complemented by an analysis of the contingency funding plan, which is the plan for surviving under stressful environments during 3- to 6-month periods for each country and for the bank as a whole. This is done by analyzing liquidity, assuming that some assets may not be collected, some liabilities may be withdrawn early, and fully committed uses and sources of funds are paid or received. If a bank is not able to survive under this plan, the net cumulative outflow may require borrowing from the central bank, which should be avoided on a planned basis and occur only in emergencies. MCO limits should be cut to force more conservative funding.

Trading Liquidity

At the beginning of this chapter we identified two types of liquidity risk. We then described *funding* liquidity risk (the risk that a bank cannot meet its contractual liabilities), the tools used to manage it, and the cost associated with it. This section examines the impact of *trading* liquidity on funding liquidity and the risks associated with trading liquidity.

What Is Trading Liquidity?

Trading liquidity is the ability to instantly liquidate price risk positions without

- Changing market prices
- Attracting the attention of other market participants
- Compromising on counterparty quality

If we want to sell 100 shares of IBM at the New York Stock Exchange, we can do it without changing the market prices and without attracting the attention of other market participants, particularly the central bank. We do not want to be seen in the market as making huge waves that are causing others to say, "Oh, MegaBank is selling." We also do not want to be in the position of having to deal with normally unacceptable counterparties just to be able to liquidate a price risk position.

Trading liquidity affects funding liquidity because trading liquidity gives a bank the capacity to convert assets into cash easily. If it turns out that for one reason or another assets cannot be sold quickly and easily, substandard trading liquidity may hurt funding liquidity.

In addition to solving funding problems, it may be necessary to liquidate an asset to protect earnings. For example, suppose we have a position in securities or foreign exchange and our market intelligence tells us the price is going down. Although we want to liquidate the position, we may find out that the position is too large to sell or that the market has one-sided liquidity. In this case we lack trading liquidity and therefore are stuck with a position we no longer want.

The impact on price risk of not having trading liquidity can be compared to sitting on the railroad tracks, seeing the train coming, and not being able to jump off.

How Is Trading Liquidity Achieved?

Trading liquidity is achieved by avoiding price risk positions with specific characteristics that relate to the size of the position relative to a marketable amount. It cannot be stated that a $2 million position is always too big, because it depends on the situation. There are some characteristics of price risk positions that can be avoided to help preserve trading liquidity:

- Large percentage of market share

  This can mean market share of the total market or market share of a specific trading month in futures (open interest indicates how many contracts are outstanding in a given trading month). If we have a very large percentage of the market share, it means that very few people will want to take the other side.

- Infrequently traded currencies and instruments

- Tenors of unusual length

- One-sided liquidity in the market

  Some commodities and financial contracts are very easy to buy but difficult to sell; others are very easy to sell but difficult to buy. If a position can be built up easily in the market, we may believe the market is liquid; then, when we try to liquidate the position, we find out that the liquidity was really one-sided. It is easy to lose a sense of proportion.

- Maturities at an exposed time of the day, week, month, or year

  A very large position maturing on Friday before a long weekend decreases trading liquidity because most traders have left for the weekend or are on vacation and the markets are not particularly active.

Trading liquidity is achieved through good credit standing. It is important to be perceived as a good counterparty so that other people will want to provide lines for trading activities.

What Is the Risk of Not Having Trading Liquidity?

Obviously, there are risks associated with not having trading liquidity. These risks include price risk, the risk of adverse changes in the marketplace; funding liquidity risk, the risk that we will be unable to liquidate a position at any price; and franchise risk, the risk that we will attract the attention of the central bank by liquidating a large position.

Not having trading liquidity can affect the ability to do business. For example, derivative, distant-date products are often the key to the price quoted for an entire customer package. The package may include floating a bond issue for the customer, swapping the proceeds for another currency, and perhaps using another type of interest rate (derivative product) and then buying a company in Europe. The customer wants to know how much the package of services will cost. If another bank has a better credit rating and can do the cross-currency interest rate swap at a better price than our bank can, it may make the difference between our getting the entire deal and not getting it.

Summary: Trading Liquidity

Trading liquidity is the capacity to convert assets into cash easily without changing market prices, attracting the attention of other market participants, or compromising on counterparty quality. Substandard trading liquidity can hurt funding liquidity.

Having trading liquidity means taking risk positions that avoid specific characteristics relating to the size of the position. It is necessary to maintain a good image as a counterparty to assure access to credit lines for trading activities. Not having trading liquidity can hinder a bank's ability to do business.

Notes

1. This happened in early 1995 in Latin American and Asian emerging markets after the Mexican devaluation at the end of 1994. Financial managers assumed that the Mexican "tequila disease" could spill over into those financial markets. In 1997 financial problems began in Thailand and spilled over to other Asian countries and, to a lesser extent, Latin America.

2. Golfers and tennis players, particularly when they are not very good at these sports, know exactly what the sweet spot is. Once in a while they hit the ball exactly right. There is no resistance; it feels very easy, and the ball goes exactly where it is supposed to go. The same is true for the sweet spot in the capital ratio. It is just right—not too much and not too little.

13

Balance Sheet Management

In the discussion of capital adequacy in Chap. 1, we assumed a regulatory requirement of 5 percent equity capital in the balance sheet and also assumed that all assets require the same amount of capital support. We used these assumptions to emphasize the need to think in terms of risk versus return. This chapter will discuss the capital/asset ratio in greater detail to more accurately reflect reality in terms of regulatory requirements.

Risk-Weighting System

For the capital/asset ratio to reflect capital adequacy accurately, it is necessary to adjust the value of assets on and off the balance sheet to account for the amount of risk they represent. Regulators mandate a minimum capital/asset ratio based on risk-adjusted assets and require the application of a standardized risk-weighting system to those assets.

On-Balance-Sheet Risk-Weighting Categories

In 1988, under the auspices of the Bank for International Settlements (BIS) in Basle, Switzerland, central bankers met to develop a standardized system for accurately reflecting risk in the balance sheet. The result was the Agreement on International Convergency of Capital Measurement and Capital Standards, commonly known as the Basle Accord. This agreement provides standardized risk-weighting categories and classification crite-

Risk-Weighting Category	Classification Criteria
0%	– Cash in vault – Claims on, or unconditionally guaranteed by, OECD central government, including central banks and government agencies – Local currency claims on, or unconditionally guaranteed by, non-OECD central governments that are funded by local currency liabilities
20%	– Claims on, or guaranteed by, OECD banks – Claims collateralized by OECD government securities or cash – Claims on, or conditionally guaranteed by, OECD governments, including central banks and government agencies – Claims on, or guaranteed by, OECD country, state, and municipal governments
50%	– Performing first-lien mortgage loans secured by residential real estate – Public-purpose, local-government revenue bonds
100%	All other claims not qualifying for a lower risk weighting, including: – Premises and equipment – Investments in unconsolidated subsidiaries – Claims on commercial enterprises

Exhibit 13-1. Risk-weighting categories and selected classification criteria.

ria for adjusting assets to reflect the amount of risk associated with them; the adjusted assets are referred to as *risk assets.*

With this system, different percentages of risk weighting are applied to different types of assets. Cash and claims on governments have 0 percent risk weighting and therefore are not counted as risk assets. Claims on banks in countries that are members of the Organization for Economic Cooperation and Development (OECD) are considered 20 percent risk assets. (A list of OECD countries follows.) First-lien residential mortgages are calculated as 50 percent risk assets, and commercial loans as 100 percent risk assets. Exhibit 13-1 provides a more detailed summary of the risk ratings and their classification criteria.

The following countries are members of the OECD:

Australia	Iceland
Austria	Ireland
Belgium	Italy
Canada	Japan
Czech Republic	Luxembourg
Denmark	Mexico
Finland	New Zealand
France	Norway
Germany	Netherlands
Greece	Portugal

Saudi Arabia	Switzerland
Singapore	Turkey
Spain	United Kingdom
Sweden	United States

Off-Balance-Sheet Credit Conversion Categories

In addition to risk-weighting categories and classification criteria for assets, the Basle Accord provides off-balance-sheet credit conversion percentages for commitments and letters of credit as well as foreign exchange and interest rate contracts. These credit conversion percentages and the classification criteria for each category, which are summarized in Exhibits 13-2 and 13-3, convey the basic idea of risk adjusting. The details may vary periodically, and therefore the categories and criteria presented may not be totally accurate.

The table in Exhibit 13-3 contains the credit conversion percentages used as the measure of additional credit risk for foreign exchange, other commodities, and interest rate contracts. These corresponding amounts must be added to the sum of the positive mark-to-market values of the portfolio. (If the mark-to-market value is ignored, a completely different set of conversion factors must be used.)

The treatment of FX, other commodities, and interest-rate-related items requires special attention because banks are not exposed to credit risk for the full face value of these contracts. They are exposed only to the potential cost of replacing the contracts (for contracts showing positive value) if the counterparty defaults.

Credit Conversion Categories	Classification Criteria
Commitments and Letters of Credit	
100%	• Direct credit substitutes • Financial guarantees • Sales with recourse • Financial standby letters of credit
50%	• Commitments beyond one year • Performance-related standby letters of credit
20%	• Commercial letters of credit
0%	• Commitments up to one year • All unconditionally cancelable commitments

Exhibit 13-2. Credit conversion categories for off-balance-sheet commitments and letters of credit.

Credit Conversion Categories	Classification Criteria
Foreign Exchange Contracts (including Gold)	
1%	Remaining life up to one year
5%	Remaining life from one year to five years
7.5%	Remaining life over five years
Other Commodities Contracts	

Equity	Precious Metal (excl. gold)	Other Commodities	
6%	7%	10%	Remaining life up to one year
8%	7%	12%	Remaining life from one year to five years
10%	8%	15%	Remaining life over five years

Interest Rate Contracts	
0%	Remaining life up to one year
0.5%	Remaining life from one year to five years
1.5%	Remaining life over five years

Exhibit 13-3. Credit conversion categories for off-balance-sheet foreign exchange, other commodities, and interest-rate-related contracts.

The Basle Accord approached this in a manner similar to the loan equivalent methodology that was presented in Chap. 9. For each transaction, the corresponding mark-to-market value (or current loan equivalent amount) must be added to an amount that represents the potential loan equivalent amount. This potential loan equivalent amount is derived by multiplying the notional amount by the appropriate conversion factor from the table in Exhibit 13-3. The BIS calls this sum the credit equivalent amount. However, there are some differences between the BIS approach and the approach used by major market participants. The analysis is always done transaction by transaction, and without a specific netting agreement with a given counterparty, a negative mark-to-market is not allowed to offset a positive potential loan equivalent amount.

The loan equivalent amount is weighted according to the category of the counterparty, as shown in Exhibit 13-1. However, since most counterparties in these markets (particularly for long-term contracts) tend to be first-class names, the Basle Accord calls for the application of a 50 percent weight to counterparties which normally would attract a 100 percent weight. As the capital ratio based on risk-adjusted assets becomes more important, many countries will raise specific questions concerning the classification of the transactions on their books. The information in this book is intended to give you the general idea of risk adjusting. For specific details, check with the financial controller of your institution.

Volatility-based conversion factors estimate potential loan equivalent amounts over the life of the contract, whereas the BIS percentages are used to ensure that banks currently have adequate capital. The volatility substitutes of the Basle Accord are considerably lower than the volatilities that prevail in the marketplace. While I do not know why this is so, I would like to share my personal thoughts. The main objective of the regulators was to implement some type of risk adjustment because before the Basle Accord, the risk of some cash assets (government bonds) was overstated and many contingent risks, particularly those from financial forward trading, were not captured at all. The financial industry probably lobbied against the regulators' intentions but had to admit that there was credit risk in forward trading. I assume that the regulators decided on almost unrealistically low volatility substitutes to get the job done at all. Also, at the end of the 1980s not all banks were financially as strong as they are today and might not have been able to absorb risk assets based on market volatilities. All this probably contributed to the low volatility substitutes that are currently in place. It would not be surprising if these percentages were increased gradually over time, something that partially occurred when higher volatility substitutes were implemented for foreign exchange and interest rate contracts beyond 5 years.

Risk-Adjusted Assets

Now that you are familiar with the on-balance-sheet risk-weighting categories, the off-balance-sheet credit conversion categories, and their respective classification criteria, let us look at an example that demonstrates how total on-balance-sheet assets are reduced when any of the assets qualify for risk ratings below 100 percent. The example also shows how a fraction of the contingent risk indicated in the footnote (off the balance sheet) is converted into risk assets and moved from the area below the line to the area above the line in the balance sheet.

We begin the discussion by looking at a simplified balance sheet with total assets and total liabilities of 1000 (Exhibit 13-4). You also can see two types of contingent risk in the footnote below the line.

ASSETS		LIABILITIES	
Cash & Due from Banks	150	Miscellaneous Liabilities	910
Securities	170	Liabilities (Tier II)	47
Loans	680	Equity / Retained Earnings (Tier I)	43
Total Assets	1,000	Total Liabilities	1,000
FOOTNOTE			
Commitments & Letters of Credit		900	
FX & Interest Rate Contracts		25,000	

Exhibit 13-4. Balance sheet.

	Amount	Risk Weighting	Risk Adjusted
Cash & Due from Banks			
Cash	2	0%	0
Reserves with Central Bank	38	0%	0
Due from OECD Banks	100	20%	20
Due from Non-OECD Banks	10	100%	10
	150		30
Securities			
OECD Government Bonds	130	0%	0
Corporate Bonds	40	100%	40
	170		40
Loans			
Unsecured Loans	350	100%	350
Loans Secured by OECD Government Bonds	300	20%	60
Commercial Mortgages	10	100%	10
Residential Mortgages	20	50%	10
	680		430
TOTAL	1000		500

Exhibit 13-5. Risk-adjusted assets.

Risk-Adjusted Assets above the Line

Let us look at the same balance sheet after the assets above the line have been adjusted for risk. The process for converting unadjusted assets into adjusted assets is shown in Exhibit 13-5.

The item "Cash and Due from Banks" is divided into "Cash," "Reserves with Central Bank," "Due from OECD Banks," and "Due from Non-OECD Banks." We see that with the application of different risk weightings, unadjusted assets of 150 are reduced to risk-adjusted assets of 30.

A similar process is applied to "Securities," where unadjusted assets of 170 are reduced to risk-adjusted assets of 40. In this case, 130 of the 170 unadjusted assets are "OECD Government Bonds," which carry a risk rating of 0 percent. Finally, "Loans" of 680 are broken down by type and adjusted to 430 because of the lower risk weighting of "Loans Secured by OECD Government Bonds" and "Residential Mortgages." The bottom line of the balance sheet shows that risk-adjusted assets equal half the unadjusted assets.

Risk-Adjusted Assets below the Line

Now we have to adjust the contingent risk below the line of the balance sheet. Let us begin with commitments and letters of credit (Exhibit 13-4) and see how this number is broken down and adjusted for risk (Exhibit 13-6).

	Amount	Risk Weighting	Risk Adjusted
Commitments / Direct Credit Substitutes for Customers	200	100%	200
Commitments Beyond One Year			
• To Corporate Customers	100	50%	50
• To OECD Banks	300	50% / 20%	30
Performance-Related Standby L/Cs	100	50%	50
Commercial L/Cs	100	20%	20
Commitments Up to One Year	100	0%	0
	900		350

Exhibit 13-6. Commitments and letters of credit adjusted for risk.

We see that 200 represents the nominal amount of assets in "Direct Credit Substitutes for Customers," which carries a 100 percent risk weighting; therefore, risk-adjusted assets also equal 200 (see "Standby Lines" in Chap. 12). Of the "Commitments Beyond One Year," 100 are commitments to corporate customers that carry a 50 percent risk rating, resulting in risk-adjusted assets of 50.

The 300 in "Commitments to OECD Banks" is risk-weighted at 50 percent, which yields risk-adjusted assets of 150. The difference is that these 150 risk-adjusted assets are commitments to OECD banks which require only a 20 percent risk weighting. Therefore, *double weighting* is applied to these assets. In other words, there are two types of risk adjustment: counterparty-related risk adjustment and product-related risk adjustment. First they are 50 percent risk-adjusted and are reduced to 150 because they represent commitments beyond 1 year. Then an additional 20 percent risk weighting is applied to these already risk-adjusted assets of 150 because the commitments beyond 1 year are to OECD banks. The final result of the double weighting is a risk-adjusted amount of 30, as illustrated in Exhibit 13-7.

Finally, we see that the total nominal amount of 900 in commitments and letters of credit translates into risk-adjusted assets of 350.

Now let us look at foreign exchange (FX) and interest rate contracts. Exhibit 13-8 shows the credit conversion factors needed to convert notional amounts into risk-adjusted assets.

To determine the total foreign exchange and interest rate risk-adjusted assets, we first identify the current mark-to-market of these transactions. The sum of all these current loan equivalent amounts (CLEAs) is converted into current risk-adjusted assets. In this case the base amount is the extent to which a contract rate is more attractive than the market rate. This amount is then risk-adjusted, reflecting the type of counterparty we dealt

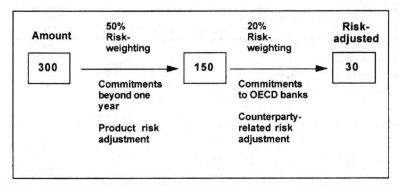

Exhibit 13-7. Double weighting of "Commitments Beyond One Year to OECD Banks."

	Notional Amount	Risk Weighting	Risk Adjusted	
Forward FX Contracts (Remaining Life 1-5 Years)				
• Corporate Customers	600	5% / 50%	15	
• OECD Banks	1,000	5% / 20%	10	25
Forward FX Contracts (Remaining Life Up to 1 Year)				
• Corporate Customers	800	1% / 50%	4	
• OECD Banks	3,000	1% / 20%	6	10
Interest Rate Contracts (Remaining Life 1-5 Years)				
• Corporate Customers	2,000	0.5% / 50%	5	
• OECD Banks	10,000	0.5% / 20%	10	15
Interest Rate Contracts (Remaining Life Up to 1 Year)				
• Corporate Customers	2,000	0%	0	
• OECD Banks	5,600	0%	0	0
SUBTOTAL	25,000			50
CLEA from "In the Money" Contracts	120	50%	60	
• Corporate Customers	200	20%	40	100
• OECD Banks				
TOTAL	25,320			150

Exhibit 13-8. FX and interest rate contracts adjusted for risk.

with by using the risk-weighting factors in Exhibit 13-1. Thereafter, the potential risk-adjusted assets are calculated by multiplying each notional amount by the corresponding conversion factor (see Exhibit 13-3) and through the corresponding counterparty-related risk weighting (see Exhibit 13-1). The addition of current and potential risk-adjusted assets represents the total risk-adjusted assets for these off-balance-sheet transactions. For example, we see "Forward FX Contracts with a Remaining Life of One to Five Years." The 600 outstanding with corporate customers receive a credit conversion percentage of 5 percent to produce an initial risk-adjusted asset of 30, which is then weighted by 50 percent to produce a final risk-adjusted asset of 15. The 1000 outstanding with OECD banks, which also are converted at 5 percent, initially produces risk-adjusted assets of 50. However, since the counterparties are OECD banks, we take only 20 percent of these risk-adjusted assets, producing a final risk-adjusted asset of 10.

The last two lines ("In the Money Contracts with Corporate Customers" and "OECD Banks") represent the add-on of all positive current marks-to-market for FX and interest rate contracts. As you can see, the current loan equivalent amount of 120 for contracts with corporate customers is risk-weighted at 50 percent to produce a risk-adjusted asset of 60 and the current loan equivalent amount of 200 for contracts with OECD banks is risk-weighted at 20 percent to produce a risk-adjusted asset of 40. The result is a total current risk-adjusted asset of 100.

A similar conversion process is applied to the other distant-date contracts outstanding. Short-dated interest rate contracts have zero weighting. The bottom line shows that a notional amount of 25,000 with a current loan equivalent amount of 320 in miscellaneous distant-date products translates into risk-adjusted assets of 150.

Note that corporate customers are weighted at 50 percent instead of 100 percent. If you recall, the BIS called for the application of a 50 percent weight to counterparties that normally would attract 100 percent weight, basically because most counterparties in these markets tend to be first-class names.

Let us see how the risk-adjusted assets from above and below the line apply to the simplified balance sheet in Exhibit 13-4.

Summary: Asset Analysis

Exhibit 13-9 summarizes the asset analysis for both unadjusted and adjusted assets. "Cash and Due from Banks" is reduced from 150 to 30, "Securities" is reduced from 170 to 40, and "Loans" is reduced from 680 to 430. You also can see that the 900 in "Commitments and Letters of Credit" and the 25,000 in "FX and Interest Rate Contracts" are converted into 350 and 150 risk assets, respectively. All this produces a risk-adjusted balance sheet of 1000.

We arrived at the risk-adjusted 1000 by converting unadjusted 1000 cash items (on the balance sheet) into risk-adjusted assets of 500 and converting 25,900 contingent risk below the line (off the balance sheet) into another risk-adjusted asset of 500 above the line.

Assets	Unadjusted off-balance	Unadjusted on-balance	Risk-adjusted	Liabilities	
Cash & Due from Banks		150	30	Misc. liabilities	910
Securities		170	40	Liabilities (Tier II)	47
Loans		680	430	Equity / Retained Earnings (Tier I)	43
Commitments & L/Cs	900		350		
FX & Interest Rate Contracts	25,000		150		
	25,900	1,000	1,000		1,000

Exhibit 13-9. Summary of asset analysis.

In the real world, the total risk-adjusted assets of most banks may be higher or lower than the total assets above the line before adjustments are made. The extent to which the risk-adjusted assets differ depends on the degree of activity in the derivatives market and the makeup of a bank's assets.

Capital/Asset Ratios

Now you are familiar with how assets and contingent risks are categorized and risk-adjusted. Obviously, these risk adjustments affect the two types of capital on the liability side of the balance sheet and the regulator-mandated capital/asset ratios that are based on risk-adjusted assets.

Capital Requirements per the Basle Accord

Chapter 1 included a footnote about tier 1 and tier 2 capital. Now we will expand this concept and relate it to capital requirements resulting from the Basle Accord. We described how the Basle Accord reduces cash assets on the balance sheet to a smaller amount of risk-adjusted assets and demonstrated how a small percentage of miscellaneous contingent liabilities, including distant-date contracts booked below the line on the balance sheet, are moved above the line as risk-adjusted assets. The Basle Accord also stipulates capital requirements related to these adjustments. There are two types of capital—tier 1 and tier 2—and these newly defined types of capital must represent minimum ratios of the newly defined risk-adjusted assets.

Tier 1 capital, also called *core* capital, consists of stockholders' equity and retained earnings. Tier 2 capital, or *supplementary* capital, consists of perpetual preferred stock, bonds with mandatory conversion to equity, and a percentage of the loan loss reserve that is specifically defined for each bank by its central bank. The minimum ratio for tier 1 capital is at least 4 percent of risk-adjusted assets. Also, the total of tier 1 and tier 2 capital must be at least 8 percent of risk-adjusted assets. In the tier 1 and tier 2 combined ratio (minimum 8 percent) at least half must be made up of tier 1 capital.

Armed with this information, let us return to Exhibit 13-9 and look at the liability side of the balance sheet. In addition to "Miscellaneous Liabilities" of 910, we see tier 1 capital of 43 and tier 2 capital of 47. This means that the tier 1 capital ratio is 4.3 percent, which is well above the required minimum of 4 percent of assets. The total tier 1 and tier 2 capital ratio is 8.6 percent, which is above the required minimum of 8 percent of assets.

You will notice that the amount of eligible tier 2 liabilities is 47. Tier 1 capital of 43 added to eligible tier 2 capital of 47 results in total capital of 90, or 9 percent of assets. Remember, however, that half the combined tier 1 and tier 2 capital must be tier 1 capital. Even though we have 47 in eligible tier 2 capital, only 43 of that 47 can be used for official capital ratio purposes. Therefore, in this example the official capital/asset ratio for risk-adjusted assets is 8.6 percent (2 × 4.3 percent).

In addition to requiring capital to cover the credit risk-adjusted assets described in the previous section, the BIS recently approved a requirement for capital allocation to cover value at risk-price risk for trading portfolios (Chap. 6). The full requirement became effective on January 1, 1998. The interest rate risk of the whole accrual balance sheet (earnings at risk) also has been identified as a risk that will require capital allocation. However, a capital allocation proposal to cover this risk has been deferred to a later date.

Principles for Managing the Balance Sheet

Each bank should have a designated area (probably ALCO) that is responsible for managing the Risk-Adjusted Asset Principles (RAAP) assets for sweet spot management purposes and the Generally Accepted Accounting Principles (GAAP) balance sheet for liquidity purposes. In order to facilitate the management of RAAP toward the targeted capital ratio sweet spot and the management of GAAP to provide appropriate funding liquidity, it is important that the annual budget includes targets and limits for assets and liabilities. Specifically, the maximum of permitted risk-adjusted assets must be stated, which includes the risk-adjusted cash assets such as loans and securities, and the risk-adjusted assets-equivalent of contingent risks such as distant-date contracts, commitments, guarantees, and letters of credit. As a result, business managers will have a budget of revenue and expense targets and a limit for risk assets with which these revenues must be achieved.

For example, in the past, a manager might have said that she would generate revenues of $2 million from assets of $200 million. It then may have turned out that she could not get a spread of 1 percent on her loans but instead only a $\frac{1}{2}$ percent spread. She would then lend a total of $500 million at $\frac{1}{2}$ percent spread and generate revenues of $2.5 million, which is better than her budget of $2 million. This behavior makes it impossible for a bank to manage toward a targeted capital ratio sweet spot. Today, managers must respect the limits established for risk assets in the budget and achieve the forecasted revenues without exceeding the established ceiling for risk assets.

In addition, risk-adjusted assets must be screened periodically to identify "lazy assets." These are assets and investments that are underperforming from a yield viewpoint and should be replaced by higher-yielding assets for which there otherwise might not be space on the balance sheet. Often one or more senior managers are in love with those assets and resist their elimination. In such situations there must be a strong hand demanding action. One successful manager of an industrial company is said to demand in such cases: Fix it! If you cannot fix it, sell it! If you cannot sell it, close it! In other words, within a specific period of time the situation must be eliminated from the problem list.

The annual funding plan must include the volumes, types, and maturities of assets and liabilities planned for the coming year. This will allow the treasurer to manage the GAAP balance sheet to the targeted level of funding liquidity. It will indicate whether there are sufficient liquid assets and whether the liabilities meet the desired criteria in terms of diversification of sources and instruments, market shares, and most importantly, sufficiently long maturities.

Note the difference in terms of "holy cow effect" when somebody puts a large amount of government bonds on the balance sheet. The manager may say, "Don't you worry. This does not require any capital." This is correct, but the bank must have the cash to pay for those bonds, and the management and planning of liquidity in the GAAP balance sheet assures that the bank has the money.

Summary

Using the categories and criteria set forth in the Basle Accord, assets in the balance sheet are adjusted to reflect risk. This process involves applying different percentages to different types of assets and reducing them to risk-adjusted assets. Contingent risk below the line is converted into risk-adjusted assets above the line.

Capital on the liability side of the balance sheet consists of tier 1 capital and tier 2 capital. Tier 1 capital must account for at least 4 percent of risk-adjusted assets, and tier 1 plus tier 2 capital must equal at least 8 percent of risk-adjusted assets.

The balance sheet must be managed in terms of GAAP and RAAP because compliance with both sets of principles is necessary for the managing, forecasting, and tracking of liquidity and capital ratios.

14
Organizational Structure

Organizational Chart

In examining the organization of a bank or any financial institution that engages in trading, we are particularly interested in the basic reporting structures of the trading, risk management, operations, audit, and corporate treasurer functions.

Front Office: Trading

The trading function may be independent or may be combined with the corporate business. An independent structure positions the traders in a straight-line organization all the way to the top, where the most senior trading person reports to a member of the board of managers. In the other possible structure, the corporate business is combined with the trading function, where the most senior person in the corporate banking world is responsible for the trading function as well as the relationship with the customers to whom commercial and industrial loans are made. In this scenario, trading, traditional customer-related banking business, and corporate finance are together.

The structure for the business side is a decision the bank has to make, and it depends on how much the bank wants to focus on the trading function. As with all choices, there are pros and cons. If a bank *combines* the overall corporate relationship with customers with the proprietary and customer trading functions under one person, the advantage is that there is less competition and profit-center thinking between the traders and the corporate people. As a result, there probably will be a more harmonious climate between banking functions and the delivery of the product to the customers will be smoother. The disadvantage is that there may be less of a focus on the trading function. Often corporate bankers and credit people become the senior people in this kind of organization, and consequently, the trading function may receive less attention. If a bank *separates* the trading function from the relationship management and corporate finance functions, trading will receive more attention and the traders will have direct representation on the board of managers, which is an advantage. The disadvantage is that there can be a lot of bickering about who gets the earnings and so forth when it comes to the customer relationship.

Middle Office: Risk Management

In terms of the risk management function, it is mandatory that checks and balances prevail and that the market risk management function or middle office be separate from the reporting lines related to trading. In other words, the people who control the risk taking, and in particular those who set the limits for risk taking, have to be independent from the risk takers. Some banks have a whole credit risk management line that reaches up to the highest level and culminates in a credit policy committee and a market risk management line that culminates in a market risk policy committee. The important point here is that the people who set limits must have a reporting line different from that of those who assume the risk within those limits.

Back Office: Operations

A third and separate function is the operations and processing area, which often is referred to as the back office.

Audit Function

Separate from these three areas (front office, middle office, and back office) is the all-important audit function, which should report directly to the board of directors. The audit function is extremely important in today's financial institutions. Given the pace of change and the complexity of the business, audit personnel must strive to be up-to-date and professional. Ideally, there are career auditors and functional specialists who rotate through the audit function for a couple of years. The functional specialists should be stars in their respective fields and should be assured of good jobs once they leave the audit function and return to the line. The audit function should not be a dumping ground for people who did not make it in their line jobs.

At the end of each audit there should be a written report detailing the corrective action required. These reports should not be vague but should clearly communicate a pass or no-pass grade for the audited unit. For example, a bank can establish a scale from 1 to 5 with 1 the highest and 5 the lowest and make it clear that 3 is a no-pass grade. This type of system sends a clear signal that the bank is serious about a sound process, particularly if all no-pass audits are copied to the board of directors. Units with substandard audit results should focus on the corrective action process and then reinvite the auditor to confirm that the problems have been eliminated. No-pass audits should lead to limit reductions, and the previously prevailing limits should not be reinstated until the corrective action process has been completed.

One reason for the importance of a strong audit function is increasing evidence that there is a direct relationship between credit ratings and shareholder value (price of the stock) on one side and the market's perception of the quality of an organization's internal controls on the other side.

Assume that you have a brother who usually ignores stop signs and red lights when he drives and often drives under the influence of alcohol. However, he has never had an automobile accident. Would you let your children drive with your brother? The answer is no. Even though he never has had an accident, given this substandard driving habit, the probability is very high that he will have a serious accident. The analogy is clear. Rating agencies and investors shy away from organizations that lack internal controls. Even though there may not have been large losses yet, they are afraid of the high probability that such losses will occur soon.

> *A reputation for having a strong audit function and good internal controls enhances shareholder value.*

Corporate Treasurer

In the context of this book, the important message from the organization chart in Exhibit 14-1 is that the front office, middle office, and back office are independent of each other and have *separate* reporting lines to the board of managers. The same is true for the corporate treasurer, whose responsibilities include the management of funding liquidity

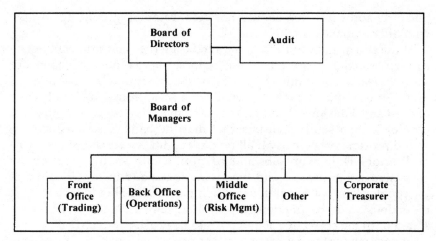

Exhibit 14-1. Organization chart focused on trading-related functions.

(see Chap. 12). The corporate treasurer also should have responsibility for managing the balance sheet. As was stated in Chap. 13, there are volumes and types of assets and liabilities that should be part of the budget, and the corporate treasurer must sign off on those budgeted items. When this procedure is used, there is a central awareness of what the balance sheet will look like in the future. Decentralized decision making is acceptable for purposes of price risk, business strategies, and earnings, but for liquidity purposes there can be no decentralization. That is why the corporate treasurer, supported by the president, has to cut across all reporting lines and business segments within a bank. The corporate treasurer has to make sure that the bank's liquidity remains as it is outlined in the business plan and that the future appearance of the balance sheet is built into the funding plan and is part of the budget.

It is worth repeating that the front office, middle office, back office, and corporate treasurer must be independent of each other and have separate reporting lines to the board of managers. The audit function reports directly to the board of directors.

Centralized versus Decentralized Trading Function

Within the front office, management can choose between a centralized and a decentralized management approach. This is a critical decision when larger, possibly international and/or global organizations are involved. The larger the organization is, the more attractive a decentralized decision-making approach may be. Specifically, what is meant here is centralized limit setting, decentralized decision making (deciding on the types of price risk positions within preapproved limits), and centralized monitoring of the results. Centralized monitoring requires a strong and independent financial control function.

Independent decision making has many advantages. Through this management style, the bank attracts the best people out of school, the entrepreneurial types who enjoy a challenge. Independent decision making and the freedom to act are instrumental in accelerating the learning curve. This enhances the employee's self-esteem, which is good for the employee, and attracts more customers, which is good for the bank. Also, these types of people tend to be more loyal to the organization because they enjoy what they do. They may be guided by the following poem:

I was sleeping and dreaming

That life was fun.

I woke up and saw

That life is work.

I did the work,

and the work was fun!

Even if a bank uses a structure of decentralized decision making in terms of price risk taking, it has become increasingly popular to establish global responsibilities for products and/or activities such as foreign exchange trading, securities trading, equities, and derivatives. These global management responsibilities do not interfere with, for example, the foreign exchange traders' freedom to take independent action in terms of buying or selling a specific currency at a particular time. Instead, the global management approach is focused on customer relationships, systems development, and human resources.

Senior Management

In addition to segregating responsibilities, institutions active in financial trading should have trading and market-risk-related expertise represented among the most senior staff. Specifically, at least two members of the board of managers and at least one of the outside directors should have an advanced understanding of financial trading and market risk management.

This type of senior management will have the capacity to understand new products and weigh the assumption of value at risk, including the associated confidence levels, against actual and expected trading revenues. (Recall the analogy in Chap. 5 between risk and return that related the probability of being on a crashing plane to the convenience of flying.)

This management strategy, combined with well-trained market-tested traders, a sound focus on customers, and a reliable audit and risk reporting process, should assure sustainable earnings growth from the trading function. Implementing all these factors means taking to heart the advice given by Alan Greenspan, the chairman of the Federal Reserve Board: "We must all guard against a situation in which the designers of financial strategies [traders] lack the experience to evaluate the attendant risks and their experienced senior managers are too embarrassed to admit that they do not understand the new strategies."

15

Internal Controls: Protecting against Errors and Fraud

In addition to managing and controlling price risk, credit risk, and liquidity risk, it is very important to control the risks inherent in operating a business and processing transactions. Most of the control techniques explained in this chapter are applied to protect a business against human error and intended wrongdoing, i.e., fraud. It is important to explain to traders that they are among the most trusted employees of the bank, but it is a good business practice to have these controls in place. Also, do not forget the old saying *that the good ones can be just as bad as the bad ones if the good ones have a chance to be bad.* No single control device provides 100 percent protection against error and fraud, but if a bank has all the known control techniques in place, the probability is very high that at least one of them will activate a red flag and bring problems to light.

Product Programs

Two people meet at 5:30 in the elevator of their bank and agree to have a quick drink together before going home. After the joke of the day has been told, they start talking about the business. One of them has a customer with a problem for which the bank does not have a product. After a couple of beers, the two imaginative bankers come up with a new idea/product that is likely to help the customer.

So far everything is wonderful. The trouble begins the following morning, when they actually do the deal using the new product they developed the previous evening. The back office does not know how to book it, and chances are that some fine points of a regulatory or legal nature have been overlooked.

This story emphasizes the need for financial institutions to develop product programs before a new product is used either with customers or in proprietary trading. This has been standard procedure for many years with all bank customers irrespective of which industry they are in. In most companies the board of directors gets involved before a new product is introduced. The problem arises when there is a willing customer for a new product and a delay in the availability of that product defers satisfaction for the customer and earnings for the bank. However, just as companies in the pharmaceutical industry have to test a new medication for months or years for negative side effects before it is approved for sale, this is a price banks have to pay.

A product program is a manual consisting of maybe 30 to 60 pages, depending on the complexity of the product. The process x-rays the product for all risks irrespective of their nature.

Product programs x-ray products for all risks.

It begins with a comprehensive description of the product, including the identification of all the market factors it contains (how much salt is in the kitchen; see Chap. 6) and all other risks. In addition, there is a detailed discussion of the target market, the development cost, the likely volume expressed in dollars and numbers of transactions, and the budgeted earnings. There also is a detailed discussion of the following:

- Risk/return evaluation
- Risk management approval process
- Accounting procedures
  Revenues recognition
  Balance sheet treatment
  Reporting requirements
  Sample booking and month-end entries for a complete transaction
- Operating and control procedures
  Procedures critical for implementation
  Special systems needed for management or production
  A step-by-step outline and detailed flowcharts of operating procedures

Highlighting of controls and contingency plans
Ongoing monitoring of risks against limits

- Approved documentation
A copy of counsel-approved legal documentation
A copy of related legal opinions

- Accounting and tax approvals
Written opinions from local consultants on specific aspects of complex products
A special focus on local and foreign taxes

- Legal and regulatory approvals
Summary of and reference to all regulations applying to the product
Local and relevant foreign regulations
Written opinions from a local counsel ensuring compliance with laws and regulations
Specification of restrictions resulting from the corporate structure

- Authorized legal vehicles for booking the product
A list of all eligible legal vehicles
Preference determination for each transaction
Detailed reasons for the choice of vehicle

- Standardized presentation
A format that facilitates updating
Dates of the original issue and the latest revision
Numbering of all the pages

The product program also indicates additional limits that may be required and describes the chain of approvals for the product as a whole. For each of the indicated areas, the ranking officer must indicate his or her approval, such as the legal counsel approving the legal aspects of the product.

Product programs are extremely unpopular with staff members because initially they require a lot of work that slows down the business process. However, after the first annual review things flow much more quickly, and soon the product becomes routine. The key to a speedy process is the quality of the initial memorandum describing the product. If everybody involved can understand quickly and easily what the product is about and if there are no problems, the whole process can be approved within a couple of days. If there are flaws, it is better to identify them before billions of dollars have been booked. In many cases, flaws can be corrected and the product can be used after a brief delay. If the flaw turns out to be fatal for the product, it is better to discover it sooner than later. If a bank rushes into a new product that is unfit for use and the bank is lucky, it will cost only money to reverse the action. If the bank is not lucky, it will find itself having violated regulatory or legal constraints, and this will lead to problems (possibly public) with the authorities. A publicized lack of internal controls is likely to hurt the price/earnings ratio and shareholder value.

Many banks allow up to five deals to be closed without going through the product program process. This gives a bank time to determine whether these are one-of-a-kind transactions or whether the bank really has developed a totally new product.

Another way to reduce the product-program-related work load is to create well-prepared standard boilerplate product programs for a few frequently used products within product families such as foreign exchange, securities trading, equity trading, and funding and gapping. The intent here is to provide transactors with a ready-made product program in situations where some features of a specific new product differ from the boilerplate standard and approval is required only for the new features.

Before getting upset with the work load or the time wasted on product programs, remember this: If a well-known international organization which suffered substantial losses because of a lack of internal controls could magically create a situation in which nobody would ever know what happened, it would be willing to pay twice the amount of money that was lost. In other words, in most cases the loss of reputation associated with mishaps resulting from inadequate internal controls and processes is much more painful and causes more damage in the long run than does the financial loss.

Do not economize on allocating resources to internal controls. Most companies that have suffered large losses because of inadequate internal controls would gladly pay twice the amount of money lost if they could turn back the clock and ignore the fact that it ever happened and that the public and regulators know about it.

Segregation of Responsibility

Segregation of responsibilities is the best protection against errors and fraud. This has been mentioned at various points in this book, and this section will repeat a few of the highlights. There must be segregation of the front office, middle office, and back office. The audit function must report to the board of directors. Confirmations of transactions must be received and processed by people not connected with the dealing function. The people who have the final say on risk limits and loss limits must be different from the management line that controls the traders. In short, when in doubt, it is better to segregate responsibilities than to have them combined under one manager. All of the above-mentioned elements and the control elements that are discussed later in this chapter must be applied without exception. This also applies to the most senior people and the biggest money makers in the organization.

Unusual losses are always investigated and examined in great detail. When there are unusual profits, it is important that this desirable situation be investigated and examined with the same rigor and enthusiasm. Supervisors must understand all the pertinent details that made the unusual earnings possible.

Absolutely No Exceptions

Segregation of responsibilities, as well as all other internal controls, must be applied to all personnel without exception. This no-exception rule must be observed by all personnel regardless of how senior and important they are, how much money they make, and whose brother or sister they are.

Taping of Phone Lines

It is highly desirable to tape all telephone lines on which financial trading is conducted. Most countries require that counterparties be advised when conversations are taped, and it is important to adhere to this. Management should make sure that recorded tapes are used only for the resolution of misunderstanding and disputes, not for other purposes, such as training new personnel.

Important as the taping of phone lines is, there is no need to keep the tapes for long periods. The tapes should be destroyed after transactions have been properly confirmed and all the related documentation has been completed. Usually there is no need to keep the tapes for longer than 6 months.

Off-Premises Dealing

In a global business it may be unavoidable that certain personnel transact business when they are not in the office, particularly when they are at home at night. This activity should be clearly approved in a separate memorandum. In particular, it should be made clear which individuals are allowed to transact business when they are not in the office and whether those transactions may increase the bank's risk positions or are limited to the liquidation or reduction of existing risk positions. Banks with branches in other time zones sometimes limit off-premises trading to transactions with their own offices. In any case, any off-premises trade should be reported immediately to a tape on a dedicated office phone with all details, including the time of day when it was recorded. The taping of an employee's home phone is not an acceptable substitute for recording the information on the office phone.

Aggregate Contract Trigger

An aggregate contract trigger for each product is not a limit on credit risk, price risk, or funding liquidity risk. In fact, it is not a limit at all but a trigger. It is simply a volume indicator that serves as a signal for management when there is a change in the volume of activity in a given product. For example, a bank may record the total volume of all unliquidated foreign exchange contracts and monitor the record for changes in the level of business activity.

Suppose that customers switch their business from spot to forward hedging or that a bank makes a conscious decision to expand its marketing to customers that require forward hedging. These situations will produce an increase in the volume of forward business and total exchange contracts outstanding, which is not bad because there is a good reason for it. However, if outstanding volumes are higher and there are strong signals that the number of errors, operating expenses, and telephone expenses are up while profits are down, this may mean that the traders are overtrading.

Aggregate contract triggers should be established for each product/instrument category, such as foreign exchange contracts, FRAs, and interest rate swaps. The trigger should be set comfortably above the currently prevailing outstanding volume, perhaps 20 to 25 percent higher, depending on the level of magnitude of outstandings. The intent is to force a hit of the trigger if there is an expansion of business activity that management should know about. If the trigger is set too low, there will be unnecessarily frequent hits, and if the trigger is set too high, the expansion of the business can be substantial without activation of the trigger. The trigger is never a constraint for a trader. It is acceptable for a trader to pass the trigger for a day or two as long as the discussion and explanation with management take place. After all, that is why it is a trigger and not a limit.

> *Aggregate contract triggers are very simple control devices which do not require rocket science technology. Several of the well-publicized mishaps and bankruptcies of the past might not have occurred if those institutions had employed this control device.*

An aggregate contract trigger is a good additional tool to have as a red flag for business activity volume and expansion. An institution wants to be alerted to change in business activity and find out if it is occurring for the right reasons.

Processing Controls

It is also very important to control the risks inherent in the back office activities required to process transactions.

Numbered Forms

Sequentially numbered forms should be used not only for confirmations but also for deal slips and similar material in the context of trading. If a form is inadvertently destroyed or lost, the responsible person should report this so that the loss can be considered in the process of reconciling the use of numbered forms.

Time Stamp

To the extent that the closing of a transaction is not automatically documented by the communication system, handwritten deal slips should be time-stamped immediately after a transaction has been completed. There should be enough time-stamp devices in a dealing room that each dealer can reach them without rising from her seat. This is important because otherwise tickets will accumulate until it is convenient to time-stamp them all at the same time. Knowing at which time a transaction has been closed can be helpful in reconstructing the details of a deal, particularly the price at which it was closed.

Confirmations

For all transactions, confirmations must be sent to counterparties and incoming confirmations must be reconciled with copies of the outgoing confirmations. This process must be separate from the dealing function

and represents one of the more prominent ways of detecting unauthorized trades. One of the problems for banks is that customers often
refuse to confirm their financial trades. For competitive reasons, it is difficult for banks to put pressure on their customers and demand confirmations. It should be explained to customers that a confirmation not
only accommodates the bank's control process but also can represent a
major contribution to the customer's internal control process.

Model Validation

The exaggerated introductory story is that a trader brought a screw-
driver to the office, opened the door of the computer, and turned the
screw a little to the right. As a result, the computer produced numbers
that were more convenient for the trader. In other words, financial models have been tampered with.

Model validation should be performed for all systems with mathematical models that result in postings to the books and records of a bank
or produce risk management reports. This means that a model should
be validated if one or both of the following two questions can be
answered with a yes:

1. Does the model update the books of the bank?
2. Does the model produce risk management reports that are used by
   management to measure risk or prepare financial statements?

For example, a spreadsheet that calculates gaps for an earnings at risk
(EAR) report or one that calculates the cost to close should be validated.
The mark-to-market revaluation of trading portfolios and the sensitivity calculation of the value of a portfolio to a specific change in a market
variable also should be validated. These examples answer either question 1 or question 2 with a yes. However, a spreadsheet done by a trader
to analyze the shape of the yield curve or check the prices implied in
financial instruments for arbitrage opportunities does not require validation. With these two examples, both questions would be answered
with a no.

Validation Responsibility

Line managers, in conjunction with the associated risk managers,
should be responsible for the model validation process. They should
select a competent validator who is independent of the unit which
developed the model in question. The experience and sophistication of
the validator should be consistent with the financial and mathematical

complexity of the model. In most cases the validator should be an outsider, such as a professor at a well-known academic institution.

The following points should be among those examined during the validation process:

- Appropriateness of the input market data based on the purpose for which the data are being used

- Accuracy of any algorithm (formula) used to transform the input market data, if necessary, for the revaluation process, such as the formula for converting interest rates into zero-coupon rates

- Correctness of the revaluation algorithms, such as the premium calculation for options

- Accuracy of the factor sensitivity measurements for trading accounts and gap calculations for accrual accounts

- Reasonableness of the assumptions which are functionally inherent to the model, such as the assumption that interest rates typically are modeled as log-normal distributions (a specific probability distribution)

Testing

After analyzing all these issues during the validation process, the validator should perform a test and keep the results. This test is done by entering test transactions into the model and comparing the output with any calculated expected or theoretical results. Since this type of testing also is required for a user's acceptance test of the system, the user's acceptance test may be used in part to satisfy the testing requirement for model validation.

If a material change occurs in a model that already has been validated, a revalidation is required. A material change is *any* change in the issues listed above; for example, if, in place of using cash rates (interest rates from cash markets) as input market rates, both cash and future rates (interest rates derived from futures markets) are used. Also, the addition of a new product module to the system obviously requires the validation of the new module. In any case, models should be revalidated every 12 to 18 months. The risk management function should keep a record of all validated models, including an aging schedule.

For all models, there should be adequate written documentation to support their validity. This includes

1. A detailed description of what was validated

2. A discussion of the validation methodology

3. A record of tests and test results

In addition to validating price-risk-related models, a bank uses financial models in other areas, and those models also must be validated in the same way as described above. These other areas include

- Liquidity management where there is a need to convert from contractual maturities to actuarial maturities
- Presettlement counterparty risk where we calculate the conversion factors with which we convert meaningless volume and notional amounts into meaningful potential loan equivalent amounts
- Volatility discovery based on historical data where we attempt to predict the future volatility levels on the basis of what happened in the past

Rate Reasonability Process

Rate reasonability is an issue that continues to capture an increasing amount of attention from the senior management in most banks because of its potentially significant implications. Significant means up to a potential bankruptcy, as has occurred with some key market participants.

The rate reasonability process is designed to ensure that all trading room transactions are executed and revalued at the prevailing market rates. The way to achieve this assurance is to require an independent verification of the prices at which transactions are executed and booked. Because of its importance, this process should be documented and approved by the most senior level of the risk management function and should be subjected to an audit.

The following example will help explain the concept of rate reasonability. A trader buys stock X for $100 at 11 a.m. in the over-the-counter (OTC) market. At the end of the day, the transaction is revalued at $101 and a profit of $1 is recorded. The question is whether this $1 profit is reasonable. Can line management be sure that this is the correct profit? Let us look at the following potential situations:

- At 11 a.m. the market quotes 99.5 for the same stock, but because there was no control at inception, the trader buys at $100. There may be many reasons for doing this. One is to share the difference with the counterparty; another is to transfer profits to a counterparty and expect the same consideration in a "bad" month. In this case the bank could obtain a mark-to-market profit of $1.5, but the books will reflect only $1. In fact, $1 may represent a good profit, and the trader may even receive a good bonus.

- At 11 a.m. the market quotes 100, and so the trader buys at the prevailing market rate. However, at the end of the day the closing price is 99.6. Since there is no independent verification of the revaluation rates, the trader decides to revalue at $101. The real loss of $1.4 will be booked, and a fictitious profit of $1 will be recorded. Again, the trader may even receive a bonus.

The first case shows the danger of a lack of control at inception, in other words, a lack of control at the moment the transactions are executed. The second case shows the danger of a lack of control at the moment of revaluation. Both put the bank at risk and should be considered very serious.

Many real examples can be used to illustrate the importance of the rate reasonability process. One involves an investment bank where a trader was responsible for the full mark-to-market process of a bond portfolio and the stripping activity (segregating the coupons of the bond and selling them separately). It turned out that the trader had actually suffered losses of tens of millions of dollars instead of the profits of hundreds of millions of dollars he had reported.

In another case an important investment bank was trading futures. A single trader was responsible for the trading, accounting, mark-to-market process, and settlements of the futures margins. He had a strong view of the market and positioned accordingly. When the market went in the opposite direction, he falsified the revaluation and duplicated the bet to cover the losses. The same strategy was followed until he ran out of money. At that time real losses exceeded the capital of the investment bank, which went bankrupt.

There are many more examples. In all cases experience has shown that if management does not pay attention to this issue, it may be putting at risk an unknown amount with unknown implications. Consequently, institutions engaged in trading must assure that the execution of transactions at inception and the revaluation (mark-to-market) of price risk positions on an ongoing basis occur at the prevailing market rates. When these situations are discovered, the damages may total several millions of dollars.

Independence for the purpose of rate reasonability may be assured in one of the following two ways:

- By separation of functions
  This is achieved when, for example, every price at which a transaction is closed by a trader is verified for reasonability by operations and any revaluation price is set by operations or financial control *independently* of the traders. (See also "Input from Outside Vendors" on pp. 67–68.)

- By separation of levels of responsibility within the line business

  This usually is the case when prices are not available in the market or from third parties. In such situations, the revaluation may be done internally by the trader and may be reviewed by a specified person at a management level above the trader. This type of person is often called a "designated officer" (see the discussion of the marked-to-market process in Chap. 3).

For liquid products such as FX and money markets, where prices are readily available, operations can compare the prices of the closed transactions with the prevailing market prices. If possible, this should be done on an automatic basis. Any transaction closed outside a certain parameter should be analyzed and discussed with the head trader. Exhibit 15-1 illustrates this procedure in more detail. We see that the process begins when the trader in the front office inputs information into the front-end system. From there it moves to the back office for rou-

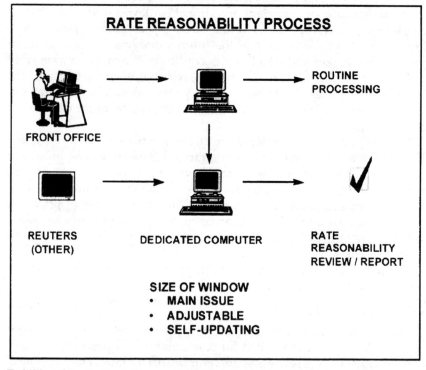

Exhibit 15-1. Analyzing transactions closed outside certain parameters.

tine processing. However, the information also is sidetracked (in the exhibit, downward) to a specially dedicated computer. This computer is updated continuously with market rates from a reliable source such as Reuters. Programmed into the computer is a window for market bid and offered rates. The rates at which the trader completed the transaction must fit through this window to pass the rate reasonability test. Otherwise, the transaction will be captured and the trader will be questioned during the rate reasonability review. The window is self-updating. For example, if the market rate is 50 bid and 60 offered, the risk management function may have programmed into the computer a window of 45 bid and 65 offered. If the market moves from 50–60 to 70–80, the window will automatically move to 65–85; i.e., it is self-updating. The size of the window can be adjusted in accordance with the prevailing volatility in the marketplace. The challenge is to have the right size for the window. If it is too small, we get false alarms, and if it is too wide, we may not recognize the fact that a transaction was closed at an off-market rate.

Let us discuss a process that sometimes is viewed as a rate reasonability test but is definitely not acceptable. In this case the risk manager waits until the end of the day, when the range of market prices that have prevailed during the day is known. For example, the low may have been 20 while the high was 80. The risk manager then checks all the tickets to verify that contract rates are not lower than 20 or higher than 80. This does not constitute satisfactory control. The trader may have transacted at 30 while the market was 70, and therefore, management should not rely on this type of system.

For illiquid products such as long-term options, the independent verification of the appropriate volatility price may be done by operations, financial control, or the designated officer.

For the daily accounting mark-to-market process, operations or financial control can provide the revaluation rates from independent sources. If that is not possible, all trader-provided market rates must be reviewed and approved by operations or financial control.

Under no circumstances may traders have sole responsibility for the mark-to-market process. The reasonableness of the prices used in this process must be confirmed by another person and/or unit that is not connected with the dealing room. It must be clear to everyone that this independent person is ultimately responsible for making sure the mark-to-market rates are the prevailing market rates. Failure to do so must have the most severe disciplinary consequences for the trader and the independent individual (see "Marking-to-Market the Trading Portfolio" in Chap. 3).

Historical Rate Rollover

There are foreign exchange swap transactions which are economically *on* the market, but the two legs making up the transactions are *off*-market rates. This situation occurs when a customer buys, for example, dollars 3 months forward against yen at 200. Three months later the market drops to 180 yen to 1 dollar. The customer does not want to take delivery of the dollars but instead would like to *roll over* the maturing forward purchase for an additional 3 months. Common practice would be for the customer to consummate the rollover through a spot sale of dollars at 180 and a corresponding 3-month forward purchase. In a historical rollover situation, the customer would want to sell the spot dollars at 200 yen to 1 dollar, the same exchange rate at which the dollars originally were bought 3 months forward. Most customers do not mark-to-market forward exchange contracts and use this process to defer recognizing the 20-yen loss.

This is a dangerous practice from the bank's viepoint. The customer's management may be unaware of these transactions. Once these deals are discovered, the customer may hold the bank responsible for the accumulated losses because, the customer will argue, without the bank's cooperation, the customer/trader could not have maintained the unauthorized position and deferred the loss. The bank often has to choose between absorbing the loss and losing its relationship with the customer. Historical rate rollovers also involve more credit risk for the bank because there is already a current loan equivalent amount at the moment the deal is done. Also, in this example the bank is effectively lending 20 yen for 3 months without an explicit interest charge. Such a charge would have to be built into the swap rate applied to the historical rate rollover.

Overall, historical rate rollovers are a very bad practice and should be avoided if possible. The Foreign Exchange Committee of the Federal Reserve Bank of New York issued a memorandum in December 1991 describing the problem and recommending procedures to be followed if the customer insists on a historical rate rollover. This memorandum is shown in Exhibit 15-2. A bank should sit down with a customer's most senior level of management that can be reached and explain the risks involved in this practice. It is hard to imagine that a truly senior representative of the customer company would still wish to engage in historical rate rollovers once she understood the dangers involved and the unfavorable image it creates for her company.

The ultimate solution to historical rate rollovers and other related problems is to force nonfinancial institutions to mark-to-market their off-balance-sheet risk positions just as financial institutions have been required to do for a long time, at least in the United States. This require-

COMMITTEE LETTER ON HISTORICAL-RATE ROLLOVERS

Historical-Rate Rollovers: A Dangerous Practice   December 26, 1991

Dear Sir / Madam:

The Foreign Exchange Committee's recently revised *Guidelines for the Management of Foreign Exchange Trading Activity* (December 1990) raised questions about the use of historical rates in pricing forward contracts. The Committee recommended that nonmarket rates should not be permitted in interbank dealing and should be permitted in other circumstances only with strict management oversight.

In recent Committee discussions, however, members have concluded that the risks involved in rolling contracts at historical rates are often not fully appreciated in the marketplace, notwithstanding well-publicized problems involving the use of such rollovers. At a time when market practices and risk controls are the subjects of increased focus in the financial community, the Committee has decided to draw attention to the potential dangers of historical-rate rollovers and to suggest ways to help management limit the risks, should they continue to provide such services to their customers.

Historical-rate rollovers involve the extension of a forward foreign exchange contract by a dealer on behalf of his customer at offmarket rates. In a typical rollover, the customer will ask his dealer to apply the historical rate of a maturing contract to the spot end of a new pair of contracts which, in effect, extends the maturing contract, thereby deferring any gains or losses.

Historical-rate rollovers virtually always involve the extension of credit by one party to the other. If the customer has a loss on the maturing contract, the rollover would in effect represent a loan by the dealer to his customer. If the customer has a profit, the dealer would in effect be borrowing from the customer. The resulting loan or borrowing amount and associated interest rate charges are typically built into the forward points the dealer quotes his customer. While accounting conventions do not require that these amounts be recognized in the books as loans or borrowings, proper risk control requires that they be treated as such.

Certain uses of historical-rate rollovers may be justified, as when used by a company seeking to hedge the currency risk of a commercial or financial transaction with an uncertain date. Companies, for example, may hedge the currency risk of a purchase of foreign goods based on an estimated delivery date, but subsequently "roll" the hedge out or in, so as to coincide with the actual date of the delivery. In this way, corporate treasurers can avoid the cash flows which might occur if the gain or loss on the forward hedge does not coincide with the currency gain or loss on the underlying commercial transaction.

However, because rollovers could be used to shift income from one institution to another or from one reporting period to another, they can also serve illegitimate purposes. A dealer who routinely offers to roll over his customers' maturing contracts at historical rates could unwittingly participate in efforts to conceal losses, evade taxes, or defraud his or another trading institution. His involvement in these efforts could potentially subject him and his bank to legal action, not to mention damage his and his institution's reputation.

Even a dealer who carefully examines each request for off-market trades may face serious problems if senior management at both the corporate counterparty and his own institution have not fully evaluated and approved of the transaction. At the counterparty firm, failure to insure that senior management has understood and signed off on the deal may risk the possibility that the terms of the transaction come into dispute. This is particularly com-

mon if the trader who arranged the deal has left the customer firm. At the dealer institution, failure to record the implied loan or borrowing amount in an historical-rate extension could threaten centralized control over the management of interest rate and credit risks.

Thus, use of historical-rate rollovers introduces risks above and beyond those normally faced by dealing institutions in the day-to-day trading of foreign exchange, including: (i) the risk that the dealer institution unknowingly aids and abets illegal or inappropriate activities; (ii) the risk that customer management is unaware of the special nature of the transaction and/or of the associated credit exposures; and (iii) the risk that management at the dealer institution is unaware of the special nature of the transaction and/or of the associated credit exposures.

Recommendations of the Foreign Exchange Committee

The Foreign Exchange Committee believes that rolling contracts at historical rates is a dangerous practice which should be avoided absent compelling justification and procedural safeguards. Because of the special risks, the Committee urges dealers that continue to accommodate customer requests for historical-rate rollovers to take the following three steps: (i) inquire about the customer's motivation in requesting an off-market rate trade to gauge the commercial justification; (ii) make sure that senior customer management is aware of the transaction and the special risks involved; and (iii) obtain the informed consent of one's own senior management to take on the additional risk and any effective credit extension.

The Committee further recommends that all dealer institutions have written procedures for historical-rate rollovers. An example of procedures that satisfy the above conditions would include the following:

(a) A letter from senior customer management (treasurer or above) should be kept on file explaining (i) that the customer will occasionally request to rollover contracts at historical rates; (ii) the reasons why such requests will be made; and (iii) that such requests are consistent with the customer firm's internal policies: this letter should be kept current.

(b) The dealer should solicit an explanation from the customer for each request for an off-market rate deal at the time the request is made;

(c) Senior management and/or appropriate credit officers at the dealer institution should be informed of and approve each transaction and any effective extension of credit;

(d) A letter should be sent to senior customer management immediately after each off-market transaction is executed explaining the particulars of the trade and explicitly stating the implied loan or borrowing amount; and (e) Normally, forward contracts should not be extended for more than three months, nor extended more than once; however, any extension of a rollover should itself meet the requirements of (b), (c) and (d) above.

Attached is the 1991 membership list for the Foreign Exchange Committee. Please feel free to contact myself, members of the Committee, or the Committee's Executive Assistant with any questions or comments regarding this letter.

> Very truly yours,
>
> John T. Arnold
> Chairman

Exhibit 15-2. Foreign Exchange Committee memorandum on historical rate rollovers.

ment would eliminate the incentive for historical rate rollovers because any loss avoided in spot would be revealed at the forward maturity through the mark-to-market process. Since nonfinancial institutions are increasingly using distant-date products for both hedging and trend anticipation (an elegant word for speculation), mandatory marking-to-market also is desirable for these types of transactions.

Customer Appropriateness

Customer appropriateness must be one of senior management's main focuses, especially, in dealing with nontraditional or not widely known products (mainly related to derivatives). Customer appropriateness involves the analysis of the suitability of a customer to a product the bank is offering. When a financial institution sells a product to a customer, the bank is responsible for making sure the customer

- Understands the fundamental mechanics, logic, and intent of the product.

- Understands whether the product increases or decreases his price risk. In other words, is the reason for buying the product to reduce existing price risk (hedge) or to intentionally assume more price risk/speculate?

- Understands any leveraging the product may entail. For example, the customer may have $1 million to invest but instead borrows an additional million and thus invests a total of $2 million. Such leveraging will double the profits if things work out but will double the losses if the market moves the wrong way.

- Fully understands what the financial impact of adverse changes in market prices will be. This should include 2SD price changes and stress testing involving price changes of up to 5SD.

- Has systems that allow daily marking-to-market of the product. In the absence of this ability, the bank must provide mark-to-market information in writing on a daily basis.

- Understands whether the bank has been officially hired as an adviser or whether the relationship is at arm's length ("consenting adults" per *Euro Money* magazine).

- Has the financial capacity to absorb negative results from adverse changes in market prices.

The most senior management (CEO) must clearly understand all these points.

If a bank is not sure about one of these points, the product should not be sold to the customer. The consequences may be harmful for the customer and the bank in terms of dollars and image.

To examine a real-world example of these consequences, take the case of a well-known bank that specializes in derivative products (Bank Y). This bank entered into a complex swap transaction with a less sophisticated customer. The product included protection against lower interest rates. However, interest rates went up, and the negative impact on the customer's earnings increased exponentially. The customer subsequently sued Bank Y, stating that he did not understand the implications of the product and that the decision to enter into the transaction was based on the bank's assumed expertise and the customer's long-standing good relationship with the bank: "We never thought that a product recommended by you could have such a negative impact on us." As a consequence, Bank Y had to settle with the customer by paying an undisclosed amount of money. For Bank Y this problem had not only a negative economic effect but also a negative image effect, because the issue was very well publicized. In fact, it caught the attention of U.S. regulators.

Authority to Deal

In operating a bank account, it is common practice to allow only people whose signatures are on file with the bank to issue payment instructions. The same protocol should be applied to traders and their authority to engage in transactions. Financial trading has become so complex and the value at risk equivalent of transactions has risen so high that banks should require customers to establish in writing who among a customer's personnel has the authority to trade on behalf of the company and designate the types of trades in which it may engage. This authorization may be broken down into special categories, as indicated in Exhibit 15-3. For example, the customer can set specific limits per individual for the size of transactions in terms of volume amounts or value at risk. The same authorization would designate individuals who are allowed to trade from their homes or any other place outside the office. Banks also should communicate to their counterparties the types of transactions their dealers are authorized to conduct. To be effective, trading authorizations for the bank and its counterparties must be updated constantly.

The bank will have to initiate this process and explain that it is in the customer's interest to establish the authority to deal in writing. All this information could be provided on a computer on-line in real time so that before a trade can be consummated, the bank's trader has to check not

```
┌─────────────────────────────────────────────┐
│            AUTHORITY TO DEAL                  │
│   •  Similar to a bank account                │
│   •  Requires written advise to the bank      │
│   •  Requires constant updating               │
│   •  Authorization by categories              │
│        *  Spot                                │
│        *  Forward                             │
│        *  Size (volume or VAR)                │
│        *  Off-premises dealing                │
│        *  Transfer instructions               │
│   •  Bank must:                               │
│        *  Initiate                            │
│        *  Monitor compliance                  │
└─────────────────────────────────────────────┘
```

Exhibit 15-3. Recommendations for authority to deal.

only the availability of credit limits for the counterparty and price risk limits for himself but also the authorization of his counterparty to deal.

Monitoring Broker Relationships

The relationship between traders and brokers has a high potential for conflicts of interest. Consequently, banks should pay close attention to all interfaces with brokers and establish a written policy on that subject. The policy should include an initial approval process before the services of brokers are employed and an annual review of those relationships. There also should be monthly monitoring of the total size of brokerage and a breakdown of the total brokerage for each broker; for example, a concentration of brokerage on a single broker should be avoided.

The use of what is known in the industry as points should be strongly discouraged. This is a situation in which the broker offers to sell, for example, at 50 and the bank wishes to buy at 50 but it turns out that the market has changed and the broker can offer the commodity only at 55. To avoid arguments with the bank, the broker suggests that they close the transaction at 55 and says, "And I owe you 5 points." The intent is to make up those 5 points in a later transaction, when the bank will be prepared to buy at 70 and the broker instead will sell to the bank at 65. This is an extremely poor practice, and regulators in many countries do not tolerate it.

Entertainment received from brokers should be closely monitored by management in terms of frequency, style, and expense. Many banks keep logs of broker-supplied entertainment. Others do not accept such entertainment at all; instead, they arrange dinners with brokers to foster "warm and friendly" relationships at the bank's expense.

Annual Memorandum on Corporate and Trader Behavior

In addition to intentional wrongdoing, traders may engage unintentionally in undesirable activities and behavior. These situations occur because traders do not know that a particular practice is not tolerated by the employer or do not appreciate the severity of the wrongdoing.

An institution engaged in financial trading should develop a comprehensive document in which the institution-specific policies are clearly explained and laid out. The documents also should include seemingly obvious policies, rules, and behavior guidelines.

The objective of this process is to avoid a situation in which the trader can say after an undesirable incident occurred, "I did not know that this was wrong," or "I knew that it was wrong, but I did not know that it is viewed as serious." Most of the points that should be covered in such a document can be found in this section and in the guidelines for foreign exchange trading activities in Appendix A, *Guidelines for Foreign Exchange Trading Activities*, issued in 1996 by the Foreign Exchange Committee of the New York Federal Reserve Bank. What must be added are each bank's specific policies on the various issues.

This document should be signed by the traders upon employment and thereafter on an annual basis. Each trader should sign it twice, once to confirm that he or she has read the document and once to confirm that the content of the memorandum was understood.

Mandatory and Minimum Vacation

Some well-publicized mishaps at major financial institutions in the past would not have occurred if the key personnel involved in hiding losses and covering up other wrongdoing had been away from the bank for several days. These people usually must be physically present to keep all the balls in the air.

Because of these experiences, banks must have a mandatory vacation policy that requires employees to be away from the office for a minimum of 2 continuous weeks a year. Seminars and similar educational programs can satisfy this requirement provided that the employee is not functionally in touch with the office. For example, it is all right to phone the secretary and congratulate him on his birthday, but this phone call may not be used to issue functional instructions affecting the business.

As is the case with almost all other control-related policies, it is critical that there be no exceptions to this vacation policy. In particular, very senior people, key personnel who seem indispensable, and major money makers cannot be exempt. Regrettably, the past has shown that if there is any wrongdoing at all, it is this category of people that is most likely to be involved. Therefore, one more time, no exceptions for anyone!

General Thoughts

Traders must understand that playing by the rules and passing audits are more important than making money. It is dangerous for a bank to tolerate a situation in which dealers who generate substantial earnings are allowed to depart from established control practices or to exceed limits without prior approval. In the long run this is poison for the organization and should not be allowed. At the beginning of this book we established the fact that the ultimate goal is to increase the price of the stock. There is ample evidence in the marketplace that organizations with substantial earnings but, rightly or wrongly, a reputation for a lack of internal controls may suffer in terms of the price/earnings ratios the market allows them and may be downgraded by rating agencies.

Unusually high earnings must be investigated and analyzed with the same rigor and attention to detail that would be applied if there had been a large loss. Management must understand which market factors had to change to create the unusually large profit and what would have happened if a particular market factor or another feature of the risk position had moved against the bank.

Traders should clearly understand that with a budget of $10 million, it is better to make $11 million and pass audits than to make $15 million and not play by the rules.

Appendix A reprints a document issued periodically by the New York Federal Reserve Bank's Foreign Exchange Committee. Readers should review this document carefully. The guidelines are very useful even if one does not trade in foreign exchange and even if the dealing room is not in the United States. Finally, managers should be serious about enforcing all the controls employed by their banks. Each control mechanism is useful only if it is adhered to at all times, without exception.

It is critical to create and adhere to a control ethic.

Final Advice

Remain creative, receptive to new ideas, mentally young!

Try to understand what you are doing and why you are doing it!

Try to understand what other people are saying and why they are saying it!

Question what is, and why things are the way they are!

Curiosity is the mother of invention.

Do not resist change in products, processes, and techniques!

Time without change produces only age.

Don't resist change—remain professionally eternally young!

Appendix **A**

Guidelines for Foreign Exchange Trading Activities

The New York Foreign Exchange Committee
January 1996

Introduction

The main objective of the *Guidelines* is to clearly and concisely document issues that should be considered by institutions active in the foreign exchange market. These recommendations are based on the views of representatives from a number of commercial banks, investment banks, and brokerage firms participating in the foreign exchange market. The guidelines are primarily directed to managers and line personnel in the institutions actively trading foreign exchange (including commercial/investment banks and other wholesale market participants) and also to managers and staff of foreign exchange brokerage firms. Others may also find the discussion useful as much of the material can be applied generically to financial market activities. These guidelines should clarify common market practices and assist individuals in conducting their daily business activities.

This is the Committee's fourth revision of a paper first published in 1980. The Committee has published numerous "good practices" recommendations in the three years since the last revision of these guidelines. This version of the *Guidelines* reflects the Committee's work on several issues affecting the conduct of foreign exchange trading activities. Many of these are referenced in the document and included in the appendices.

The Foreign Exchange Committee encourages wide distribution of the *Guidelines.* To that end, foreign exchange professionals are encouraged to duplicate and distribute the document freely. Interested parties may also obtain current copies of these guidelines by contacting the Executive Assistant, Foreign Exchange Committee, 33 Liberty Street, New York, NY 10045/telephone 212/720-6651 and facsimile 212/720-1655.

Ethical Issues for Management

Confidentiality

Confidentiality and customer anonymity are essential to the operation of a professional foreign exchange market. Market participants and their customers expect to have their interest and activity known only by the other party to the transaction and an intermediary if one is used. It is inappropriate to disclose, or to request others to disclose, information relating to a counterparty's involvement in a transaction except to the extent required by law.

A trader may have access to a considerable amount of confidential information, including the trades he or she prices and confidential material prepared within the organization or obtained from those with whom the institution does business. Such information might pertain directly to the foreign exchange market or to other financial markets. Although not explicitly stated to be confidential, it may not be publicly available.

Managers should expect that their employees will not pass on confidential information outside of their institution except with the permission of the party or parties directly involved. Nor should a trader or broker distribute confidential information within his or her institution except on a need-to-know basis. Managers should not tolerate traders or brokers utilizing confidential material for personal benefit or in any manner that might compromise their institution. In the event that confidentiality is broken, it is the role of management to act promptly to correct the conditions that permitted such an event to occur.

Management should be alert to the possibility that the changing mechanics of foreign exchange trading might jeopardize their efforts to preserve confidentiality. As technological innovations are introduced into the trading environment, managers should be aware of the security implications of such changes. For example, the use of two-way speaker phones has largely been abandoned or controlled to safeguard confidentiality. Ongoing advances in telecommunications systems, computer networks, trade processing systems and market analysis systems, and the integration of these systems within an institution can lead to inadvertent breaches of security. The potential loss of confidentiality represented by complex systems—with multiple users, multiple locations, and ongoing data base or operating program changes—may be further complicated when the central processing unit or software is managed by an outside vendor.

Managers should also act to protect sensitive information when visitors are present in trading rooms or brokerage operations. There is always the possibility that visitors will be exposed to confidential information such as: names of transaction participants, amounts of trades, and currencies traded. Whether or not disclosed information is put to use, and however unintentional disclosure may be, the fact that confidentiality between counterparties has been violated is grounds for concern. Visits should be prearranged and visitors should be accompanied by an employee of the host institution. A visitor from another trading institution should not be permitted to trade for his or her own institution from the premises of the host.

Trading for Personal Account

In general, managers should expect traders to give their full attention to their employing institution's business activities without being distracted by their own personal financial affairs. Managers should also expect traders to fulfill their institutional responsibilities objectively, unbiased by their own financial position.

Managers should be aware that a conflict of interest or an appearance of a conflict of interest may arise if traders are permitted to deal for themselves in those commodities or instruments closely related to the ones they deal for their institution. Such conflict could be detrimental or embarrassing to the institution, the trader, or both. It is management's responsibility to develop and disseminate a clear institutional policy on these matters and to establish procedures to avoid actual conflicts of interest. At a minimum, an institution should require senior management to give traders explicit permission to engage in trading for personal account and require traders to execute such transactions in a manner that allows monitoring by management. Some institutions have recently taken steps to prohibit traders from any trading for personal account that could give rise to the appearance of a conflict of interest.

Traders should recognize that they, too, have a responsibility to identify and avoid conflicts and the appearance of conflict of interest. A trader should bring to management's attention any situation where there is a question of propriety. In no instance should a trader use his or her institutional affiliation, or take advantage of nonpublic or exclusive foreign exchange transaction information involving a third party to create trading opportunities for personal gain.

Entertainment/Gifts

Management should assure themselves that their institution's general guidelines on entertainment and the exchange of gifts are sufficient to address the particular circumstances of their employees. Where appropriate, such general guidelines should be supplemented for trading personnel to help them avoid the dangers of excessive entertainment. Special attention needs to be given to the style, frequency, and cost of entertainment afforded traders. Many trading institutions have mechanisms in place to monitor entertainment. Although it is customary for a broker or trader to occasionally entertain market contacts at lunch or dinner, entertainment even in this form becomes questionable when it is underwritten but not attended by the host.

Foreign exchange market personnel should conduct themselves in such a way as to avoid potentially embarrassing situations and the appearance of improper inducement. They should fully understand their institution's guidelines on what constitutes an appropriate gift or entertainment as well as the bounds of law and reasonable propriety. They should also be expected to notify management regarding unusual favors offered traders by virtue of their professional position.

Fiduciary Responsibility/Appropriateness

Management should act honestly and in good faith when marketing, transacting, and administering its foreign exchange trading activities. Firms should take care to determine that the client has the capability (either internally or through independent professional advice) to understand the nature and risk of foreign exchange activities and that the client is not relying on recommendations or advice of the firm when entering into foreign exchange activities (unless a written advisory agreement has been signed by both parties). Consideration should be given to the making of risk disclosures in connection with foreign exchange trading activities. Firms should maintain policies and procedures that identify and address circumstances that can lead to uncertainties, misunderstandings, or disputes with the potential for relationship, reputational, or litigation risk. A more detailed discussion of the issues relating to fiduciary responsibility/appropriateness is contained in Principles and Practices for Wholesale Financial Market Transactions, August 1995.

Human Resource Issues for Management

As a result of the rapid growth and increasing complexity of the financial markets, trading rooms are operating on frontiers of earnings and risk, business mission and business policy. Skillful, capable people are a prerequisite for success in this demanding environment. It is a primary management responsibility to recruit, develop, and lead individuals and teams tasked to operate in this atmosphere.

The work environment for trading personnel has some very important characteristics. Trading room situations are positions of great trust. The pace of work is intense. Traders operate under strong internal pressures to make profits in a market that is open twenty-four hours a day. At the same time, the process of developing a trader has become compressed. Today, traders are either hired from other institutions or selected internally from individuals thought to have the work experience or academic training that would prepare them quickly for market-making, position-taking, or sales-related activities.

Selection

The process of selecting new employees is an important management responsibility. Managers should ensure that prospective trading room staff meet predetermined standards of aptitude, integrity, and stability for trading room jobs at all levels. Managers should exercise caution in delegating hiring decisions. To the extent possible, job candidates should be interviewed by several staff members of the institution and references should be checked. The managers' expectations concerning a trader's responsibilities, profitability, and behavior should be discussed thoroughly before a candidate is hired.

Training

The mobility of trading personnel within the financial industry has a material effect on traders' perceptions of their relationship to their employers. In some cases, it may be possible for an employee to begin trading an instrument for an institution although he or she does not have an intimate knowledge of the traditions and practices of that market or of the traditions and corporate culture of his or her current employer. This situation can give rise to misunderstandings about management's expectations of traders.

Managers should ensure that each trader is fully acquainted with the policies, procedures, and style that their institution chooses to employ in the conduct of its business. Management should consider providing complete orientation procedures for new employees at all levels and formal procedures to ensure periodic review of the institution's rules and policies by each trader. An awareness of and respect for market procedures and conventions should be encouraged.

Roles, responsibilities, and authorities should be unambiguous. Procedures, technologies, and contingencies should be thoroughly explained. Risk measurements and risk reporting should be understood by all involved in trading activities.

Compensation

Compensation systems should encourage appropriate behavior, reflecting institutional goals and reinforcing organizational values.

Stress

Stress may lead to job performance problems. Managers need to be able to identify symptoms of stress among trading personnel and then act to mitigate problems. Management should consider educating trading room staff in personal stress-management techniques.

Substance Abuse

Managers should educate themselves and their traders or brokers about the signs of drug use and the potential damage resulting from the use of drugs and other forms of substance abuse. Policies should be developed and clearly announced for dealing with individuals who are found to be substance abusers.

Gambling

Gambling among market participants has obvious dangers and should be discouraged.

Trading Practices

The smooth functioning and integrity of the interbank market, whether through direct dealing or electronic or voice brokers, depends on trust, honesty, and high standards of behavior by all market participants.

Traders' Responsibility for Prices

It is a management responsibility to ensure that traders who are authorized to quote dealing prices are aware of and comply with policies and procedures that apply to foreign exchange dealing.

In the interbank market, dealers are expected to be committed to the bids and offers they propose through brokers for generally accepted market amounts unless otherwise specified and until the bid or offer is (1) dealt on, (2) canceled, (3) superseded by a better bid or offer, or (4) the broker closes another transaction in that currency with another counterparty at a price other than that originally proposed. In the cases of (3) or (4), the broker should consider the original bid or offer no longer valid unless reinstated by the dealer.

If one counterparty is unacceptable to the other because of limited credit line availability, the broker may propose to substitute a "clearing institution." If both counterparties agree, this use of "switches" is an acceptable practice, but it entails certain risks. Management is encouraged to adopt the recommended principles and procedures for broker switches outlined in the Foreign Exchange Committee Letter on Name Substitution, September 23, 1993.

Electronic Trading Vehicles

In utilizing electronic trading vehicles, dealers are expected to be clear and precise in their use of dealing terminology, and alert to potential educational and structural issues or problems inherent in the adaptation of new technology. Management should actively monitor the introduction of such systems to insure proper training, timely dispute resolution, and appropriate interaction with vendors in order to refine and enhance these dealing tools. Opportunities for trade disputes are inevitable when using new systems. Users should govern themselves according to established market conventions and any departure from those conventions should be agreed upon at the time a deal is transacted.

Need to Avoid Questionable Practices

When markets are unsettled and prices are volatile, opportunities may arise for traders to engage in practices that may realize an immediate gain or avoid a loss but may be questionable in terms of a trader's reputation (as well as that of the trader's institution) over the long run. There are many kinds of questionable practices. For example, perpetrating rumors may reflect adversely on the professionalism of the trader. Reneging on deals may give rise to liability. The profitability of a given forward transaction may be distorted by delayed or inconsistent establishment of the appropriate spot rate. In the latter case, it is recommended that management adopt the standard of the middle rate at the time of the transaction.

It is unethical to manipulate market practice or convention to gain unfair competitive advantage. Management should be alert to any pattern of complaints about a trader's behavior from sources outside the institution such as customers, other trading institutions, or intermediaries. Information available within the organization should be reviewed to determine if individual traders or brokers become frequently involved in disputes over trades or tend to accept deals at rates that were obvious misquotes, accidental or otherwise, by counterparties. Complaints about trading practices may be self-serving, however, and should be handled judiciously.

Off-Market Rates

Dealers may occasionally face requests from customers to use "off-market" exchange rates. Such requests should be accommodated only after resolving issues concerning credit policy and propriety.

"Historical-rate rollovers" are an important example of off-market rate transactions. (See Foreign Exchange Committee Letter "Historical-Rate Rollovers: A Dangerous Practice," December 26, 1991.) Historical-rate rollovers involve the extension of a forward foreign exchange contract by a dealer on behalf of his customer at off-market rates. The application of nonmarket rates can have the effect of moving income from one institution to another (perhaps over an income reporting date) or of altering the timing of reported taxable income. Such operations, in effect, result in an extension of unsecured credit to a counterparty.

The use of historical-rate rollovers involves two major risks: (1) either counterparty could unknowingly aid illegal or inappropriate activities, and (2) either counterparty could misunderstand the special nature of the transaction and the associated credit exposures. Given these risks, the rolling over of contracts at historical rates is a dangerous practice that should be avoided absent compelling justification and procedural safeguards. While the nature of certain commercial transactions may justify the use of historical rates with some customers, use of historical rates with other trading institutions should not be permitted. Even when used with customers, historical-rate rollovers are appropriate if (1) customers have a legitimate commercial justification for extending the contract, and (2) senior management of both the customer and the dealer institutions are aware of the transaction and the risks involved.

All dealer institutions permitting requests for historical-rate rollovers should have written procedures guiding their use. An example of such procedures is as follows:

a. A letter from the customer's senior management (treasurer or above) should be kept on file explaining (1) that the customer will occasionally request to roll over contracts at historical rates; (2) the reasons why such requests will be made; and (3) that such requests are consistent with the customer firm's internal policies. This letter should be kept current.

b. The dealer should solicit an explanation from the customer for each request for an off-market rate deal at the time the request is made.

c. Senior Management and/or appropriate credit officers at the dealer institution should be informed of and approve each transaction and any effective extension of credit.

d. A letter should be sent to senior customer management immediately after each off-market transaction is executed explaining the particulars of the trade and explicitly stating the implied loan or borrowing amount.

e. Generally, forward contracts should not be extended for more than three months, nor extended more than once; however, any extension of a rollover should itself meet the requirements of (b), (c), and (d) above.

Stop-Loss/Profit Orders

Trading institutions may receive requests from customers, branches, and correspondents to buy or sell a fixed amount of currency if the exchange rate for that currency reaches a specified level. These orders, which include stop-loss and limit orders from trading counterparties, may be intended for execution during the day, overnight, or until executed or canceled. The growing incidence of such orders is due to widening acceptance of technical trading concepts, and increasingly sophisticated and disciplined risk management in spot, forward and derivative foreign exchange products. Fluctuations in market liquidity, multiple price discovery mechanisms, and evolving channels of distribution obscure transparency and may complicate the execution of such business. As a result, management should ensure clear understanding between their institution and their counterparties of the basis on which these orders will be undertaken. In accepting such an order, an institution assumes an obligation to make every reasonable effort to execute the order quickly at the established price. However, a specified rate order does not necessarily provide a fixed-price guarantee to the counterparty. Specifically, dealers may wish to inform customers that stop-loss orders will remain valid only from Monday 6:00 a.m. Sydney through Friday 5:00 p.m. New York, the time frame presently specified in the barrier option addendum to the foreign exchange and option master agreement.

When a dispute arises between institutions as to whether an order should have been executed, brokers are often asked to confirm the high/low price of the day. Brokers are not the market per se and can only be used as an information source. A brokering company is one representative of the market and can therefore give trading ranges seen from within their institution, which may not be indicative of the entire market range. Consequently, that information should be treated with discretion. Management should also ensure that their dealers and operations department are equipped to attend to all aspects of the frequently complex nature of these orders during periods of peak volume and extreme volatility. These complexities may include: conditional provisions, transaction notification, and cancellation or forwarding instructions.

Trader-Trader Relationship

A current practice among trading institutions is to deal directly with each other, at least at certain agreed-upon times during the dealing day. The nature of the direct dealing relationship will vary according to the interests of the two parties. Management should ensure that the terms of each relationship are clearly understood and accepted by both institutions and that these terms are respected in practice.

A possible element of a direct dealing relationship between two institutions is reciprocity. That is, each institution in a direct dealing pair may agree to provide timely, competitive rate quotations for marketable amounts when it has received such a service from the other. Differences in institutions' relative size, expertise, or specialization in certain markets, will influence what is perceived by the two parties as equitable.

In the brokers' market, traders should not renege on a transaction, claiming credit line constraints, in an effort to "settle" a personal dispute. Instead, senior management should be made aware of a problem so that both institutions may act to address it. In all cases and at all times, traders should maintain professionalism, confidentiality, and proper language in telephone and electronic conversations with traders at other institutions.

Traders should also be certain that their market terminology is clear and understood by their counterparty. They should take steps to avoid using confusing or obscure market jargon that could be misleading or inaccurate.

Management should analyze trading activity periodically. Any unusually large concentration of direct trading with another institution or institutions should be reviewed to determine whether the level of activity is appropriate.

Trader-Broker Relationship

Senior management of both trading institutions and brokerage firms should assume an active role in overseeing the trader-broker relationship. Management should establish the terms under which brokerage service is to be rendered, agree that any aspect of the relationship can be reviewed by either party at any time, and be available to intercede in disputes as they arise. Management of both trading institutions and brokerage firms should ensure that their staffs are aware of and in compliance with internal policies governing the trader-broker relationship. Ultimately, the senior management at a trading institution is responsible for the choice of brokers. Therefore, senior management should periodically monitor the patterns of broker usage and be alert to possible undue concentrations of business. Brokerage management should impress upon their employees the need to respect the interests of all of the institutions served by their firm.

Name Substitution

Brokers are intermediaries who communicate bids and offers to potential principals and otherwise arrange transactions. In the traditional foreign exchange market, the names of the institutions placing bids or offers are not revealed until a transaction's size and exchange rate are agreed upon; even then, only the counterparties gain this information. If one of the counterparties is unacceptable to the other, the substitution of a new counterparty may be agreed on.

"Name substitution" (the practice of interposing a new counterparty or clearing bank between the two original parties) developed because before names are introduced in the course of a transaction each counterparty has already committed to the trade and its details. Many institutions believe that once they have revealed confidential information, they should complete a trade with the same specifications.

A name substitution in a spot transaction is an acceptable practice provided that:

- both counterparties receive the name of an acceptable counterparty within a reasonable amount of time;

- the clearing bank is fully aware of the trade; and

- the clearing bank is operating in accordance with its normal procedures and limits.

Under these circumstances, the bank's risk does not differ from any other trades involving the respective trading institutions. When transactions cannot be completed expeditiously, risks increase and disruptions can occur. Therefore, foreign exchange managers should clearly establish with their brokers the approach their institution will generally follow in handling specific name problems. Managers should provide their brokers with the names of institutions with which they are willing to deal or, alternatively, the names of the institutions they will virtually always reject. Brokers should use this information to try to avoid name problems. If a broker proposes a transaction on behalf of an institution not usually regarded as an acceptable counterparty, it is appropriate for that broker to make a potential counterparty aware that the transaction may need to be referred to management for credit approval (that is, the counterparty may be "referable") before the trade can be agreed to.

Name substitutions rarely occur in the brokered forward market. Participants in this market recognize and understand that a broker's forward bids and offers, even though firm, cannot result in an agreed trade at matching prices unless it comes within the internal credit limits of each counterparty. Forward dealers should not falsely claim a lack of credit to avoid trades or to manipulate prices.

Missed Prices and Disputes

Difficulties may arise when a trader discovers that a transaction thought to have been entered, was not completed by the broker. Failure to complete a transaction as originally proposed may occur for a variety of reasons: the price was simultaneously canceled, an insufficient amount was presented to cover dealers' desired transactions, or an unacceptable counterparty name might be presented. Disputes may also arise over misunderstandings or errors by either a trader or a broker.

Whenever a trade is aborted, managers and traders must recognize that it may be impossible for the broker to find another counterparty at the original price. Managers should ensure that their staffs understand that it is inappropriate to force a broker to accept a transaction in which a counterparty has withdrawn its interest before the trade could be consummated—a practice known as "stuffing."

For their part, brokerage firm management should establish clear policies prohibiting position-taking by brokers and require that any position unintentionally assumed be closed out at the earliest practical time after the problem has been identified.

Avoiding Disputes

The management of both trading institutions and brokerage firms should take steps to reduce the likelihood of disputes. This can be accomplished when management assumes a key role in training new employees. Training may extend to the use of proper, clear, and common terminology; awareness of standard market practice; and adherence to the procedures of their institution. Trading institution management should also consider implementing frequent intraday reconciliations with other counterparties, including those arranged through brokers; once-a-day checks may be inadequate.

Even if these procedures are followed, disputes are inevitable and management should establish clear policies for resolution. Informal dispute resolution practices, which sometimes develop in the market, can be inconsistent with sound business practices.

Resolution of Disputes

When disputes arise or differences occur, the following guidelines for compensation apply:

Differences should be routinely referred to senior management for resolution, thereby changing the dispute from an individual trader-broker issue to an inter-institutional issue. All compensation should take the form of a bank check or wire transfer in the name of the institution or of adjustment to brokerage bills. The settlement of differences should be evenhanded, allowing for compensation to go both ways.

All such transactions should be fully documented by each firm. Once a resolution has been reached, an institution should make restitution by check or some other noncash mean (for example, reduction of brokerage bill). When differences occur between a broker and dealer, the dealer is strongly urged to accept compensation directly from the brokering company and not to insist on a name at the original price.

For more detailed suggestions on the resolution of differences and disputed trades, see: 1989 Foreign Exchange Committee Annual Report pp. 16–17; the Federal Reserve Bank of New York "Policy Statement on the Use of 'Points' in Settling Foreign Exchange Contracts," August 1, 1990; and the "Committee Letter on Confirmation and Dispute Resolution Practices," December 22, 1993.

Trader-Customer Relationship

Issues may develop in the relationship between trading institutions and their customers. As a consequence, the management of customer relationships requires a high degree of integrity and mutual respect as well as effective communication of each party's interests and objectives. Disputes that may arise between a trader and a customer concerning the terms of a transaction should be referred to the appropriate level of management for resolution.

It is a normal practice for nonfinancial organizations to delegate trading authority formally to specific individuals within the organization and to advise their bankers accordingly. At the same time, trading institutions are obliged to make reasonable efforts to comply with corporate dealing authorization instructions. Trading personnel who deal with customers should be familiar with current corporate instruction, and those instructions should be readily accessible. Sales and trading personnel should bring to management's attention changes in counterparties trading patterns, significant book profits or losses, or any unusual requests.

Undisclosed Counterparties

"Know your customer" has long been a golden rule for most non-arms length financial transactions. The recent increases in the volume of foreign exchange transactions conducted through funds managers/investment dealers has resulted in substantial numbers of deals where the principal counterparties are not known at the time of transaction. Dealers should identify counterparties as soon as possible following a deal.

Management at financial institutions engaged in trading on this basis needs to be aware of the risks involved, particularly with respect to credit exposure and money laundering.

Operational Aspects of Trading

Risk Management

Institutions should be duly aware of the various types of risk to which they are exposed when engaging in foreign exchange transactions, including:

- *Market Risk:* The risk of loss due to adverse changes in financial markets (exchange rate risk, interest rate risk, basis risk, correlation risk, etc.).

- *Credit Risk:* The risk of loss due to a counterparty default (settlement risk, delivery risk, sovereign risk).

- *Liquidity Risk:* The risk that a lack of counterparties will leave a firm unable to liquidate, fund, or offset a position (or to do so at or near the market value of the asset).

- *Operational/Technology Risk:* The risk of loss from inadequate systems and controls, human error, or management failure (processing risk, product pricing risk, valuation risk, etc.).

- *Legal Risk:* The risk of loss due to legal or regulatory aspects of financial transactions (suitability risk, compliance risk, etc.).

There are also overall business risks that fall outside these categories such as reputation risk, event risk and fraud.

Sound management controls to monitor and evaluate the risk exposures associated with foreign exchange and related trading operations can help keep these exposures within management's specifications. Management needs to reinforce information tools with effective mechanisms for monitoring compliance.

Many different approaches are used by financial institutions to measure and manage the various risks arising from foreign exchange transactions. Risk Management methodologies vary in complexity. At the simple end of the spectrum one finds notional value limits by product type, by customer, and by country for controlling credit and settlement risk exposures as well as the market risk exposures incurred. On the more sophisticated end, an institution may use a combination of real time measures of value-at-risk (VAR) and scenario analysis. VAR is calculated by using often complex statistical models and simulation techniques for predicting rate volatility. These also take into account cross-currency and cross-market correlations, liquidity factors, and (in the case of credit risk) expected counterparty default rates. Management should ensure that the risk management techniques employed in their institutions are commensurate with the levels of risk incurred and the nature and volume of the foreign exchange activity being undertaken.

There are important aspects of risk management that go beyond the measurement of market and credit risk. These include:

- adherence to company-approved accounting policies and standards for all products;

- periodic independent reviews by internal auditors and daily oversight role of an independent risk management/compliance unit; annual review by external auditors and annual or more frequent examinations by the regulators;

- segregation of trading room and back-office functions for deal processing, accounting and settlement;

- independent verification of revaluation rates and yield curves used for risk management and accounting purposes;

- documented and regularly tested disaster recovery and back-up procedures involving both systems (front and back office) and off-site facilities;

- sufficient human resources and systems support to ensure that deal processing and risk reporting remain timely and accurate;

- independent verbal and/or written confirmation of all trades;

- independent daily reporting of risk positions to senior management;

- daily reporting of traders' profit/loss to senior management;

- new product approval and implementation procedures, which include sign-offs by legal, tax, audit, systems, operations, risk management, and accounting departments;

- an independent valuation-model testing and approval process;

- well-documented and appropriately approved operating procedures;

- independent approval of customer credit limits and market risk position limits;

- independent monitoring of credit and market risk limits; and

■ exception reporting and independent approval of limit excesses

Risk management is not a substitute for integrity or awareness. Management should be aware of the assumptions used in its risk assessments and the need to develop the discipline, depth, and experience that ensure survivability. Risks should be weighed against potential returns and longer term organizational goals.

Accounting for Forward Transactions

Net present value accounting (NPV) is the preferred approach for marking foreign exchange forward books to market. NPV more accurately reflects the true market values of unsettled forward contracts. The well known theory of "covered interest rate arbitrage," which is the financial underpinning of forward foreign exchange markets, takes into account the time value of money. Discounting or deriving the NPV of the forward cash flows is required to evaluate the financial viability of a forward transaction. It requires the linking of the forward and spot pieces of a forward transaction while taking into account the funding costs of a forward position.

A firm's choice of accounting methods is management's prerogative; however, if management does not use NPV for valuing their foreign exchange books, an alternative means of controlling the inherent risks must be devised. These risks include:

■ taking "unearned" profits on the spot portion of the forward deal into income immediately and delaying the recognition of trading losses until some point in the future. NPV accounting evaluates the spot and forward pieces of a forward deal together and allows a firm to identify losses earlier.

■ inappropriate economic incentives resulting from inconsistencies between the accounting treatment applied to cash instrument transactions and other off-balance sheet instrument transactions. Variances in accounting methods may inadvertently provide an inappropriate financial incentive for a trader to engage in transactions that provide no economic value (or even negative economic value) to the firm.

■ collusion between traders who work at institutions that practice NPV accounting methods and traders at those institutions that do not. The early closeout of a forward transaction (which would be based on a discounted value) could result in an immediate and unanticipated gain or loss being realized in the books of a firm not practicing NPV accounting methods.

Netting

Interest in foreign exchange netting has increased as institutions have sought to reduce counterparty credit risk exposure, interbank payments, and the amount of capital allocated to foreign exchange activity. While netting arrangements may have operational similarities, they can differ significantly in their legal and risk-reduction characteristics. Some forms of netting reduce the number and size of settlement payments while leaving credit risk at gross levels. The masking of risk, however, is not consistent with sound banking practice. Other forms of netting, such as netting by novation, can reduce credit risk as well as payment flows by legally substituting net obligations in place of gross obligations. In 1994 the Foreign Exchange Committee published the paper, *Reducing Foreign Exchange Settlement Risk*, which defines settlement risk and offers several best practices recommendations.

Since the 1994 paper, several commercial ventures providing netting services to market participants have been launched. These ventures vary in their approach to and method for reducing settlement risk. The Committee recommends that firms considering joining or subscribing to a netting service evaluate their options carefully to insure that it will provide the anticipated level of risk reductions for the firm.

The Foreign Exchange Committee has held a long-standing interest in foreign exchange netting. Further information about the types of netting arrangements are found in the Committee's Annual Report for 1988 (p. 9), and for 1989 (p. 8). Other sources of information are the *Report of the Committee on Interbank Netting Schemes of the G-10 Central Banks* published by the Bank for International Settlements (BIS) in November 1990, and *The Supervisory Recognition of Netting for Capital Adequacy Purposes* published by the BIS in April 1993.

New Product Development

The growing complexity of new financial instruments and services requires that detailed research and documentation, together with internal cross-functional reviews and personnel training, be completed before a product is marketed. Formal programs to control the introduction of a new product help verify that the new activity is likely to be sufficiently profitable, that associated risks will be manageable, and that all legal, regulatory, accounting, and operating requirements are met. While many requirements must be fulfilled before the introduction of a product, the existence of formal, new product programs can actually speed and facilitate the product development cycle. (For further discussion, see *1988 Foreign Exchange Committee Annual Report*, p. 11.)

Taping of Telephone Conversations

Many trading institutions record all telephone lines used for trading and confirmation. Taping conversations in foreign exchange trading rooms and confirmation areas helps resolve disputes quickly and fairly. Whether or not traders need access to untaped lines in order to carry out unrecorded conversations on sensitive topics is a matter of management preference.

Access to tapes containing conversations should be granted only for the purpose of resolving disputes and should be strictly limited to those personnel with supervisory responsibility for trading, customer dealing, or confirmations. Tapes should be kept in secure storage for as long as is sufficient for most disputes to surface. When taping equipment is first installed, trading institutions should give counterparties due notice that conversations will be taped.

Deal Confirmations

Institutions active in the foreign exchange market should exchange written confirmations of all foreign exchange transactions—including both interbank and corporate, spot, and forward. Any use of same-day telephone confirmations should be followed with written confirmations through means of immediate communication. Such timely confirmations can be provided by telex, SWIFT, fax transmissions, as well as by various automated dealing and confirmation systems. These forms of communication are more appropriate than mailed confirmations, which, particularly on spot transactions, may not arrive in time to bring problems to light before the settlement date. Trading institutions have found that the sooner a problem is identified, the easier and often less expensive it is to resolve. Prompt and efficient confirmation procedures are also a deterrent to unauthorized dealing.

In the United States brokered foreign exchange market, when both parties to a transaction are offices of institutions located in the United States, the counterparties—and not the broker—are responsible for confirming the transaction directly to one another. However, when a broker arranges an "international" transaction, where either one or both of the parties does not have a U.S. "address," it is the broker's responsibility to provide each of the counterparties with written confirmations of the transaction. Brokers should ensure that confirmations of spot transactions are given on the same day that a trade is consummated. Trading institutions have the responsibility to check that the confirmations provided by brokers are received and reconciled on a timely basis. They also are responsible for promptly reconciling the activity going through their nostro accounts with their trading transactions.

For further discussions, see: the "Committee Letter on Confirmation and Dispute Resolution Practices," December 22, 1993; and the Foreign Exchange Committee Letter of June 1995.

Documentation

It is in the market's best interest that participants use and support the development of market standard documentation. In addition, firms should maintain explicit policies on documentation requirements and procedures for safeguarding executed documents. Policies may address how to handle specific documents, including, but not limited to, the following:

- corporate resolutions;
- certificates of incumbency;
- delegation of authority;
- industry standard agreements;
- risk disclosures; and
- confirmations.

Third-Party Payments

Management should have a clear policy for traders concerning the appropriateness of honoring requests for "third-party payments." A third-party payment is a transfer of funds in settlement of a foreign exchange transaction to the account of an institution or corporation other than that of the counterparty to the transaction. A subsidiary of the counterparty is a legally separate third party, but a foreign branch of an institution is not.

The normal payment risk inherent in foreign exchange—the risk that funds are paid out to a counterparty but not received—is most acute when the funds, in either local or foreign currency, are transferred to a party other than the principal to the transaction. These third-party payments are more susceptible than normal transactions to: (1) fraud perpetrated by a current or former employee of the counterparty who is diverting payment to a personal account, (2) fraud perpetrated by an employee of the bank who is altering the payment instructions, or (3) misinterpretation of the payment instructions whereby the funds are transferred to an erroneous beneficiary. In many cases, the ability to recover the funds paid out will depend upon the outcome of legal proceedings.

As a matter of policy, many institutions establish special controls for this type of transaction. The control procedures appropriate to address the associated risks include various measures to authenticate or verify third-party payments, such as:

- requiring the counterparty to provide standing payment and settlement instructions;
- requiring an authenticated confirmation on the transaction date;
- requiring the counterparty to submit a list of individuals authorized to transact business and to confirm deals; or
- confirming by telephone all deals on the transaction date to the individual identified by the counterparty.

Importance of Support Staff

Management's attention to a foreign exchange trading operation is usually directed toward establishing trading policies, managing risk, and developing trading personnel. Equally important is an efficient "back office" or operating staff. Details of each trading transaction should be accurately recorded. Payment instructions should be correctly exchanged and executed. Timely information should be provided to management and traders. The underlying results should be properly evaluated and accounts quickly reconciled. Time-consuming and costly reconciliation of disputed or improperly executed transactions mar the efficiency of the market, hurt profitability, and can impair the willingness of others to trade with the offending institution.

Accordingly, management must be aware of its responsibility to establish a support staff consistent with the scope of their trading desk's activity in the market. In addition, management should ensure that trading is commensurate with available back office support. It is also essential that management and staff of the back office are sufficiently independent from the traders and trading management in terms of organizational reporting lines. Finally, the incentive and compensation plans for back office personnel should not be directly related to the financial performance of the traders.

Audit Trail

Management should ensure that procedures are in place to provide a clear and fully documented audit trail of all foreign exchange transactions. The audit trail should provide information identifying the counterparty, currencies, amount, price, trade date, and value date. Such information should be captured in the institution's records as soon as possible after the trade is completed and should be in a format that can be readily reviewed by the institution's management as well as by internal and external auditors. These procedures should be adequate to inform management of trading activities and to facilitate detection of any lack of compliance with policy directives.

Recent technological innovations in trading and execution systems tend to improve data capture and allow for the creation of more precise audit records. For example, some electronic dealing systems independently generate trade data that serve as an effective audit trail. Trades executed via telex, automated dealing systems, or an internal source document provide better verification than trades executed over the telephone. An accurate audit trail significantly improves accountability and documentation and reduces instances of questionable transactions that remain undetected or improperly recorded. Management may therefore wish to emphasize such systems when considering trading room configuration and mechanics for dealing with counterparties.

Twenty-Four Hour Trading

With foreign exchange trading now taking place on a continuous twenty-four-hour basis, management should be certain that there are adequate control procedures in place for trading that is conducted outside of normal business hours—either at the office or at traders' homes. Management should clearly identify the types of transactions that may be entered into after the normal close of business and should ensure that there are adequate support and accounting controls for such transactions. Management should also designate and inform their counterparties of those individuals, if any, who are authorized to deal outside the office. In all cases, confirmations for trades arranged off-premises should be sent promptly to the appropriate staff at the office site.

Twenty-four-hour trading, if not properly controlled, can blur the distinction between end-of-day and intraday position risk limits. Financial institutions involved in twenty-four-hour trading should establish an unofficial "close of business" for each trading day against which end-of-day positions are monitored.

Increasingly, during the U.S. workday, institutions in the United States receive requests to trade from overseas traders who are operating outside their own normal business hours. Management should consider how they want their traders to respond. It is possible that, for selected counterparties, arrangements can be discussed in advance and a procedure can be established to accommodate the counterparty's needs while still identifying and protecting all parties to the transaction.

Conclusion

The intersection of all these topics, issues, and guidelines occurs on the trading floor. On the floor risk is assumed, clients are served, business potential is realized and principle becomes practice. As financial markets grow increasingly dynamic and the global environment increasingly complex, the role of the trading room manager has evolved beyond revenue and expense management. Individuals should be carefully chosen and empowered. The demands, responsibilities and importance of this role should not be underestimated by senior management.

Trading Practices Subcommittee

The Foreign Exchange Committee's *Guidelines for Foreign Exchange Trading Activities* was revised by the Trading Practices Subcommittee, chaired by Richard Mahoney from Bank of New York and John Nixon from Tullett & Tokyo Forex International Limited. The following members of the Subcommittee provided invaluable assistance to this project:

Lloyd C. Blankfein	Goldman, Sachs & Co.
James P. Borden	The Chase Manhattan Bank
Anthony Bustamante	Midland Bank
Kikou Inoue	The Bank of Tokyo, Ltd.
David Puth	Chemical Bank
Jamie K. Thorsen	Bank of Montreal

In addition, the Subcommittee would like to thank the following people for their contributions:

David L. Carangelo	Federal Reserve Bank of New York
Christopher Kelson	Lasser Marshall
Matthew Lifson	The Chase Manhattan Bank

The Subcommittee would also like to acknowledge the contributions of the following individuals, who, through their participation in the Head/Chief Dealer Working Group, helped refine and edit this revision.

Nick Brown
John Caccavale
Keith Cheveralls
Paul Farrell
Scott Gallopo
Geoff Gowey
David Harbison
Stephen Jury
Akihiko Kagawa
James Kemp
Howard Kurz

Nathaniel J. Litwak
Donald J. Lloyd
Varick Martin
John Miesner
David O'Reilly
David Ogg
Steven M. Peras
Salvatore Provenzano
Ivan Sands
Jens-Peter Stein

Additional Information

These *Guidelines* are regularly reviewed and updated. The Trading Practices Subcommittee welcomes your comments and suggestions. In addition, the Subcommittee stands ready to provide further guidance on the issues presented in the *Guidelines*. If you would like to discuss particular issues with a member of the Subcommittee or you have a suggestion on how to improve the *Guidelines*, please contact the Trading Practices Subcommittee, c/o Executive Assistant, Foreign Exchange Committee, 33 Liberty Street, New York, NY 10045, telephone: 212/720-6651 and facsimile: 212/720-1655.

Glossary

Actual Loss MAT: Management action trigger that is activated when there are modest losses irrespective of the size of position sensitivities.

Actuarial Maturities: Maturity dates estimated by analyzing historical withdrawal patterns and the rollover behavior of investors and borrowers.

Aggregate Loan Equivalent Amount: Current loan equivalent amount plus potential loan equivalent amount in a forward contract.

Asset Securitization: Process of combining comparable assets into a newly created negotiable instrument that legally represents the underlying assets and can be sold and/or traded in the financial markets.

Asset Trading: Buying and selling securitized assets.

Basis Point: 0.01 percent p.a. (e.g., the difference between 6.50 percent p.a. and 6.51 percent p.a.).

Basis Risk: See *interest-rate-differential-sensitive position.*

Business Plan: Written plan developed by management describing the current and expected political, economic, and regulatory environment, customers, products, and positioning activity as well as expected revenues, necessary limits, and human resource requirements. Departmental business plans should be integrated in the overall business plan of a country or region.

Capital: Stockholder's equity plus retained earnings. Also see *tier 1 capital* and *tier 2 capital.*

Capital/Asset Ratio: Ratio for measuring capital adequacy in which capital is expressed as a percentage of risk assets.

Contingency Funding Plan: Written plan for maintaining liquidity under adverse conditions on the basis of assumptions about possible environmental abnormalities.

Counterparty Risk: Risk that a counterparty will default on a contract.

Covariance: Degree of similarity between the movements of exchange rates, interest rates, and volatility.

Credit Conversion: Off-balance-sheet risk adjustment for commitments and letters of credit, foreign exchange contracts, and interest rate contracts.

Current Loan Equivalent Amount: Contract rate is more attractive than the prevailing market rate. Calculated as the differential between the contract rate and the market rate derived from the mark-to-market process.

Defeasance Period: The time needed to liquidate a price-risk position.

Delta-Neutral Hedge Position: A hedge position in which the hedge percentage equals the percentage of probability that the option will be exercised.

Derivatives: Off-balance-sheet forwards, futures, and options contracts for interest rates and commodities, including foreign currencies. Contracts involve either no cash or a small percentage of the transaction amounts and values are "derived" from underlying cash or spot contracts.

Double Weighting: The process of applying two risk-weighting percentages in the risk adjustment process to an asset that fits into two different categories, for example, *counterparty*-related risk adjustment and *product*-related risk adjustment.

Earnings at Risk Limit: Maximum allowable negative variance in interest rate accrual risk.

Earnings per share: Corporate earnings divided by the number of shares outstanding.

Forward Interest Rate Agreement (FRA): Hedge instrument used to lock in interest rates.

Funding Liquidity Risk: Risk that the bank cannot meet its contractual obligations at maturity.

Futures Contract: Contract at organized exchanges for interest rates, equities, and commodities, including foreign currencies, that requires margins and is standardized in terms of quantity, quality, and maturity.

Gamma: Sensitivity of the delta-hedge ratio of an option to changes in the spot price of the underlying asset.

Gap: Mismatch of tenors between deposits/borrowings, loans/placements, and their respective derivative contracts to create an interest-rate-level-sensitive position.

Historical Database: Source of information about changes in market prices observed in the past that are used to estimate future volatility.

Interest-Rate-Differential-Sensitive Position: Price risk position in anticipation of a change in the interest differential between two instruments for the same maturity or a change in the interest differential for the same instrument maturing on two different dates.

Interest-Rate-Level-Sensitive Position: Price risk position in anticipation of a change in the level of interest rates.

Instrument Spread: Interest differential between two different instruments with the same maturity.

Leverage: Use of credit to enhance speculative capacity.

Liquidity Risk: Risk that a bank will be unable to fulfill its contractual obligations when they are due.

Loan Equivalent Amount: Current replacement cost of a forward contract plus the amount by which the replacement cost may increase during the life of that contract.

Management Action Trigger (MAT): Dollar figure that defines management's tolerance for accepting risk-related losses. Reaching an MAT requires the involvement of the next level of management. An MAT is not a limit.

Margin: Percentage of a transaction amount in a futures contract. Collateral to protect the broker against counterparty risk. The size of the initial margin depends on volatility. Daily marking-to-market produces the size of variation margins. These are also called maintenance margins because they maintain the initial margin at the intended level.

Market Share: Size of a unit's activity expressed as a percentage of the total market. Used to indicate the relative size of an activity.

Marking-to-Market: Valuing price risk positions at current market rates; simulating the liquidation of such positions.

Maturities: Settlement dates for transactions.

Maturity Buckets: Categories of tenors on the yield curve that are based on a reasonable commonality in volatility percentages.

Maturity Spread: Interest differential for the same instrument maturing on two different dates.

Maximum Cumulative Outflow (MCO): Maximum cumulative negative cash flows for a time period. Used as a limit for liquidity risk.

Negative Gap: A long placement combined with a short borrowing to position for declining interest rates.

Net Position: An imbalance between assets and unliquidated purchases of a currency and liabilities and unliquidated sales of that currency.

Notional Amount: Amount on which a forward rate agreement or swap agreement is based.

Off Balance Sheet: Record of transactions that does not appear above the line on the balance sheet. Instead, it appears as an indication of contingent risk below the line of the balance sheet.

On Balance Sheet: Record of assets and liabilities that provides a financial picture of a company at a given time.

Option Premium: Price an option buyer pays up front in cash to the seller for the right granted by the option.

Option: Right to buy or sell an asset on a given date at a given price.

Payment Risk: Risk from acting as a clearing or correspondent bank for customers when they use their accounts with the correspondent bank to receive funds purchased or borrowed and to make payments to settle their obligations.

Positioning: Deliberate assumption of price risk to benefit from expected changes in market rates. Also known as *speculating*.

Positive Gap: A short placement combined with a long borrowing to position for rising interest rates.

Potential Loan Equivalent Amount: Risk that the contract rate is more attractive than the expected future market rate. Results from multiplying the appropriate expected volatility percentage by the transaction amount of a contract.

Presettlement Risk: Risk that a trading partner will fail before the maturity date and the market rate will change, resulting in a contract rate that is more attractive than the prevailing market rate.

Present Value: Value of future cash flows that have been discounted to current value.

Price/Earnings Ratio: Relationship of the price of a stock to the amount of earnings per share. Indicates the multiple of earnings per share that equals the price of the stock, for example, price of stock (50), earnings per share (5), price/earnings ratio (10). This ratio also is referred to as the true price of a stock.

Price Risk: Risk resulting from one or several financial contracts of such a nature that a change in financial market prices would affect the profit and loss statement.

Return on Equity: Profitability ratio obtained by expressing earnings as a percentage of net worth.

Risk-Adjusted Assets: Result of risk-adjusting assets and contingent risk. Basis for calculating capital ratios.

Risk Weighting: Converting assets on the balance sheet and contingent risk off the balance sheet into risk-adjusted assets that reflect an estimate of the size of the expected risk. The process is based on the classification criteria of the Basle Accord and specific modifications by central banks.

Sensitivity Limits: Limit for the dollar equivalent of a 1-unit change in a market price (e.g., 1 basis point for interest rates, 1 percent flat for commodity prices including foreign currencies, and 10 basis points for volatility).

Settlement Risk: Risk that a counterparty will fail on the maturity date of a contract involving an exchange of assets. Specifically, the risk is that one will deliver but not receive delivery. Usually longer in time and larger in amount than is commonly assumed.

Speculating: See *positioning*.

Spread Trading: See *instrument spread* and *maturity spread*.

Standard Deviation: Statistical measure of the percentage of time during which the change in the market price will or will not exceed the estimated future volatility. Measure of confidence level in reported risk amounts.

Strike Price: Price at which an option holder will buy or sell the underlying asset if an option is exercised; also called the exercise price.

Tier 1 Capital: Capital that consists of stockholders' equity and retained earnings; also called core capital.

Tier 2 Capital: Capital that consists of perpetual preferred stock, bonds with mandatory conversion to equity, and a percentage of the loan loss reserve; also called supplementary capital.

Trading Liquidity Risk: Risk that a bank cannot liquidate assets quickly enough when cash is needed or liquidate price risk positions when an adverse price change is expected.

Universal Maximum Cumulative Outflow (MCO) Limit: MCO limit for net cash flows irrespective of currency; applies to highly liquid, easily converted currencies.

Value at Risk: Amount that potentially can be lost on a price risk position if a 2SD adverse move in the market rate occurs. It is *not* the maximum risk or the worst that can happen.

Value-at-Risk MAT: MAT activated when there are small actual losses combined with large value at risk amounts resulting from existing price risk positions. The amount is often equal to the value at risk sublimit for the same risk-taking unit.

Volatility Implied in Options: Market price quoted as a percentage per annum among professional traders, representing an amount by which the market price of the underlying asset of an option is expected to move up or down.

Yield Curve: Level of interest rates for different maturity dates. The shape may be positive (upward-sloping), flat, or inverted (downward-sloping), depending on the expectations of market participants about the trend of future interest rates.

Index

About the Author

Heinz Riehl, one of the world's leading experts in managing risk in treasury and derivatives, is founder and president of *Riehl World Training & Consulting, Inc.*, a risk-management consulting firm which advises international banks, central banks, and multinational corporations worldwide. Additionally, he is Adjunct Professor of International Business and Finance at New York University's Stern School of Business. He also serves as expert witness in disputes about financial trading. In 1996 he retired after 35 years of service from Citibank New York, where he was a senior vice president and both a cofounder and member of the Market Risk Policy Committee. Riehl was also for many years a member of the New York Federal Reserve Bank's Foreign Exchange Committee and chairman of its Risk Management subcommittee. Riehl is coauthor of McGraw-Hill's *Foreign Exchange & Money Markets*.